Topic relevant selected content from the highest rated entries, typeset, printed and shipped.

Combine the advantages of up-to-date and in-depth knowledge with the convenience of printed books.

A portion of the proceeds of each book will be donated to the Wikimedia Foundation to support their mission: to empower and engage people around the world to collect and develop educational content under a free license or in the public domain, and to disseminate it effectively and globally.

The content within this book was generated collaboratively by volunteers. Please be advised that nothing found here has necessarily been reviewed by people with the expertise required to provide you with complete, accurate or reliable information. Some information in this book maybe misleading or simply wrong. The publisher does not guarantee the validity of the information found here. If you need specific advice (for example, medical, legal, financial, or risk management) please seek a professional who is licensed or knowledgeable in that area.

Contents

Articles

References

Article Licenses

Chris Evans (actor)

Chris Evans

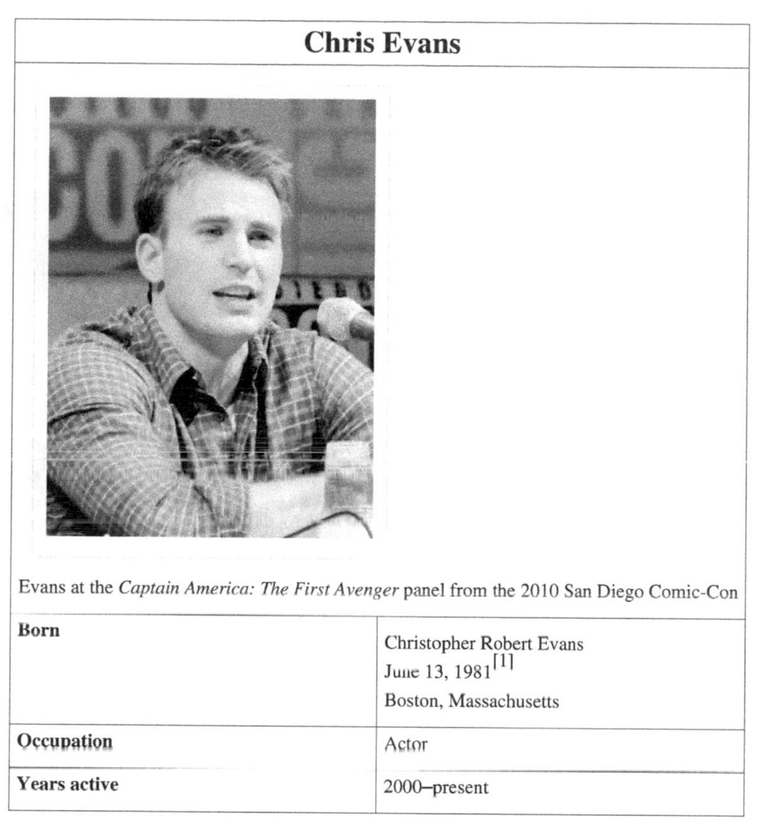

Evans at the *Captain America: The First Avenger* panel from the 2010 San Diego Comic-Con

Born	Christopher Robert Evans June 13, 1981[1] Boston, Massachusetts
Occupation	Actor
Years active	2000–present

Christopher Robert "Chris" Evans (born June 13, 1981) is an American actor. He played Cary Baston on the television series *Opposite Sex*, and transitioned to a film career, starring in several hits, including *Not Another Teen Movie* (2001), *Fierce People* (2005), *Fantastic Four*, sequel *Fantastic Four: Rise of the Silver Surfer* (2007), and *Captain America: The First Avenger* (2011).

Early life

Chris Evans was born in Boston, Massachusetts[2] and raised in the Boston suburb of Sudbury.[3] His mother, Lisa Marie (née Capuano), is an artistic director at the Concord Youth Theater, and his father, G. Robert "Bob" Evans III, is a dentist.[4] [5] [6] He is the nephew of U.S. Congressman Mike Capuano, who is his mother's brother.[7] [8] He has two sisters, Carly, a graduate of New York University's Tisch School and a high-school drama and English teacher,[4] Shanna, and a younger brother, Scott,[5] who was featured on the ABC soap opera *One Life to Live*. His mother is of half Italian and half Irish ancestry.[9] [10] [11] Evans was raised Catholic,[9] and graduated from Lincoln-Sudbury Regional High School.[3]

Career

After filming wrapped on *Not Another Teen Movie*, Evans landed lead roles in *The Perfect Score* and *Cellular*, and then starred in two independent films in Chicago: Dirk Wittenborn's *Fierce People*, playing the sinister Bryce, and *London*, playing a strung-out drug user with relationship problems. He then played Johnny Storm, the superhero the Human Torch, in the 2005 comic book adaptation *Fantastic Four*, leading to his being named a Male Superstar of Tomorrow at the 2005 Young Hollywood Awards. Evans reprised the role of the Human Torch in the 2007 sequel *Fantastic Four: Rise of the Silver Surfer*. That year he also starred as engineer turned astronaut Mace in Danny

Boyle's science-fiction film *Sunshine*.

In 2008, Evans appeared in *Street Kings*, co-starring Keanu Reeves, and the Tennessee Williams play adaptation *The Loss of a Teardrop Diamond*, co-starring Bryce Dallas Howard and Ellen Burstyn. The following year he appeared in the science-fiction thriller *Push*, with Dakota Fanning and Camilla Belle. Evans performed his own fight scenes, which took weeks to film, and was bruised during filming.[12] Also that year, Evans was ranked 474th in Forbes' "Star Currency" rankings, based on films' global box-office performance.[13]

In 2010, he completed filming on co-directors Mark Kassen and Adam Kassen's *Puncture* in Houston, Texas. The film was selected to debut at the 2011 Tribeca Film Festival as one of the Spotlight projects for the 10th anniversary of the festival. Also that year, Evans appeared in Sylvain White's *The Losers*, an adaptation of the comic-book series from the DC Comics imprint Vertigo.[14] Evans then appeared in another comic-book adaptation, Edgar Wright's *Scott Pilgrim vs. the World*, where he portrayed Lucas Lee, one of Ramona Flowers' seven exes.[15] Evans played the Marvel Comics character Captain America in *Captain America: The First Avenger*, and will reprise the role in the film *The Avengers* and at least two sequels to *Captain America*.[16]

Evans with Stan Lee at the 2011 San Diego Comic-Con

Evans starred in the film *What's Your Number?*, a romantic comedy co-starring Anna Faris.[17]

With actress Evan Rachel Wood, he is part of the advertising campaign for the perfume Gucci Guilty,[18] and the cologne Guilty pour Homme.[19] Evans is a supporter of gay rights.[20]

Feature Films

Year	Title	Role	Notes
2000	*The Newcomers*	Judd	Film debut
2001	*Not Another Teen Movie*	Jake Wyler	
2003	*The Paper Boy*	Ben Thomas	Short film
2004	*The Perfect Score*	Kyle	
2004	*Cellular*	Ryan	
2005	*Fierce People*	Bryce Langley	
2005	*Fantastic Four*	Jonathan "Johnny" Storm / Human Torch	Nominated — MTV Movie Award for Best On-Screen Team
2005	*London*	Syd	
2007	*TMNT*	Casey Jones	Voice
2007	*Sunshine*	Mace	
2007	*Fantastic Four: Rise of the Silver Surfer*	Jonathan "Johnny" Storm / Human Torch	• Nominated — Teen Choice Award for Choice Movie Actor: Action Adventure • Nominated — Teen Choice Award for Choice Movie: Rumble
2007	*The Nanny Diaries*	Hayden aka "Harvard Hottie"	
2007	*Battle for Terra*	Stewart Stanton	Voice
2008	*Street Kings*	Detective Paul Diskant	

2008	*The Loss of a Teardrop Diamond*	Jimmy Dobyne	
2009	*Push*	Nick Gant	
2010	*The Losers*	Jake Jensen	
2010	*Scott Pilgrim vs. the World*	Lucas Lee	Nominated — Detroit Film Critics Society Award for Best Ensemble Nominated — Scream Award for Best Vilain (shared with Satya Bhabha, Brandon Routh, Mae Whitman, Shota Saito, Keita Saito and Jason Schwartzman)
2011	*Puncture*	Mike Weiss	
2011	*Captain America: The First Avenger*	Steven "Steve" Rogers / Captain America	Nominated — Teen Choice Award for Choice Summer: Movie Actor Scream Award for Best Superhero
2011	*What's Your Number?*	Colin Shea	
2012	*The Avengers*	Steven "Steve" Rogers / Captain America	

Television

Year	Title	Role	Notes
2000	*Opposite Sex*	Cary Baston	Lead Role
2000	*The Fugitive*	Zack Lander	Episode: "Guilt"
2001	*Boston Public*	Neil Mavromates	Episode: "Chapter Nine"
2002	*Eastwick*	Adam	TV film
2003	*Skin*	Brian	Episode: "Pilot"
2008	*Robot Chicken*	Gobo Fraggle / Human Torch / Teacher / Pilot (voice)	Episode: "Monstourage"

Video Games

Year	Game	Role	Notes	Country
2005	*Fantastic Four*	Johnny Storm / The Human Torch		U.S.
2011	*Captain America: Super Soldier*	Steven "Steve" Rogers / Captain America		U.S.

|+ Voice

References

[1] "World news" (http://www.guardian.co.uk/world/feedarticle/8556516). *The Guardian* (London). January 23, 2008. .

[2] Itzkoff, Dave (July 8, 2011). "Chris Evans in 'Captain America: The First Avenger'" (http://www.nytimes.com/2011/07/10/movies/chris-evans-in-captain-america-the-first-avenger.html). *The New York Times*. .

[3] Pai, Tanya. "America's Most Wanted" (http://www.bostonmagazine.com/arts_entertainment/articles/americas_most_wanted_chris_evans_is_captain_america/), *Boston*, June 2011. WebCitation archive (http://www.webcitation.org/5zxBHb81H).

[4] Marotta, Terry (July 19, 2007). "*Grease* is the word" (http://www.wickedlocal.com/sudbury/columnists/x580418862). Gatehouse News Service via Wicked Local Sudbury. . Retrieved July 19, 2010.

[5] Keck, William (September 9, 2004). "Chris Evans' career ready to sizzle" (http://www.usatoday.com/life/people/2004-09-09-chris-evans_x.htm). USA Today. . Retrieved December 10, 2007.

[6] (http://pqasb.pqarchiver.com/boston/access/1996898972.html?FMT=CITE&FMTS=CITE:AI&type=historic&date=Jul+31,+1977&author=&pub=Boston+Globe+(1960-1979)&desc=WEDDINGS&pqatl=google)

[7] "Capuano to be joined by actor nephew at "Open Mike" Nov. 9" (http://www.wickedlocal.com/somerville/town_info/government/x1156078852/Capuano-to-be-joined-by-actor-nephew-at-Open-Mike-Nov-9). *Wicked Local Somerville*. Nov 6, 2009. . Retrieved July 19,

2010.
[8] Stickgold, Emma (July 21, 2010). "Rita Capuano; campaigned with vigor for husband, son; at 90" (http://www.boston.com/bostonglobe/obituaries/articles/2010/07/21/rita_capuano_campaigned_with_vigor_for_husband_son_at_90/). *Boston Globe*. . Retrieved July 22, 2010.
[9] "Meet curious Chris" (http://web.archive.org/web/20070929125532/http://www.deccanherald.com/Content/May272007/enter200705263888.asp). *Deccan Herald*. May 27, 2007. Archived from the original (http://www.deccanherald.com/Content/May272007/enter200705263888.asp) on 2007-09-29. . Retrieved June 8, 2009.
[10] . http://articles.boston.com/2010-07-21/bostonglobe/29300213_1_italian-fare-soda-bread-husband.
[11] "Sunshine - Chris Evans interview" (http://www.indielondon.co.uk/Film-Review/sunshine-chris-evans-interview). IndieLondon.co.uk. . Retrieved June 8, 2009.
[12] "*Push* Comes to Shove for Chris Evans" (http://www.parade.com/celebrity/celebrity-parade/archive/chris-evans-push-comes-to-shove.html?npId=171). *Parade*. February 4, 2009. . Retrieved July 19, 2010.
[13] "Chris Evans: Star Currency (2009)" (http://star-currency.forbes.com/celebrity/chris-evans). Forbes.com. . Retrieved August 23, 2009.
[14] Billington, Alex (July 13, 2009). "Complete Look at the Full Cast of Sylvain White's The Losers" (http://www.firstshowing.net/2009/07/13/complete-look-at-the-full-cast-of-sylvain-whites-the-losers/). *FirstShowing.net*. . Retrieved July 13, 2009.
[15] Fischer, Russ (January 20, 2009). "A Handy Cast Guide To Scott Pilgrim Vs The World" (http://www.chud.com/articles/articles/17846/1/A-HANDY-CAST-GUIDE-TO-SCOTT-PILGRIM-VS-THE-WORLD/Page1.html). Chud.com. . Retrieved January 20, 2009.
[16] Graser, Marc (March 22, 2010). "Chris Evans to play *Captain America*" (http://www.variety.com/article/VR1118016757.html). *Variety*. . Retrieved March 23, 2010.
[17] Anderton, Ethan (March 8, 2010). "Casting Tidits: Anna Faris, Liv Tyler, Ryan Gosling and More" (http://www.firstshowing.net/2010/03/08/casting-tidits-anna-faris-liv-tyler-ryan-gosling-and-more/#ixzz0hgFCFbBt). FirstShowing.net. . Retrieved August 3, 2010.
[18] Rosenblit, Rachel. "Chris Evans and Evan Rachel Wood Promote Guilty" (http://www.elle.com/Fashion/Fashion-Spotlight/Chris-Evans-and-Evan-Rachel-Wood-Promote-Guilty), *Elle*, August 12, 2010.
[19] "Gucci Guilty Pour Homme To Launch" (http://www.realstylenetwork.com/index.php/beauty/5255/), RealStyleNetwork.com, January 10, 2011.
[20] Voss, Brandon (January 6, 2009). "A List: Chris Evans" (http://www.advocate.com/Arts_and_Entertainment/Film/A_List__Chris_Evans/). *The Advocate*. . Retrieved July 20, 2010.

External links

- Chris Evans (http://www.imdb.com/name/nm262635/) at the Internet Movie Database
- "Chris Evans box office breakdown and upcoming movies" (http://www.boxofficemojo.com/people/chart/?id=chrisevans.htm). *Box Office Mojo*. Retrieved 2010-09-24.
- Chris Evans video interview (http://www.stv.tv/content/out/film/displayHotnow.html?id=opencms:/out/hotnow/films/Chris_Evansx_Fantastic_Four_2_interview) with stv.tv/movies, for *Fantastic Four: Rise of the Silver Surfer*

Not Another Teen Movie

Not Another Teen Movie	
Theatrical release poster	
Directed by	Joel Gallen
Produced by	Neal H. Moritz Phil Beauman Mike Bender Buddy Johnson
Written by	Mike Bender Adam Jay Epstein Andrew Jacobson Phil Beauman Buddy Johnson
Starring	Chyler Leigh Chris Evans Jaime Pressly Eric Christian Olsen Eric Jungmann Mia Kirshner Deon Richmond Cody McMains Sam Huntington Samm Levine Cerina Vincent Ron Lester Lacey Chabert Riley Smith
Music by	Theodore Shapiro
Cinematography	Reynaldo Villalobos
Editing by	Steven Welch
Studio	Original Film
Distributed by	Columbia Pictures
Release date(s)	December 14, 2001
Running time	89 minutes
Country	United States
Language	English
Budget	$15 million

Box office	$66,468,332[1]

Not Another Teen Movie is a 2001 American comedy film directed by Joel Gallen, released on December 14, 2001 by Columbia Pictures. It is a parody of teen movies which have accumulated in Hollywood over the last few decades. While the general plot is based on *Pretty in Pink*, *She's All That*, and *10 Things I Hate About You*, the film also filled with allusions to numerous other films including *Bring It On*, *American Pie*, *Cruel Intentions*, *American Beauty*, and *The Breakfast Club*. A single was released alongside the movie titled "Prom Tonight" and reached #86 on the Billboard Top 100.

Plot

In the stereotypical high school community of John Hughes High in Southern California, sexy Priscilla (Jaime Pressly), a popular cheerleader, separates from her football star boyfriend, Jake Wyler (Chris Evans). After Jake discovers that Priscilla is now dating strange and socially inept Les (Riley Smith) just to spite him, one of Jake's friends, Austin (Eric Christian Olsen), suggests seeking retribution by making Janey Briggs (Chyler Leigh), a "uniquely rebellious girl", the prom queen. Jake attempts to court Janey's love, but faces adversity from his own sister, Catherine (Mia Kirshner), who is sexually attracted to him; Janey's unnoticed admirer and best friend, Ricky (Eric Jungmann); and memories from his past football career. Catherine eventually helps her brother by slightly altering Janey's appearance (taking away her glasses and ponytail), instantly making her drop dead gorgeous.

Meanwhile, Janey's little brother, Mitch (Cody McMains), and his friends, Ox (Sam Huntington) and Bruce (Samm Levine), make a pact to lose their virginity by Graduation even though they are still in their Freshmen year. Mitch tries to impress his longtime crush, the beautiful yet perverted Amanda Becker (Lacey Chabert) with a letter professing his love for her. Ox says that he does not have a chance with her.

As the prom draws near, Jake draws infamy among his peers after he fails to lead his football team to victory at the state championship game the year before. The situation is further worsened when Austin tricks Jake into telling Janey about his plan to spite Priscilla by pretending to whisper the secret bet in Janey's ear, causing her to immediately leave Jake. During prom night, Austin and Janey go together; a jealous Jake and Catherine have a dance off with Austin and Janey, with Catherine dancing in a sexual manner. Janey runs off crying.

Meanwhile, Mitch and his friends are having a lousy time at the prom until Amanda Becker arrives and Mitch gives her the letter and Ox later hooks up with Catherine.

Jake is awarded prom king and the principal reads out that the votes for prom queen are tied. Everyone thinks that it is between Janey and Priscilla, but they are shocked to find that Kara and Sara Fratelli (Samaire Armstrong and Nectar Rose), twins conjoined at the head, win prom queen. During the traditional prom king and queen dance, Janey supposedly left with Austin to go to a hotel. Jake goes to the hotel room where he finds Austin having wild sex with a girl but is shocked to find that it is Priscilla not Janey while the weird Les videotapes with his pants down supposedly having an erection, Austin tells Jake that Janey *"ran home to her daddy"*. Jake angrily punches Austin and Priscilla for what they had done to Janey, then punches Les for "being really weird" (He also punches a plastic bag that happens to be floating next to Les); afterwards he runs to Janey's house only to learn from her father (Randy Quaid) that she is going to Paris for art school.

Jake arrives at the airport and confronts her before she can board the plane, and uses a plethora of clichéd lines from other movies (such as *She's All That*, *Cruel Intentions*, *American Pie*, *The Breakfast Club*, and *Pretty in Pink*) to convince her to stay in America. His final (and first original) speech suggests they would be better off apart, but Janey mistakenly believes he is quoting *The Karate Kid*, and she decides to stay with him.

List of movies parodied

- *10 Things I Hate About You*
- *American Beauty*
- *American Pie*
- *Better Off Dead*
- *The Breakfast Club*
- *Bring It On*
- *Can't Buy Me Love*
- *Can't Hardly Wait*
- *Cruel Intentions*
- *Dazed and Confused*
- *Detroit Rock City*
- *Fast Times at Ridgemont High*
- *Ferris Bueller's Day Off*
- *Full Metal Jacket*
- *Grease*
- *Jawbreaker*
- *The Karate Kid*
- *Lucas*
- *Never Been Kissed*
- *Porky's*
- *Pretty in Pink*
- *Risky Business*
- *Road Trip*
- *Rudy*
- *Save the Last Dance*
- *She's All That*
- *Sixteen Candles*
- *Varsity Blues*

Cast of characters

- Chyler Leigh as Janey Briggs ("The Pretty Ugly Girl")
- Chris Evans as Jake Wyler ("The Popular Jock")
- Jaime Pressly as Priscilla ("The Nasty Cheerleader")
- Eric Christian Olsen as Austin ("The Cocky Blond Guy")
- Mia Kirshner as Catherine Wyler ("The Cruelest Girl in School")
- Deon Richmond as Malik Token ("The Token Black Guy")
- Eric Jungmann as Ricky Lipman ("The Obsessed Best Friend")
- Ron Lester as Reggie Ray ("The Stupid Fat Guy")
- Cody McMains as Mitch Briggs ("The Desperate Virgin")
- Sam Huntington as Ox ("The Sensitive Guy")
- Samm Levine as Bruce ("The Wannabe")
- Lacey Chabert as Amanda Becker ("The Perfect Girl")
- Cerina Vincent as Areola ("The Naked Foreign Exchange Student")
- Riley Smith as Les ("The Beautiful Weirdo")
- Ed Lauter as The Coach
- Randy Quaid as Mr. Briggs
- Joanna Garcia as Sandy Sue
- Beverly Polcyn as Sadie Agatha Johnson
- Robert Patrick Benedict as Preston Wasserstein
- Josh Radnor as "Tour Guide"/"Ted"
- Paul Goebel as "The Chef Who Ejaculated Into Mitch's French Toast"

Cameos

Many stars of recent teen movies as well as those highlighting the 1980s decade make credited and uncredited appearances. These include:

- Molly Ringwald as "The Rude, Hot Flight Attendant" - Ringwald starred in many '80s teen movies such as *Pretty in Pink, Sixteen Candles* and *The Breakfast Club*.
- Mr. T as "The Wise Janitor" - *The A-Team*'s opening sequence music is playing at the end of his speech.
- Kyle Cease as "The Slow Clap Guy" - Cease played Bogey Lowenstein in *10 Things I Hate About You*.
- Melissa Joan Hart as "Slow Clapper's Instructor" - Hart can also be seen in the teen movies *Can't Hardly Wait* and *Drive Me Crazy*. The commentator at the football game praises Joan Hart and *Sabrina the Teenage Witch*.
- Lyman Ward as Mr. Wyler - Ward played Ferris Bueller's father in *Ferris Bueller's Day Off*.
- Paul Gleason as Richard "Dick" Vernon - Gleason played Vernon in *The Breakfast Club*.
- Sean Patrick Thomas as "The Other Token Black Guy" - Thomas appeared in teen movies *Cruel Intentions* and *Save the Last Dance*.
- Good Charlotte as "The Band" - The band playing at the prom.

Extra footage

Alternate footage

- Three scenes that appear on the R-rated trailer are not included in the film: a scene that spoofs *Save the Last Dance* where a girl is dancing at the big party, a scene that spoofs *Never Been Kissed* during the football game with Sadie standing on the football field with a microphone before the entire football team runs her down (the person she was waiting for - one of the school teachers - gets up out of the bleachers just before she is run down and then sits immediately after she is trampled), and a small scene with Areola asking the principal if her breasts are perky (this scene does appear in the unrated cut of the film).
- In the trailer for the film, Jake wears boxer shorts during the whipped cream bikini scene, whereas during that same scene in the film, he wears no shorts; his bare crotch is covered with whipped cream instead.

Footage during credits

The film has three extra scenes at the end:

- Mitch, Ox, and Bruce talking about what they learned from the whole experience. (This scene comes only in the unrated cut.)
- Mr Briggs, in a parody of a scene from "American Pie", talks about a "three-way" while holding two pies. (This scene comes only in the rated cut.)
- The albino folk singer sings about being blind, and her corneas being burned out by the sun. (This scene comes after all the credits have finished.)

Box office

The film opened at number 3 at the US box office taking $12,615,116 in its opening weekend behind *Vanilla Sky*'s opening weekend and *Ocean's Eleven (2001 film)*'s second weekend.

DVD release

The R-rated version of the film was released on DVD on April 30, 2002 with the original 89-minute cut with special features including:

- *School's in Session*: 3 behind-the-scenes featurettes
- "Tainted Love" unrated music video by Marilyn Manson
- *Car Ride*: Director Joel Gallen's first short film
- *Test Your Teen Movie IQ* trivia game with the cast and crew
- Auditions montage
- Meet the cast promos
- *The Yearbook*: The cast looks back at their high school years
- 9 bonus previews

The Unrated Extended Director's Cut was released July 26, 2005 with all of the original special features including an added 11 minutes to the film adding up to 100 minutes.

Reception

The film received generally negative reviews. Most critics dislike the excessive scatological humor and feel that it follows the movies it parodies too closely. The film received a 28% rating on Rotten Tomatoes[2] and 32% on Metacritic.[3]

Soundtrack listing

The soundtrack for the film features metal, punk and rock artists from the 1990s and 2000s, mostly covering songs from the 1980s, and this CD was released by Maverick Records in 2001.

1. "Tainted Love" (Gloria Jones) - Marilyn Manson - 3:21
2. "Never Let Me Down Again" (Depeche Mode) - The Smashing Pumpkins - 4:01
3. "Blue Monday" (New Order) - Orgy
4. "The Metro" (Berlin) - System of a Down
5. "But Not Tonight" (Depeche Mode) - Scott Weiland
6. "Message of Love" (The Pretenders) - Saliva
7. "Bizarre Love Triangle" (New Order) - Stabbing Westward
8. "99 Red Balloons" (Nena) - Goldfinger
9. "I Melt with You" (Modern English) - Mest
10. "If You Leave" (OMD) - Good Charlotte
11. "Please Please Please Let Me Get What I Want" (The Smiths) - Muse
12. "Somebody's Baby" (Jackson Browne) - Phantom Planet
13. "Let's Begin" - Bad Ronald
14. "Prom Tonight" - *Not Another Teen Movie* cast

References

[1] "Not Another Teen Movie" (http://www.boxofficemojo.com/movies/?id=notanotherteenmovie.htm). *Box Office Mojo*. . Retrieved August 7, 2010.

[2] "Not Another Teen Movie Reviews, Pictures" (http://www.rottentomatoes.com/m/not_another_teen_movie/). *Rotten Tomatoes*. . Retrieved December 19, 2010.

[3] "Not Another Teen Movie at Metacritic" (http://www.metacritic.com/movie/not-another-teen-movie). *Metacritic*. . Retrieved December 19, 2010.

External links

- *Not Another Teen Movie* (http://www.imdb.com/title/tt0277371/) at the Internet Movie Database
- *Not Another Teen Movie* (http://www.allrovi.com/movies/movie/v255993) at AllRovi
- *Not Another Teen Movie* (http://www.boxofficemojo.com/movies/?id=notanotherteenmovie.htm) at Box Office Mojo
- *Not Another Teen Movie* (http://www.rottentomatoes.com/m/not_another_teen_movie/) at Rotten Tomatoes
- *Not Another Teen Movie* (http://www.metacritic.com/movie/notanotherteenmovie) at Metacritic

The Perfect Score

The Perfect Score	
The Perfect Score Theatrical Poster	
Directed by	Brian Robbins
Produced by	Roger Birnbaum Jonathan Glickman Brian Robbins Michael Tollin
Written by	Marc Hyman Jon Zack Mark Schwahn
Starring	Erika Christensen Chris Evans Bryan Greenberg Scarlett Johansson Darius Miles Leonardo Nam
Music by	John Murphy
Cinematography	J. Clark Mathis
Editing by	Ned Bastille
Studio	MTV Films
Distributed by	Paramount Pictures
Release date(s)	January 30, 2004 (US)
Running time	93 minutes
Country	United States
Language	English
Box office	$10,876,805 (Worldwide)[1]

The Perfect Score is a teen heist film released in 2004 and directed by Brian Robbins. It stars Erika Christensen, Chris Evans, Bryan Greenberg, Scarlett Johansson, Darius Miles, and Leonardo Nam.

The film focuses on a group of six high school students whose futures will be jeopardized if they fail the upcoming SAT exam. They conspire together to break into the ETS building and steal the answers to the exam, so they can all get perfect scores. The film deals with the themes of one's future, morality, individuality, and feelings.

It has similarities to other high school movies, including *The Breakfast Club* and *Dazed and Confused*, which are often referenced throughout the film. However, the film was panned by most critics and performed poorly at the box office.

Plot

The film revolves around high school student Kyle (Chris Evans), who needs a high score on the SAT to get into his preferred architecture program at Cornell University. He constantly compares himself to his older brother Larry, who is now living above his parents' garage. Kyle's best friend, Matty (Bryan Greenberg), wants to get a high score so he can go to the same college as his girlfriend, but he is an underachiever who had previously received a low score on his PSAT. They both believe that the SAT is standing in the way of their futures.

The two boys realize that fellow student Francesca Curtis' (Scarlett Johansson) father owns the building that houses the regional office of ETS, where the answers to the SAT are located. Francesca initially doesn't want to help but changes her mind, saying "What the hell? It sounds like fun." Meanwhile, Kyle becomes attracted to Anna Ross (Erika Christensen), the second-highest ranked student in the school, and tells her about the plan. Anna had bombed a previous SAT and needs a good score to get into Brown University. However, Matty doesn't like the fact that she now knows about the plan and has an outburst, right in the presence of stoner Roy (Leonardo Nam), who then has to be included in the heist. And finally, Anna tells the school basketball star Desmond Rhodes (Darius Miles), who needs a score of 900 or better to join the basketball team at St. John's University.

An early attempt to break into the ETS offices fails, but the team then devises another plan. On the eve of the exam, Francesca will arrange for Kyle and Matty to have a meeting near the top floor, staying after closing. The other three will wait outside and watch the night guard until Francesca, Kyle, and Matty have successfully stolen the answers.

The first part of the plan goes well, with Francesca, Kyle, and Matty successfully dodging security cameras and the night guard. However, the answers are located on a computer, and only the technical genius Roy can crack the password; he and the other two get into the building, and Roy correctly guesses the password after seeing a photograph of an employee. Still, the answers can't be printed, so the group decides to take the test with their combined knowledge and get the answers that way. In the early hours of morning, they are finished and have all the answers written down.

Just then, the guard ascends the stairs, and they try to escape through the ceiling; however, Francesca is left behind and is about to be discovered, so Matty purposefully gives himself up in order to save her. Everyone else escapes, but each faces a certain confrontation before the exam: Kyle's brother asks him if he's really worse than a thief, Matty is bailed out by Francesca, Anna finds independence from her parents, and Desmond's mother convinces Roy to quit drugs.

Before the SAT testing begins, the group realizes that, although it will help get them what they want, they would be better off without cheating. Roy grabs the answers and distributes them in the bathroom. After the decision, Matty comments that "this whole thing was for nothing." Kyle replies, "I wouldn't say nothing," as he glances at Anna. Matty and Francesca also share a look, as they have presumably started a relationship, too. Each person eventually gets their desired test score without the answers: Kyle's dream of becoming an architect is still alive by attending Syracuse University, Desmond ends up going to St. John's, Matty becomes an actor, Francesca writes a novel (which is about six kids who conspire to steal the answers to the SAT), and Anna decides to travel Europe for awhile before starting college. As for Roy - the narrator of the movie - he earned the highest SAT in the county, and, under Desmond's mom's guidance, he gets a GED. He then puts his untapped intelligence to use through programming, becoming a successful video game designer.

Reaction

The film was panned by almost all critics, scoring an 18 percent "Rotten" rating on Rotten Tomatoes. *Slant Magazine* critic Keith Uhlich called it an "MTV film that extreme right-wing moralists can be proud of, as it posits a quintessentially American world of racial, intellectual, and sexual conformity."[2] Many compared the film unfavorably with *The Breakfast Club*, and many even called it a rip off. *Entertainment Weekly* wrote the film off as being "like *The Breakfast Club* recast as a video game for simpletons."[3] Likewise, Roger Ebert awarded the film two stars out of four, calling the film "too palatable. It maintains a tone of light seriousness, and it depends on the caper for too much of its entertainment value." Ebert's review went on to point out that *The Perfect Score* was given a wide release, but that *Better Luck Tomorrow*, a teen drama film that received much more acclaim, was given a very limited release.[4]

The movie opened in 2,208 theaters and grossed $4.8 million,[5] making for a $2,207 per-theater average. Placing fifth over the weekend, the film saw sharp declines in following weeks and ended its domestic run with $10.3 million.

References

[1] Box Office Mojo - The Perfect Score (http://www.boxofficemojo.com/movies/?id=perfectscore.htm)
[2] Slant Magazine - Film Review: The Perfect Score (http://www.slantmagazine.com/film/film_review.asp?ID=962)
[3] The Perfect Score | Movie Review | Entertainment Weekly (http://www.ew.com/ew/article/review/movie/0,6115,584306_1_0_,00.html)
[4] The Perfect Score | Movie Review| Roger Ebert (http://rogerebert.suntimes.com/apps/pbcs.dll/article?AID=/20040130/REVIEWS/401300305)
[5] The Perfect Score - Movie Reviews, Trailers, Pictures - Rotten Tomatoes (http://uk.rottentomatoes.com/m/perfect_score/numbers.php)

External links

- *The Perfect Score* (http://www.imdb.com/title/tt0314498/) at the Internet Movie Database
- *The Perfect Score* (http://www.allrovi.com/movies/movie/v284678) at AllRovi
- *The Perfect Score* (http://www.boxofficemojo.com/movies/?id=perfectscore.htm) at Box Office Mojo

Cellular (film)

Cellular	
Promotional movie poster	
Directed by	David R. Ellis
Produced by	Dean Devlin Lauren Lloyd
Screenplay by	Chris Morgan **Uncredited:** J. Mackye Gruber
Story by	Larry Cohen
Starring	Chris Evans Kim Basinger Jason Statham Eric Christian Olsen Eric Etebari Noah Emmerich William H. Macy
Music by	John Ottman
Cinematography	Gary Capo
Editing by	Eric Sears
Distributed by	New Line Cinema
Release date(s)	September 10, 2004
Running time	94 minutes
Country	United States Germany
Language	English
Budget	$25,000,000 (estimated)
Box office	$56,422,687

Cellular is a 2004 thriller film directed by David R. Ellis and starring Kim Basinger, Chris Evans, Jason Statham and William H. Macy. The screenplay was written by Chris Morgan, Larry Cohen (who also scripted *Phone Booth*, another film that evolves from a phone call) and J. Mackye Gruber (not credited).

Plot

The film opens with Jessica Martin (Kim Basinger), a high school biology teacher, talking to her son Ricky, while escorting him to the school bus. After she returns home, mysterious assailants enter her home through the back door, kill her house maid, kidnap her and confine her in the attic of their safe house. Ethan (Jason Statham), the gang leader, smashes the attic's telephone to prevent her from contacting anyone. She has no idea who the kidnappers are or what they want. She pieces together the broken phone and randomly makes a connection. She reaches the cell phone of Ryan (Chris Evans), who has just been dumped by his girlfriend, Chloe (Jessica Biel), for being too irresponsible. He believes the call is a joke, but Jessica persuades him to go to the police. At the police station, desk sergeant Mooney (William H. Macy) tells him to go to the detectives on the fourth floor. He begins to lose the signal in the stairwell, so he turns back to avoid losing the connection.

Meanwhile, Ethan returns to the safehouse and asks Jessica for something she doesn't know about. When Jessica tells him that she doesn't know, he tells her that he is going to get her son. Ryan, who overhears them, is now convinced that the kidnapping is real. After Ethan leaves, she tells Ryan to reach her son's school before they do. Unfortunately, he is too late and her son is kidnapped. Ryan hijacks a security officer's car and gives chase. Because his cell phone's battery is dying, he drives to a shop for a charger. After being repeatedly redirected from counter to counter, he uses a gun from the security vehicle to hold up the store and get the charger.

Sgt. Mooney meanwhile decides to check on the kidnapping claim that he received. He uses the Department of Motor Vehicles records to find the address of Jessica, but when he comes to her house, a woman meets him, telling him that she is Jessica and that everything is fine. Believing it to be a false alarm, he leaves. It is revealed that the woman is Dana Bayback (Valerie Cruz), an accomplice of the kidnappers.

Ethan returns to the safe house and asks Jessica for the location of a place called "The Left Field", where her husband was. He reveals that he has Ricky and threatens to kill him if Jessica does not tell him what "The Left Field" means. She tells him that "The Left Field" is a bar in Los Angeles International Airport. As Ethan leaves, she tells Ryan that they have gone to get her husband. A cross-connection between phone lines causes Ryan to grab a nearby lawyer's cell phone as well as his car after his is destroyed. Jessica urges him to find her husband, and at the airport, he tries to stop the kidnappers by planting the gun under one of their jackets. The gun trips the alarm and security intervenes, but the kidnappers flash police badges and soon apprehend Craig. After viewing a news report, Mooney identifies Ryan and calls Jessica's home. When he gets the voice mail, he notices that Jessica's voice on the answering machine is different from the woman he met.

Craig is brought into the attic and is forced to reveal the location of a videotape. He tells them that it is in a bank safe deposit box. Ethan and his friends, Dimitri and Deason, go with Craig while another kidnapper stays on guard. Ryan also reaches the bank, and when the kidnappers retrieve the video camera, Ryan grabs it, and flees to the roof. However, he accidentally drops the cell phone off the roof, smashing it to pieces. He manages to escape in a taxi, and while watching the videotape learns that Craig accidentally shot footage of Los Angeles Police Department Detectives Ethan, Mad Dog, Dimitri, Bayback, Deason, and Jack Tanner, a friend of Officer Mooney, robbing and murdering drug dealers. Ryan steals the lawyer's car again and gets back his own cellphone.

Mooney returns to the Martin residence, where Bayback shoots at him, injuring him. He retaliates and kills her but learns, to his dismay, that she was a cop too. Meanwhile, Mad Dog stumbles upon the phone line Jessica is using from the downstairs phone, and Jessica kills him by cutting his brachial artery. She attempts to escape with her son, but Ethan returns with Craig as a hostage and stops her. Before Ethan can do anything, Ryan uses his cell phone's memory to contact Ethan and makes a deal directly over the phone: the video tape in exchange for the Martin family. Upon learning of the meeting, Tanner convinces Mooney to go so that he can identify Ryan.

The deal goes down at the Santa Monica Pier. Ryan tries to handle it his way in disguise, but his ex-girlfriend accidentally exposes him, after which Mooney is able to finger him. While Tanner sends Dimitri to help Mooney get needed medical attention, he takes Ryan to Ethan. Ethan destroys the video recording and Tanner radios the order to kill the Martins, although Deason in the van suggests they wait until they get to the safe house.

However, Mooney overhears the radio transmission from Dimitri's radio and he realizes that Tanner is one of the kidnappers. Ryan escapes following a distraction by his friend Chad, while Dmitri attempts to kill Mooney, but Mooney overpowers and handcuffs him. Tanner and Ethan confront Ryan in a boathouse, where Ryan knocks out Tanner, but Ethan beats him up with his superior fighting skills until Mooney intervenes. After a brief cat and mouse game, Ryan, wounded, notices that Ethan has circled behind Mooney, and helps Mooney by calling Ethan's cell phone. The ring of the cell betrays Ethan's hiding place, and Mooney promptly shoots him dead. As Ethan falls, he looks dumbfoundedly at Ryan...and then at Ryan's cell phone "weapon" that got him killed.

While this was going on, Jessica manages to strangle Deason with her handcuff chain from the rear of their van, then frees her husband and son. But Deason was merely stunned, and aims his gun at them. Then, Ryan suddenly intervenes and smashes him around till he is unconscious.

While Ryan and Mooney are being treated by medics, Tanner is also exposed, because Ryan had made a copy of the video recording onto his cell phone, and the Martin family is set free. Jessica finally gets to meet the man who has risked his life saving her and her family. Ryan's only request is that she is never to call him again.

Cast

- Kim Basinger as Jessica Martin
- Chris Evans as Ryan
- Jason Statham as Ethan
- William H. Macy as Sgt. Bob Mooney
- Eric Christian Olsen as Chad
- Matt McColm as Deason
- Noah Emmerich as Jack Tanner
- Brendan Kelly as Mad Dog
- Eric Etebari as Dmitri
- Valerie Cruz as Dana Bayback
- Richard Burgi as Craig Martin
- Jessica Biel as Chloe
- Caroline Aaron as Marilyn Mooney
- Dat Phan as Asian Face Artist (cameo)
- Adam Taylor Gordon as Ricky Martin

Production

Cellular was filmed in Southern California, most notably in Santa Monica, Westwood, Los Angeles, Downtown Los Angeles and West Los Angeles. There were a few directorial errors throughout the film that stumped viewers.[1] Peter Sarsgaard turned down the role of Ethan (and would portray a similar role a year later in *Flightplan*), making this film Jason Statham's first film as a villain.

Reception

Box office

The film has had gross receipts of $32,003,620 in the U.S. and Canada and $24,419,067 in international markets for a total of $56,422,687 worldwide.

Critical response

Reviews on *Cellular* were mixed, currently holding an approval rating of 54% on Rotten Tomatoes.

Entertainment Weekly said this film was "pure chase-thriller excitement".[2] Claudia Puig of *USA Today* called this film a "well-paced action film in the vein of *Speed*".

Kim Basinger was nominated for a Saturn Award for Best Supporting Actress but lost against Daryl Hannah in *Kill Bill Vol. 2*.

Home media

A novelization of the film was written by Pat Cadigan and released in October, 2004 by Black Flame. *Cellular* was released worldwide in widescreen on DVD along with the VHS format on January 18, 2005.

Remakes

The film inspired a 2008 Chinese language remake by director Benny Chan. The film, *Connected*, stars Barbie Hsu and Louis Koo in the Basinger and Evans roles respectively. A Bollywood remake of this film called *Speed* was released in India in 2007 starring Urmila Matondkar, Zayed Khan, Sanjay Suri but, despite including an ensemble cast especially Urmila's appreciated performance, did not succeed like the original. A version in Tamil, Vegam, was released in 2007.The movie was remade in to Telugu as Deepavali,but the film became utter flop due to poor script ,cast and direction.

References

[1] Cellular Filming Locations (http://www.seeing-stars.com/Locations/Cellular.shtml)

[2] Owen Gleiberman (September 8, 2004). "Cellular" (http://www.ew.com/ew/article/0,,694121,00.html). *Entertainment Weekly*. . Retrieved July 31, 2010.

External links

- Official website (http://web.archive.org/web/20071107151058/http://www.cellularthemovie.com/)
- *Cellular* soundtrack information (http://www.soundtrackinfo.com/title/cellular.asp)
- *Cellular* (http://www.imdb.com/title/tt0337921/) at the Internet Movie Database

Fierce People (film)

Fierce People	
Theatrical release poster	
Directed by	Griffin Dunne
Produced by	Griffin Dunne Nick Wechsler Dirk Wittenborn
Screenplay by	Dirk Wittenborn
Based on	*Fierce People* by Dick Wittenborn
Narrated by	Anton Yelchin
Starring	Diane Lane Anton Yelchin Donald Sutherland Chris Evans Kristen Stewart
Music by	Nick Laird-Clowes
Cinematography	William Rexer
Editing by	Allyson C. Johnson
Studio	Industry Entertainment
Distributed by	Lions Gate Films Autonomous Films
Release date(s)	April 24, 2005 (Tribeca) April 28, 2006 (Canada) September 30, 2007 (Limited) November 30, 2007
Running time	111 minutes
Country	United States Canada
Language	English Tagalog
Box office	$269,755[1]

Fierce People is a 2005 drama thriller film adapted by Dirk Wittenborn from his 2002 novel of the same name. Directed by Griffin Dunne, it starred Anton Yelchin, Diane Lane, Kristen Stewart, Chris Evans, and Donald

Sutherland.

Plot

Trapped in his drug-dependent mother, Liz's (Diane Lane), Lower East Side apartment, 16-year-old Finn Earl (Anton Yelchin) wants nothing more than to escape New York. He wants to spend the summer in South America studying the Ishkanani Indians (known as the "Fierce People") with his anthropologist father whom he's never met. Earl's plan has to change after he is arrested in an effort to help Liz, who works as a massage therapist. Determined to get their lives back on track, Liz moves the two of them into a guesthouse for the summer on the country estate of her ex-client, the aging billionaire, Ogden C. Osbourne (Donald Sutherland).

In Osbourne's world of privilege and power, Finn and Liz encounter the super rich, a tribe portrayed as fiercer and more mysterious than anything the youth might find in the South American jungle. (Dirk Wittenborn, the author of the novel on which the film is based, grew up poor and feeling an outsider among the super rich in an upper-crust New Jersey enclave.[2])

While Liz battles her substance abuse and struggles to win back her son's love and trust, Finn falls in love with Osbourne's granddaughter, Maya (Kristen Stewart). He befriends her older brother, Bryce (Chris Evans); and wins the favor of Osbourne. When violence ends Finn's acceptance within the Osbourne clan, the promises of this world quickly sour. Both Finn and Liz, caught in a harrowing struggle for their dignity, discover that membership in a group comes at a steep price.

Cast

- Diane Lane as Liz Earl
- Anton Yelchin as Finn Earl
- Donald Sutherland as Ogden C. Osbourne
- Chris Evans as Bryce Langley
- Kristen Stewart as Maya Langley
- Paz de la Huerta as Jilly
- Blu Mankuma as Detective Gates
- Elizabeth Perkins as Mrs. Langley
- Christopher Shyer as Dr. Richard "Dick" Leffler
- Garry Chalk as McCallum
- Ryan McDonald as Ian
- Dexter Bell as Marcus Gates
- Kaleigh Day as Paige
- Aaron Brooks as Giacomo
- Teach Grant as Dwayne
- Dirk Wittenborn as Fox Blanchard
- Will Lyman as Voice of documentary narrator

Production

Portions of the film were shot on location in British Columbia, Canada at Hatley Castle.[3]

Release

Critical reception

Fierce People earned mixed critical reviews.[4] [5]

The film currently holds a 24% 'Fresh' rating on Rotten Tomatoes, with the consensus, "*Fierce People*'s premise of a teenager studying rich people like animals is grating and self-satisfied, and Anton Yelchin's smug performance makes the film even harder to agree with."[6]

Box office

The film received a limited release and grossed $85,410 at the box office in the US.[7]

References

[1] *Fierce People* (http://www.boxofficemojo.com/movies/?id=fiercepeople.htm) at Box Office Mojo

[2] Joy Press, "Privileged Information" (http://www.villagevoice.com/2002-06-11/books/privileged-information/), *Village Voice*, 11 Jun 2002

[3] Hatley Castle (http://www.hatleypark.ca/about-us/hatley-castle.htm)

[4] Movie Review - "Fierce People *(2006): Surviving in That Rain Forest East of the Delaware River"* (http://movies.nytimes.com/2007/09/07/movies/07fier.html), *The New York Times*, 7 September 2007, accessed 8 Jan 2010.

[5] Movie Review - *Fierce People* (2006) (http://chicago.metromix.com/movies/movie_review/fierce-people/168053/content), *chicago.metromix.com.*

[6] *Fierce People* (http://www.rottentomatoes.com/m/fierce_people/) at Rotten Tomatoes

[7] http://www.hollywood.com/movie/Fierce_People/1747663 "Fierce People"], Hollywood.com, accessed 8 Jan 2010

External links

- Official website (http://www.fiercepeoplemovie.com/)
- *Fierce People* (http://www.imdb.com/title/tt0401420/) at the Internet Movie Database
- *Fierce People* (http://www.allrovi.com/movies/movie/v306113) at AllRovi
- *Fierce People* (http://www.boxofficemojo.com/movies/?id=fiercepeople.htm) at Box Office Mojo
- *Fierce People* (http://www.rottentomatoes.com/m/fierce_people/) at Rotten Tomatoes

Fantastic Four (film)

Fantastic Four	
Directed by	Tim Story
Produced by	Avi Arad Bernd Eichinger Ralph Winter
Written by	Michael France Mark Frost
Based on	• *Fantastic Four* by • Stan Lee • Jack Kirby
Starring	Ioan Gruffudd Jessica Alba Chris Evans Michael Chiklis Julian McMahon
Music by	John Ottman
Cinematography	Oliver Wood
Editing by	William Hoy
Studio	20th Century Fox Constantin Film Marvel Studios 1492 Pictures
Distributed by	20th Century Fox
Release date(s)	June 29, 2005 (Jamaica) July 8, 2005 (United States)
Running time	106 minutes
Country	United States
Language	English
Budget	$100 million
Box office	$330,579,719

Fantastic Four is a 2005 American superhero film based on the Marvel Comics comic *Fantastic Four*. It was directed by Tim Story, and released by 20th Century Fox. It is the second live-action *Fantastic Four* film to be filmed. The previous attempt, a B-movie produced by Roger Corman only for the purpose of retaining the film rights, was never intended for a theatrical release. Despite getting major hype on its release and becoming a box office success, the film was negatively received by both critics and fans.

The film was released in the United States on July 8, 2005. It was the third superhero film of the year, after *Elektra* and *Batman Begins*.

In 2007, a sequel, *Fantastic Four: Rise of the Silver Surfer*, was released.

Plot

Dr. Reed Richards (Ioan Gruffudd), a genius but timid and bankrupt physicist, is convinced that evolution was triggered millions of years ago on earth by clouds of cosmic energy in space, and has calculated that one of these clouds is soon going to pass near Earth. Together with his friend, the gruff yet gentle astronaut Ben Grimm (Michael Chiklis), Reed convinces Dr. Victor von Doom (Julian McMahon), once his classmate at MIT and now CEO of Von Doom Industries, to allow him access to his privately-owned space station to test the effects of exposure to the cloud on biological samples. Doom agrees, in exchange for control over the experiment and a majority of the profits from whatever benefits it brings. He brings aboard his beautiful chief genetics researcher (and Reed's ex-girlfriend from MIT) Susan Storm (Jessica Alba), and her hot-headed brother Johnny Storm (Chris Evans), a private astronaut who was Ben's subordinate at NASA but is his superior on the mission.

The quintet travels to space to observe the cosmic energy clouds, but Reed has miscalculated and the clouds materialize well ahead of schedule. Reed, Susan and Johnny leave the shielded station to rescue Ben who has gone on a space-walk to place the samples, and Victor closes the shield behind them. Ben receives full exposure out in space, while the others receive a more limited dose within the station. They return home but soon begin to develop strange powers. Reed is able to stretch like rubber; Susan can become invisible and create force fields, especially when angered; Johnny can engulf himself in fire at temperatures in excess of 4000 K (erroneously described as supernova-like in the film), and is able to fly; and Ben is transformed into a large, rock-like creature with superhuman strength and durability. Victor meanwhile faces a backlash from his stockholders due to the publicity from the failed mission, and has a scar on his face from an exploding control console he was near during the cloud's pass.

Ben returns home to see his fiancee (Laurie Holden), but she cannot handle his new appearance and flees. He goes to brood on Brooklyn Bridge and accidentally causes a traffic pile-up while stopping a man from committing suicide. The four use their various powers to contain the damage and prevent anyone from being hurt. While the public cheers them for their efforts, Ben sees his fiancee leave her engagement ring on the ground and run. Reed hands a heartbroken Ben the ring and vows to find a way to turn him back to normal. The media dubs them "The Fantastic Four" for their efforts. Victor watches the news story and is told that his company is lost now, the group's fame overriding the company's fate with the media. The four move into Reed's lab in the Baxter Building to study their abilities and find a way to return Ben to normal. Victor offers his support in their efforts but blames Reed for the mission's failure, the lights flickering as he grows enraged.

Reed tells the group he will construct a machine to re-create the storm and reverse its effect on their bodies, but warns it could possibly accelerate them instead. Meanwhile Victor continues to mutate, his arm turning into an organic metal and allowing him to produce bolts of electricity, and he begins plotting to use his new powers to take his revenge. Victor drives a wedge between Ben and Reed by telling Ben that Reed has no desire to change himself back, as the group's research has allowed him to rekindle his relationship with Susan. Reed and Ben argue, Ben walking out in a rage. This motivates Reed to attempt the machine on himself, but he cannot generate the power needed to push the storm to critical mass. Doom hears Reed tell Susan this through security cameras and has Ben brought to the lab. Ben is placed in the machine and Doom uses his abilities to produce the electricity needed to power it, turning Ben back to normal and accelerating Doom's condition, causing much of his body to turn to metal. Victor knocks the human Ben unconscious and kidnaps Reed.

Victor - now calling himself 'Doom' - dons a metal mask to hide his physical disfigurations and incapacitates Reed using a super-cooling unit. Doom fires a heat-seeking missile at the Baxter Building to kill Johnny, and Johnny flies through the city to evade it, lighting a garbage barge on fire to trick it. Susan rushes to confront Doom as Ben begins to regret his decision to turn normal. Susan frees Reed and battles Doom but is outmatched - Ben arrives to save her, transformed into The Thing again by reusing the machine (speaking his signature line, "I'ts Clobberin' Time"). The battle spills into the streets, and the four assemble to battle Doom. Johnny and Susan combine their powers to wrap Doom in an inferno of intense heat, and Ben and Reed douse him with cold water, inducing thermal shock and freezing Doom in place. As an epilogue, Ben informs Reed that he has accepted his condition with the help of Alicia Masters, a blind artist for whom he has developed feelings, and the team decide to embrace their roles as superheroes and unite officially as the Fantastic Four. Reed proposes marriage to Susan, who accepts and they share a kiss. Meanwhile, Doom's statuesque remains are being transported back to his homeland of Latveria when the dockmaster's electronic manifest briefly experiences electronic interference, suggesting Doom is still alive, thus leading to the events of the sequel, Fantastic Four: Rise of the Silver Surfer.

Cast

- Ioan Gruffudd as Dr. Reed Richards / Mr. Fantastic
- Jessica Alba as Susan Storm / Invisible Woman
- Chris Evans as Johnny Storm / Human Torch
- Michael Chiklis as Ben Grimm / The Thing
- Julian McMahon as Victor von Doom / Doctor Doom
- Hamish Linklater as Leonard
- Kerry Washington as Alicia Masters
- Laurie Holden as Debbie McIlvane
- Kevin McNulty as Jimmy O'Hoolihan
- Maria Menounos as Nurse
- Michael Kopsa as Ned Cecil
- Stan Lee as Willie Lumpkin

As in almost all of the previous Marvel Comics-based films, *Fantastic Four* co-creator Stan Lee makes a cameo appearance. He is Willie Lumpkin, the postal worker who greets the team on their way to the Baxter Building elevator.[1]

Release

The film's American release was moved from July 1, 2005 to the following week, July 8, in order to avoid competition with Steven Spielberg's *War of the Worlds*.[2] It opened in 3,602 theaters, and eventually expanded to 3,619 the following week for its widest release.[3]

Critical reception

Fantastic Four received mostly negative reviews from critics. The film scored a 27% rating at the critics-aggregate site Rotten Tomatoes[4] and 40 out of 100 at Metacritic.[5] The movie was criticized for poor science, undeveloped characters, and having less action than some people would have liked. The plot was criticised for the perceived imbalance of pitting four superheroes against one villain.[6]

Box office performance

At the box office, *Fantastic Four* held the number one position with $56,061,504 in its opening weekend. By September 2005, the film had grossed over $330 million worldwide, with a domestic gross of $154 million.[7]

Deleted scenes

Among the deleted scenes included on the December 2005 DVD release:

- Three slightly modified scenes concerning the attack on Doctor Doom - one in which Reed uses his body as a funnel to direct a stream of water at Doom, one in which he doesn't, and one in which Doctor Doom's line "Is that the best you can do, a little heat?" is cut short, having the "..a little heat?" portion removed.
- Two versions of a scene with Jessica Alba and Ioan Gruffudd. The original features the pair in the planetarium, where they communicate their feelings for each other without an argumentative tone. This ends in a kiss. The second version, included in the DVD release as a bonus feature, features the two outside, looking toward the Statue Of Liberty. Similar lines are used, but it ends with Alba's Susan turning invisible before Gruffudd's Reed can kiss her. A joke was used during the line "a stronger man": Instead of Reed giving himself a square jaw (as he does in the theatrical release), he makes his skin look like X-Men's Wolverine. Actor Gruffudd breaks the fourth wall and looks directly at the camera as he does this.
- There is also a scene where Reed and Sue are in a storage room of the Baxter Building where we see on one of the shelves is a robot that is supposed to be H.E.R.B.I.E. from the 1970s Fantastic Four cartoon.

The novelization of the film contained a number of scenes not in the final cut, including a small number of scenes that developed the character of Alicia Masters.

Extended cut

In June 2007, an extended cut of the film was released, incorporating over 20 minutes of deleted scenes and also includes a preview of *Fantastic Four: Rise of the Silver Surfer.*

Sequel

A sequel, *Fantastic Four: Rise of the Silver Surfer*, was released on June 15, 2007. Director Tim Story and the cast reprised their roles for the sequel. In the film, the Fantastic Four encounter the Silver Surfer. The film had a mixed, but overall better reception.

References

[1] Matthew Kirdahy (7 February 2008). " Q&A With Stan Lee (http://www.forbes.com/leadership/2008/02/07/heroes-villains-comics-lead-cx_mk_0206stanlee.html)". *Forbes.com.* Accessed February 7, 2008.

[2] Lichtenfeld, Eric (2007). *Action Speaks Louder*. Middletown, Connecticut: Wesleyan University Press. p. 241. ISBN 0819568015.

[3] "Fantastic Four (2005) - Weekly Box Office" (http://www.boxofficemojo.com/movies/?page=weekly&id=fantasticfour.htm). . Retrieved March 22, 2011.

[4] ""Fantastic Four"" (http://www.rottentomatoes.com/m/fantastic_four/). RottenTomatoes.com. . Retrieved 2011-04-20.

[5] ""Fantastic Four"" (http://www.metacritic.com/film/titles/fantasticfour). Metacritic.com. . Retrieved 2011-04-20.

[6] Lundin, Leigh (2011-10-16). "The Mystery of Superheroes" (http://www.sleuthsayers.org/2011/10/mystery-of-superheroes.html). Orlando: SleuthSayers.org. .

[7] ""Fantastic Four"" (http://www.boxofficemojo.com/movies/?id=fantasticfour.htm). BoxOfficeMojo.com. . Retrieved 2011-04-20.

External links

- Official website (http://web.archive.org/web/20050401183827/http://www.fantasticfourmovie.com)
- *Fantastic Four* (http://www.imdb.com/title/tt0120667/) at the Internet Movie Database
- *Fantastic Four* (http://www.allrovi.com/movies/movie/v286677) at AllRovi
- *Fantastic Four* (http://www.rottentomatoes.com/m/fantastic_four/) at Rotten Tomatoes
- *Fantastic Four* (http://marvel.com/movies/movie/14/fantastic_four) on Marvel.com

London (2006 film)

London	
Theatrical movie poster	
Directed by	Hunter Richards
Produced by	Paul Davis-Miller
Written by	Hunter Richards
Starring	Jessica Biel Chris Evans Jason Statham Joy Bryant Isla Fisher Kelli Garner
Distributed by	Samuel Goldwyn Films
Release date(s)	February 10, 2006 (USA)
Running time	92 minutes
Language	English
Budget	£14,000 (estimated)
Box office	$20,361

London is a 2006 romantic drama film centering on a Manhattan party. The movie is directed and written by Hunter Richards, his first. It stars Jessica Biel, Chris Evans, Jason Statham, Joy Bryant, and Lina Esco.

Plot

Syd (Chris Evans) awakens from the latest in a long series of drug- and booze-fueled benders when he received a phone call from a friend informing him that his ex-girlfriend London (Jessica Biel) will be moving away to California with her new boyfriend in a few days, and that a going-away party is being thrown for her that evening. Although not invited to the bash, Syd decides to attend anyway, bringing along Bateman (Jason Statham), a banker who delivers cocaine to Syd as a favor to their mutual dealer.

Bateman is carrying a large supply of cocaine. After arriving at the party at the condominium belonging to the parents of a club girl Rebecca (Isla Fisher), he and Syd install themselves in the bathroom, where they snort line after line while guzzling tequila and discussing philosophical matters regarding love, sex, and emotional pain. For example, Syd was never able to tell London that he loved her, while Bateman is impotent.

The private party-within-a-party is soon joined by Maya (Kelli Garner) and Mallory (Joy Bryant), who use their cocaine and feign sympathy with Syd and Bateman. When Syd learns that London has arrived, he talks on and on until Bateman challenges him to go out and talk to her.

After a heated confrontation in the middle of the party, Syd and London decide to leave to talk somewhere more private. As they are leaving, a fight ensues in which Syd and Bateman fight the other male guests, and they barely make it out of the party. After a little while they make up in Syd's car and have sex later in London's apartment. In the last scene, at the airport, Syd says "I love you". Although this impresses London deeply, she still leaves him.

Cast

- Jessica Biel as London
- Chris Evans as Syd
- Jason Statham as Bateman
- Joy Bryant as Mallory
- Kelli Garner as Maya
- Isla Fisher as Rebecca
- Dane Cook as George

Soundtrack

London Original Movie Soundtrack	

Soundtrack album by The Crystal Method	
Released	February 24, 2006

Genre	Big beat	
Label	Reincarnate Music	
Producer	The Crystal Method	
The Crystal Method chronology		
Community Service II (2005)	***London Movie Soundtrack*** (2006)	*Drive: Nike + Original Run* (2006)

London is the soundtrack to the film of the same name by The Crystal Method.

Track listing

All songs written and performed by The Crystal Method except where noted.

1. "London"
2. "Restless" by Evil Nine featuring Toastie Taylor
3. "Smoked" (Vocals by Troy Bonnes)
4. "Fire to Me" (vs. Hyper)
5. "Roboslut"
6. "Defective"
7. "Vice"
8. "Crime" by Troy Bonnes
9. "C'mon Children" by The Out Crowd
10. "Onesixteen"
11. "Sucker Punch" by Connie Price and the Keystones
12. "Glass Breaker" (Vocals by Charlotte Martin)
13. "I Luv U"
14. "Nothing Like You and I" by The Perishers

- Track 4 is merely an instrumental edit of "Set Fire To Me" by Hyper.

External links

- *London* [1] at the Internet Movie Database
- *London* [2] at Rotten Tomatoes
- Review [3] by Roger Ebert at the *Chicago Sun-Times*

References

[1] http://www.imdb.com/title/tt0449061/
[2] http://www.rottentomatoes.com/m/1157247/
[3] http://rogerebert.suntimes.com/apps/pbcs.dll/article?AID=/20060209/REVIEWS/602090304/1023

TMNT (*film*)

TMNT	
Poster of *TMNT*	
Directed by	Kevin Munroe
Produced by	Kyle Clark Thomas K. Gray Galen Walker Steve Lumley Paul Wang
Written by	Kevin Munroe
Based on	*Teenage Mutant Ninja Turtles* by Kevin Eastman Peter Laird
Narrated by	Laurence Fishburne
Starring	Chris Evans Sarah Michelle Gellar Mako Kevin Smith Patrick Stewart Zhang Ziyi Mitchell Whitfield James Arnold Taylor Mikey Kelley Nolan North
Music by	Klaus Badelt
Cinematography	Steve Lumley
Editing by	John Damien Ryan
Distributed by	The Weinstein Company Warner Bros. Pictures
Release date(s)	March 23, 2007
Running time	87 minutes
Country	Hong Kong United States
Language	English
Budget	$34 million[1] [2]

Box office	$95,608,995

TMNT (also known as ***Teenage Mutant Ninja Turtles*** or ***Teenage Mutant Ninja Turtles 4***) is a 2007 film based on the Teenage Mutant Ninja Turtles franchise. This is the fourth and final installment in the original film series. The film sees the Turtles grow apart after their defeat of The Shredder. Meanwhile, strange things are happening in New York City. An army of ancient creatures threatens to take over the world and the Turtles must unite again to save it.

It is the first *Teenage Mutant Ninja Turtles* film made with Computer-Generated Imagery (CGI) by Imagi Animation Studios. The previous films in the series were all live-action. It is the first film in the franchise in 14 years. Chronologically, the film takes place after the original films.[3] [4] *Teenage Mutant Ninja Turtles* was released on March 23, 2007, in a number of Eastern European and Asian countries,[5] on March 23, 2007, in the United Kingdom, Canada, and the United States, and April 5, 2007, in Australia as well as subsequently in numerous other countries. It was the #1 film in the U.S. on its opening weekend, bringing in $25.45 million. It made its television debut on Cartoon Network on November 1, 2009.

The film features the four Turtles (Leonardo, Donatello, Raphael, and Michelangelo) as well as Casey Jones and April O'Neil. The main villains are Max Winters, the Stone Generals, Karai, and the Foot Clan. Voices are provided by Chris Evans, Sarah Michelle Gellar, Patrick Stewart, Zhang Ziyi, and Laurence Fishburne, who provides narration. It is also the last film starring Mako.

Plot

The film opens 3,000 years before the 21st century, during which time a powerful warlord named Yaotl and his four generals discover a portal opening into a parallel universe which is said to have a great power. Upon opening the portal, the warlord is exposed to this power and made immortal, but his four generals are turned to stone. The portal also releases 13 immortal monsters that destroy Yaotl's army, as well as his enemies. Afterwards, the monsters escape into the world, and Yaotl is left alone on the battlefield with his stone generals.

The film then cuts to the twenty first century. The Teenage Mutant Ninja Turtles have grown apart. After the defeat and demise of the Shredder, Master Splinter has sent Leonardo away to Central America for training. The rest of the Turtles have settled into lives in New York:

- Donatello works as an IT specialist and has become the de facto leader.
- Michelangelo works as a birthday party entertainer called "Cowabunga Carl".
- Raphael continues fighting crime at night while disguised as the vigilante "Nightwatcher".

April O'Neil, seemingly expanded from her antique store "2nd Time Around", now operates a company that locates rare relics and acquires them for collectors with the help of her boyfriend Casey Jones.

While on a business trip in Central America, April meets Leonardo, whom she advises to return to New York, but he is hesitant to do so out of fear that he has not completed his training. April then tells him how the other Turtles have drifted apart, then leaves Leo to ponder his next move. April returns to New York with a stone statue for her client Max Winters, the wealthy CEO of a financial empire. Leo stows away on board a plane and returns shortly afterwards. April and Casey deliver the statue to Winters at his corporate office, after they leave, Winters is then visited by Karai and the Foot Clan, whom he hires to scour the city searching for the 13 beasts, who will be drawn to New York before the reopening of the portal, scheduled to happen in days. Later, as Nightwatcher, Raph encounters Casey, who reveals his knowledge of Raph's double identity and joins him in hunting criminals (while arguing over who is the sidekick). Meanwhile, Winters reanimates his generals with advanced technology, but they remain stone.

Leo returns home to the sewer of the Turtles, where he faces Splinter. Splinter, desiring him to reunite his brothers as a family, forbids the Turtles from fighting until they can act as a team again. While training, the Turtles encounter one of the thirteen beasts battling with the Foot Clan. Seeing the Foot losing the battle, the Turtles defy Leo and Splinter's orders and engage the beast as well. The beast easily defeats the Turtles, but before it can kill them the four

Stone Generals arrive and capture the beast, spiriting it away in a disguised garbage truck. The next morning, Leo and Raph quarrel, and Splinter berates the Turtles for disobeying him after finding out about the damage they caused. Raphael leaves, clearly upset. He goes to April's apartment to get Casey. As he is about to explain what's going on to Casey, they encounter one of the monsters, and witness its capture by the Foot and the Stone Generals. The Generals spot them, and Raph is hit by a dart fired by a Foot ninja. They are pursued by one of the generals until a police helicopter chases the general off. Casey takes the unconscious Raph to the apartment, while April calls the Turtles for help. While examining Raph, they learn the identities of Winters and his Generals from April. After being revived, Raph suggests they pursue Winters. Leo denies him, saying they won't go anywhere until they get Splinter's blessing. Leo refuses to argue about Splinter's orders, so Raph quits the team. He goes out alone to investigate as the Nightwatcher.

Leo, Donny, and Mikey return to their sewer home to plan their next move, where Donny discovers the reopening of the portal will be directly over Winters' Tower. Splinter calls Leo aside and tells him that his team is not complete, and that he knows what he must do. Meanwhile, 11 monsters have been captured, and General Aguila questions Winters' actions. Believing that their leader is planning to betray them, the Generals conspire to betray Winters, wanting to remain immortal. Meanwhile, Raphael encounters one of the remaining monsters in a diner, but manages to drive it off. Leo finds the Nightwatcher at the diner, and chases him across the rooftops. He corners him, and the two engage in a fight. Leo gains the upper hand, knocking Nightwatcher's helmet off while delivering an uppercut to his face, revealing Raph. Raphael, being resentful of Leo's self-righteous authority and feeling like his brother abandoned him when he left, duels with his brother. Raph ultimately wins when he breaks Leo's swords with his sai. Raph, horrified by his own rage towards his brother, flees the scene. The Stone Generals then seize Leo, intending to substitute him for the thirteenth missing beast. Raph turns around in an attempt to save his brother, but is too late.

Raph returns to Master Splinter and reveals the fight, deciding to make amends by rescuing Leo. Thereafter Splinter and the Turtles, accompanied by Casey and April, travel to Winters' Tower. As the portal opens, Winters discovers the treachery of his generals and begs them to help him repair the damage he caused 3000 years ago, but they refuse. The Turtles, along with April, Casey, and Splinter, manage to get inside the tower. Winters is knocked out by his generals, but he quickly regains consciousness. He then reveals the truth to the heroes: he wants to return all 13 monsters to the portal so that he will be free of his curse of immortality. The Generals then reveal that they wish to preserve their immortality, but also to use the portal to bring in more monsters to finalize their conquest around the world. Having refused to betray Winters in exchange for immortality, April, Casey, and the Foot Clan decided to work together and search for the final monster while the Turtles fight off the Generals. As for Splinter and Winters, they fight off numerous other monsters emerging from the now open portal. After a long battle and a death-defying search, April, Casey, and Karai crash into the tower, with the thirteenth monster right behind them. The monster crashes into the Stone Generals, pushing them into the portal with it. The generals turn human again, screaming as they all disintegrate in the portal. The portal closes, and the heroes cheer in victory (while April and Casey kiss).

Karai warns them to enjoy their victory while it lasts, on grounds that they will soon contend with a familiar foe (implying the Shredder's return and a future sequel). She and the rest of the Foot Clan then depart. Winters, now mortal again, honors the Turtles and Splinter, thanks them for the fulfillment of his wish, and disintegrates away before their eyes to a peaceful afterlife. Later, Splinter proudly places Winter's helmet among his trophy collection, as well as Raphael's "Nightwatcher" helmet and Michelangelo's turtle costume. The collection also includes items from the previous films, including Shredder's helmet, the broken canister of the mutagenic "ooze" which gave the Turtles and Splinter their present forms, and the Time Scepter. An epilogue narrated by Raph's voice then shows the Turtles unitedly patrolling New York City, and concludes the film with the much-repeated catchphrase *"I love being a turtle!"*

Cast

- Chris Evans as Casey Jones
- Sarah Michelle Gellar as April O'Neil
- Mako as Master Splinter (see below)
- Patrick Stewart as Max Winters
- Zhang Ziyi as Karai
- James Arnold Taylor as Leonardo
- Mitchell Whitfield as Donatello
- Mikey Kelley as Michelangelo
- Nolan North as Raphael / Nightwatcher
- John DiMaggio as Colonel Santino
- Paula Mattioli as General Serpiente
- Kevin Michael Richardson as General Aguila
- Fred Tatasciore as General Gato
- Frank Welker as General Mono
- Kevin Smith as Diner Cook
- Laurence Fishburne as Narrator

Actor Greg Baldwin is credited only for providing "additional voices", but he also performed a substantial portion of Splinter's dialogue, despite Mako Iwamatsu being the only actor credited for that role. Baldwin had already mimicked Iwamatsu's voice when he took up the late actor's role as "Iroh" in the concurrently-produced cartoon *Avatar: The Last Airbender*, and used this precedent to successfully lobby to join the cast of *TMNT* as Splinter following Iwamatsu's death. [6] Other additional voices were provided by Dee Bradley Baker, Jeff Bennett, Jim Cummings, Grey DeLisle, Crispin Freeman, Chris Edgerly, Kim Mai Guest, Jennifer Hale, Jess Harnell, Phil LaMarr, Paul Michael Robinson, Tara Strong, and Billy West.

Production

The first of three films released in the TMNT franchise by New Line Cinema in the early 1990s was *Teenage Mutant Ninja Turtles*. Subsequently, *Teenage Mutant Ninja Turtles II: The Secret of the Ooze* was released in 1991, and finally *Teenage Mutant Ninja Turtles III* in 1993. A CGI *TMNT* movie was first announced in 2000, with John Woo supposedly at the helm. That movie languished in development hell, and Woo ultimately moved on to other projects.[7] *TMNT*, executive produced by Peter Laird, Gary Richardson, and Frederick U. Fierst, departs from the previous films' live action style, and is the first TMNT film to be CGI. Writer/Director Kevin Munroe, who had previously worked with video games, comics, and television animation said that he wanted to do total CGI instead of live action and CGI turtles because it would be easier for the audience to "suspend disbelief for such an offbeat story" as there would be no break in the reality between CGI and live action.[8] Producer Tom Gray explained that the decision to depart from the live action franchise was due to escalating budgets for the three films, and with each film making less than its predecessor, a CGI film became a reality.[9] For example the first film made $135.2 million on a budget of $13.5 million, and the third made $44 million on a budget of $21 million.[9] Golden Harvest's rights expired, and Gray, at an animation company, said the question arose there over a CGI TMNT film in 2004.[9]

Munroe stated in terms of the story line that ideas were floated as extreme as the Turtles being in space, but eventually it just came back to New York City, and the theme of the family that had fallen apart.[9] When developing the screenplay, Munroe wanted to take on a less lighthearted tone or "less Cowabunga" and place an emphasis on dark elements as shown in the original comics to appeal to the mature audience. "I had a very specific tone because mixing that sort of action and comedy is a very specific thing. Most people were just coming and wanting to make it too funny. I think that version of the movie could do really well, but we wanted to do something where it sort of pushes the envelope a little bit more and says that animation is more than just comedic animals bumping into each other and farting!"[10] Munroe said that in design and in the rendering of the animation, he was after the feel of a comic book.[9]

Development and pre-production for *TMNT* began in June 2005 [11] at Imagi's Los Angeles facility and then the state-of-the-art CG animation were produced in Hong Kong, followed by post-production in Hollywood.[11] In designing the New York backdrop, art director/concept artist Simon Murton stylized the familiar Manhattan skyline and urban landscapes to make them appear uniquely "TMNT." "We began with cinematic cues from certain black-and-white films from the 1940s and '50s," notes Murton. "I really wanted to push the lighting and the environments to create the look and feel of an alternate reality."[12] The animators that worked on the fight sequences were inspired by Hong Kong action films. Animation director Kim Ooi explains since it was in CG, they were able to "push and stylize beyond the limits of live action."[12] Imagi used Maya with Pixar's RenderMan for the production pipeline's back-end.[1]

The cast is new compared to the older films. Jim Cummings and Frank Welker (who voiced Tokka and Rahzar in *Teenage Mutant Ninja Turtles II: The Secret of the Ooze*) are the only past TMNT actors to appear in this film. Cummings has previously contributed voice-work in the 1987 *Teenage Mutant Ninja Turtles* series. *TMNT* was Mako Iwamatsu's last film prior to his death. Mako was announced as the voice of Splinter at the San Diego Comic-Con on July 20, 2006. He then died the next day.[13] A dedication to Mako appears at the end of the film's credits.[14] This is the second TMNT film to include a dedication, the other being *Teenage Mutant Ninja Turtles II: The Secret of the Ooze*, which was dedicated to Jim Henson.

Promotion

The first teaser-poster featured the logo of the 2003 TV series, which was eventually abandoned and then recovered in 2004. In addition to the main poster, there were several others including individual ones for each turtle.

At the 2006 Comic-Con, the TMNT panel screened an exclusive preview that contained a Splinter voice-over with shots of monsters, jungles, foot ninjas, facial tests, concept designs, muscle tests, dynamic fight tests, and some comedic scenes.[15] Also, a sneak peek booklet containing storyboards, environment designs, and character designs by comic artist Jeff Matsuda was distributed.

The teaser-trailer was released in July 2006 and was attached to *Pirates of the Caribbean: Dead Man's Chest*. It starts out with the camera moving above the buildings on a dark night. When it finally stops moving, the Turtles open their eyes and all that can be seen is the whites of their eyes against the dark background. Then, the Turtles start maneuvering across the tops of the buildings, finally jumping down and landing in a dark alleyway. As each one lands, they perform kata with their respective weapon. After Leonardo finishes with his kata, Michelangelo can be seen falling into a dumpster. As Donatello opens the dumpster, Michelangelo says "I'm okay." A police siren is heard and then the car pulls up. The officer shines his light down the alley, but the Turtles have already disappeared. The camera pans down the alley to show a manhole cover being slid back into place, with the name "TMNT" on it. The movie's full trailer was attached on December 15 to the films *Eragon* and *Unaccompanied Minors*. It is currently available on Apple Trailers, MTV.com, and Yahoo! Movies. It also debuted on the G4 show Attack of the Show!.

On February 26, two television spots debuted and began airing. Later, two more TV spots, geared specifically toward the young children demographic aired on 4Kids TV, the channel that broadcast the Teenage Mutant Ninja Turtles (2003 TV series).

In February 2007, Warner Bros. began an online campaign by creating a MySpace page for each of the Turtles . Within a week before the release date, several clips were unveiled through various websites.

The McDonald's fast-food chain promoted TMNT, having eight toys to collect with the purchase of a Happy Meal. There is a novelization based on the film.

The film was originally set for release domestically (USA and Canada) on March 30, 2007, which would have been the seventeenth anniversary of the release of the first film. The March 30 date was advertised in the teaser trailer and early posters, but the release was moved up to March 23, 2007.

Video game

- *TMNT* is the video game version of the 2007 CGI movie. It was released three days before the actual movie's release.[16] Ubisoft secured the rights and released the games on March 20. Ubisoft won the rights from Konami, who had produced all the previous games.[17] The game is available for PlayStation 2, PSP, PC, Game Boy Advance, Nintendo DS, GameCube, Wii, and Xbox 360 game systems. Reviews for the games ranged from horrible to mediocre to exemplary, due to the vastly different games produced. The home console games were identical, and given bad to mediocre ratings; the PSP and Nintendo DS games were identical to each other but not the home console versions, and were given abysmal ratings; and the Game Boy Advance version was entirely separate, but received good ratings in contrast to the other versions. It was lauded for its excellent use of the side-scrolling beat-'em-up style, which evoked nostalgia for older games in the series such as Teenage Mutant Ninja Turtles: Turtles in Time. There is no multi-player mode in the GBA version. "The *TMNT* movie is all about the emotions associated with family and teenage angst," said Nick Harper, the game's creative director. "We've taken that philosophy and turned it into gameplay mechanics that will be fun and challenging.[18] The game features collaborative team-ups between the Turtles. The game also features single-player campaigns for the brothers.
- *TMNT: Power Of Four* is the mobile game version of the 2007 CGI movie. It is produced by uclick and developed by Overloaded.

Reception

Critical response

TMNT received generally mixed reviews from film critics. SuperHeroHype.com posted a review for *TMNT* with an overall score of 7/10, stating the film had a good balance of dark aspects and kid friendliness. IGN.com also gave it 7/10, calling it "by far, the best Teenage Mutant Ninja Turtles movie yet." The film received an 8/10 from reviewers on JoBlo.com, CHUD, and Moviesonline. Despite minor problems with the overall design of the human characters, they praise the film for its unique animation style and top notch voice acting. Comic and animation related websites like Newsarama, Comic Book Resources, and Toon Zone were also favorable in their reviews. As of August 31, 2011, review aggregator Rotten Tomatoes gave the film a score of 33% based on 116 reviews.[19] Critics generally pointed to lack of originality as the film's main flaw. Richard Roeper expressed this in his review, saying, "I guess if you read the comic strip and you played the video games and you watched the TV show and dug the earlier movies, you'll dig this new version. For me, I didn't do any of that stuff."

Box office

TMNT ranked number one at the box office on its opening weekend, beating out *300* (the top film of the previous two weeks), *The Last Mimzy*, *Shooter*, *Pride*, *The Hills Have Eyes 2*, and *Reign Over Me*. Weekend estimates showed that the film made $25.45 million over the weekend of March 23-25, 2007. The film grossed over $95 million worldwide during its 91 day run in theaters.[5]

Awards

In 2008, it has been nominated for the Annie Award and Sean Song for the Best Storyboarding in an Animated Feature Production

Home media

TMNT was released on August 7, 2007, for DVD, HD DVD, and Blu-ray Disc.[20]

The DVD contains the following bonus features:[21]

- Commentary by Writer/Director Kevin Munroe
- Alternate Opening and Alternate Ending
- Deleted Scene
- Side-by-Side Comparison of Storyboard and CG
- Interviews with Voice Talent

In 2009, a quadrilogy with all four TMNT films was released to celebrate the 25th anniversary. It is also available on Blu-ray.

References

[1] Joe Strike (2007-03-23). "TMNT: The Turtles More Animated in CG" (http://mag.awn.com/index.php?ltype=pageone&article_no=3219&page=1). Animation World Network. . Retrieved 2007-03-23.

[2] Martin A. Grove (2007-03-31). "$35 million budget puts TMNT on road to profits" (http://www.hollywoodreporter.com/hr/content_display/features/columns/e3ic8a667db1a35f3a0a110d1408938c54d). Hollywood Reporter. . Retrieved 2007-03-31.

[3] Film review: TMNT - Review - Culture Shock - www.atomicmpc.com.au (http://www.atomicmpc.com.au/article.asp?CIID=77939)

[4] TMNT (2007) : HollywoodJesus.com : Movie Reviews, Trailers and Spiritual Commentary (http://www.hollywoodjesus.com/movieDetail.cfm/i/01ED9AEF-BCE5-0E4B-A1B8B8D212CE9488/ia/93EA18F1-0982-C5FF-622FCA5E04DD8206)

[5] "TMNT (2007)" (http://www.boxofficemojo.com/movies/?id=tmntcg.htm). *Box Office Mojo*. Amazon.com. .

[6] Baldwin implicitly confirms his role as Splinter while answering fans' questions at an Avatar forum (http://distanthorizons.proboards.com/index.cgi?action=display&board=avgeneral&thread=8419&page=5#306993)

[7] Brian Linder (2001-06-30). "Teenage Mutant Ninja Turtles: The Real Deal" (http://movies.ign.com/articles/301/301029p1.html). *IGN*. News Corporation. . Retrieved 2007-03-11.

[8] Anthony Breznican (2006-12-20). "Slow to return, teen Turtles are back!" (http://www.usatoday.com/life/movies/news/2006-12-20-ninja-turtles-cover_x.htm). USA Today. . Retrieved 2007-03-21.

[9] Heather Newgen (2007-01-25). "TMNT Studio Visit!" (http://www.superherohype.com/news/tmntnews.php?id=5133). Super Hero Hype. . Retrieved 2007-03-21.

[10] Martin A. Grove (2007-03-20). "Turtles live again in CGI spinoff TMNT" (http://web.archive.org/web/20070326164821/http://www.hollywoodreporter.com/hr/content_display/features/columns/e3i1e1961ef9c286a58c4bf6b958b5f3880). Hollywood Reporter. Archived from the original (http://www.hollywoodreporter.com/hr/content_display/features/columns/e3i1e1961ef9c286a58c4bf6b958b5f3880) on 2007-03-26. . Retrieved 2007-03-25.

[11] "Imagi Media Kit" (http://imagi.com.hk/corporate/pdf/MediaKit.pdf) (PDF). Imagi.com.hk. . Retrieved 2007-03-21.

[12] "TMNT Production Notes" (http://media.movieweb.com/galleries/3042/notes.pdf) (PDF). MovieWeb. . Retrieved 2007-03-17.

[13] "More Sign Up for "Ninja Turtles"" (http://www.worstpreviews.com/headline.php?id=1853). WorstPreviews. 2006-12-22. . Retrieved 2006-12-30.

[14] Anne Neumann (2007-03-06). "Kevin Munroe on TMNT" (http://www.superherohype.com/news/topnews.php?id=5296). Super Hero Hype. . Retrieved 2007-03-21.

[15] Omar Aviles (2006-07-25). "CON: WB Animation" (http://www.joblo.com/index.php?id=12201). Joblo. . Retrieved 2007-03-24.

[16] Li C. Kuo (2006-12-20). "First Details on *Teenage Mutant Ninja Turtles*" (http://gba.gamespy.com/gameboy-advance/teenage-mutant-ninja-turtles-2007/751917p1.html). GameSpy. . Retrieved 2006-12-29.

[17] Brendan Sinclair (2007-01-11). "Ubisoft gets turtle power" (http://www.gamespot.com/news/6142209.html). GameSpot. . Retrieved 2007-01-11.

[18] Brendan Sinclair (2006-12-26). "Ubisoft's Ninja Turtles emerge from the shadows" (http://www.gamespot.com/news/6163457.html?part=rss&tag=gs_news&subj=6163457). GameSpot. . Retrieved 2006-12-29.

[19] "TMNT - Movie Reviews" (http://www.rottentomatoes.com/m/tmnt_2007/). *Rotten Tomatoes*. Flixster. . Retrieved August 31, 2011.

[20] http://www.thedigitalbits.com/#mytwocents

[21] DVD Empire - Item - TMNT / DVD-Video (http://www.dvdempire.com/Exec/v4_item.asp?userid=99365754955882&item_id=1334065&tab=5&back=1&anchor=1#topoftabs)

External links

- Official website (http://tmnt.warnerbros.com/) from Warner Bros.
- Official website (http://www.ninjaturtles.com/) from Mirage Studios
- *TMNT* (http://www.imdb.com/title/tt0453556/) at the Internet Movie Database
- *TMNT* (http://www.boxofficemojo.com/movies/?id=tmntcg.htm) at Box Office Mojo
- *TMNT* (http://www.allrovi.com/movies/movie/v334940) at AllRovi
- *TMNT* (http://www.rottentomatoes.com/m/teenage_mutant_ninja_turtles/) at Rotten Tomatoes
- Director Kevin Munroe on *TMNT* (http://animated-views.com/2007/director-kevin-munroe-on-tmnt/) Animated News & Views interview
- TMNT Review (http://www.variety.com/review/VE1117933101.html) on *Variety.com*

Sunshine (2007 film)

Sunshine	
Theatrical poster	
Directed by	Danny Boyle
Produced by	Andrew Macdonald
Written by	Alex Garland
Starring	Cillian Murphy Chris Evans Rose Byrne Michelle Yeoh Cliff Curtis Troy Garity Hiroyuki Sanada Benedict Wong Chipo Chung Mark Strong
Music by	John Murphy Underworld
Cinematography	Alwin H. Kuchler
Editing by	Chris Gill
Distributed by	Fox Searchlight Pictures
Release date(s)	6 April 2007
Running time	107 minutes
Country	United Kingdom
Language	English
Budget	GB£20 million[1] / US$40 million[2]
Box office	US$32,017,803

Sunshine is a 2007 British science fiction film directed by Danny Boyle and written by Alex Garland about the crew of a spacecraft on a dangerous mission to the Sun. In 2057, with the Earth in peril from the dying Sun, the crew is sent to reignite the Sun with a massive stellar bomb with the mass equivalent to Manhattan Island. The crew is made up of an ensemble cast consisting of Cillian Murphy, Chris Evans, Rose Byrne, Michelle Yeoh, Cliff Curtis, Troy Garity, Hiroyuki Sanada, Benedict Wong, Chipo Chung, and Mark Strong.

The script was based on a scientific back-story that took the characters on a psychological journey. The director cast a group of international actors for the film, and had the actors live together and learn about topics related to their roles, as a form of method acting. To have the actors realistically react to visual effects that would be implemented in post-production, the filmmakers constructed live sets to serve as cues.

Previous science fiction films that Boyle cited as influences included Kubrick's 1968 film *2001: A Space Odyssey*, the 1972 Tarkovsky's *Solaris*, and the 1979 science-fiction horror film *Alien*. *Sunshine* was released in the United Kingdom on 6 April 2007 and in the United States on 20 July 2007. The film took £3.2 million in the UK over twelve weeks, and in the USA it was placed no. 13 in the box office on the first weekend of its wide release. With a budget of US$40 million,[2] it ultimately grossed almost US$32 million worldwide.[3]

Plot

In 2057, the failure of the Earth's Sun threatens life on the planet, compelling humanity to send a spacecraft that carries a stellar bomb payload intended to re-ignite it. The first spacecraft with the payload, the *Icarus I*, was lost seven years previously for reasons unknown, having failed in its mission. A second spacecraft with a new payload, the *Icarus II*, is sent to the Sun in a final attempt, as the Earth has been exhausted of the materials necessary to make the payload.

The design of the *Icarus* spacecraft, displayed in the opening shots of the movie, incorporates a massive heat shield made of many small positionable mirrors in an umbrella shape at the front of the vessel. This shield protects the relatively fragile main hull of the *Icarus* craft from the intense radiation and superheated particles of the solar wind, which at such close proximity to the Sun can dissolve most materials near-instantaneously. The stellar bomb is located just behind the heat shield, with the remainder of the ship, including the engines, living quarters, oxygen garden, computer core, and other structure behind a second, smaller heat shield. This second shield will be used as both protection and a solar sail during the return trip, after the payload is deployed into the Sun taking the larger shield with it.

As the movie opens, the *Icarus II* is passing into the "dead zone", beyond which the radio communications of the crew back to Earth are lost in the solar wind. Mission Physicist Capa records a last-minute message to send back to his parents on Earth, while psychiatrist Searle views the Sun's filtered light on the ship's solar observation deck, pushing the limits of the computer's safety protocols to view as much light as is allowed.

When the *Icarus II* passes Mercury on its way to the Sun, communications officer Harvey discovers the distress beacon of *Icarus I*. Capa is asked by Captain Kaneda to decide whether to change course and approach *Icarus I*. Capa runs a simulation of the bomb's deployment and detonation, which like all previous runs is inconclusive due to the unpredictable variables inherent in the physics inside a gravity well. After a risk assessment, Capa decides to rendezvous with the stricken vessel in order to acquire its payload, hopefully doubling their chances of success.

In planning the new course, navigator Trey forgets to realign the heat shield to match the new trajectory, which results in damage to some of the mirrors on the heat shield, putting the spacecraft and mission at risk. Kaneda and Capa embark on a spacewalk to make repairs while the ship is angled to shelter the damaged portion of the shield, but an unintended automatic override by the ship's computer puts the two men at risk of fatal solar exposure. Capa escapes to shelter behind the shield while Kaneda completes the vital repairs. Unable to reach safety before the shields are completely exposed to full sunlight, he turns back and stares at the Sun as the solar wind consumes him. The incident that caused the override turns out to be a fire in the ship's oxygen garden, started by sunlight reflected from an exposed part of the ship. The fire both totally destroys the garden and dangerously depletes the oxygen levels, making a return trip impossible. Trey blames himself for the losses due to his neglect, and Searle sedates him, assessing him as a suicide risk.

The *Icarus II* makes rendezvous with the *Icarus I*, and the lost spacecraft is explored by four men of the crew: Harvey, Capa, Searle, and engineer Mace. While the *Icarus I* has a functional oxygen garden, the ship's operational computer is found to be sabotaged, rendering delivery of the payload impossible. Mace finds a video left behind by Captain Pinbacker, an extremely religious man, who states the mission was purposely abandoned, thinking it was the "will of God" that humanity should die. The crew of *Icarus I* is found dead in the solar observation room, having been exposed to unshielded rays of sunlight. During the group's exploration, the airlocks inexplicably decouple, damaging the *Icarus I*'s airlock and stranding the crew members on the derelict spacecraft. In a risky move, Searle stays behind to jettison the three men using the coordinated vacuuming of the airlock to propel them to the airlock of the *Icarus II*. Harvey is knocked into space and quickly freezes to death in the near-absolute-zero temperatures of space, while Searle, trapped on the *Icarus I*, submits himself to the same fate as the original crew in the observation room, exposing himself to the full light of the Sun.

Five remain on the *Icarus II*: Capa, Mace, Trey, Cassie, and Corazon. The survivors check the *Icarus* activity file and discover that someone must have manually decoupled the airlock as there was no hardware failure. While Trey — now the prime suspect for sabotaging the airlock — is elsewhere, the four other crew members discuss that the remaining oxygen reserves would only allow them to reach the Sun to deliver the payload if there were only four people. Everyone except Cassie decides Trey must be killed, but when they go to Trey, they find he has apparently committed suicide.[A] During a final inspection some nineteen hours before the delivery point, Capa discovers with surprise from the spacecraft's computer that even without Trey the reserves will not last long enough to deploy, because of an unaccounted-for fifth person on the spacecraft. He discovers that Pinbacker is still alive and has made his way into the *Icarus II* observation room. He is the one that decoupled the *Icarus II* from the *Icarus I*. He is very badly burned because of repeated exposures to the Sun. He slashes Capa with a scalpel and seals him in an airlock.

Pinbacker attempts to sabotage the spacecraft so that it will not complete its mission, removing the Icarus mainframe computer stack from its sub-zero coolant bath, and attacking the other crew members, killing Corazon in the oxygen garden. Mace attempts to undo Pinbacker's sabotage, but is trapped in the coolant reservoir and freezes to death there. Capa, trapped in the airlock, manages to blow the airlock door off, completely decompressing most of *Icarus II*. He makes his way to the computer core and manually uncouples the bomb from the rest of the spacecraft. Capa then travels to the airlock and jumps the distance to the payload, reaching it just as the boosters ignite. This sends the bomb out of solar orbit and into the Sun's corona, which burns up the remains of *Icarus II* as Capa enters the payload's airlock. He finds Cassie in the payload section, having been pursued there by Pinbacker. Pinbacker attempts to drop Capa off a precipice within the bomb, but Cassie grabs on to Capa, their combined weight peels the skin off Pinbacker's arm and they fall, then the changing gravitational pull of the Sun arrests their fall down the cliff. Capa triggers the bomb in time to re-ignite the Sun. With the sparks of the stellar bomb multiplying, Capa watches the inner surface of the Sun burst through one wall of the payload capsule, as space and time break down, owing to the Sun's immense gravity field. He reaches out and touches it, smiling blissfully.

On Earth, Capa's sister reviews her brother's last message on video while her children build snowmen. Suddenly, the sky brightens, an indication of the mission's success. The final scene reveals that they were building snowmen on the frozen harbour near the Sydney Opera House.

Cast

- Cillian Murphy as Robert Capa:

  The physicist who operates the massive star-bomb device. Murphy described the character of Capa as a silent outsider, which was due to the fact that only Capa understood the operation and true scale of the star bomb.[4] Murphy worked with physicist Brian Cox to learn about advanced physics,[5] touring the CERN facility and learning to copy physicists' mannerisms.[6] The actor also studied the thriller *The Wages of Fear* (1953) with Boyle to gain an understanding of the type of suspense that Boyle wanted to create in the film.[7] Murphy claims that his involvement in the film caused him to change his views on religion from agnosticism to atheism.[6] [8]

- Chris Evans as Mace:

  The engineer. Evans described his character Mace as one with a military family and background. Mace has a dry and morally uncomplicated personality. Said Evans, "[He] has a very level head which enables him to operate fairly coherently under pressure-filled situations."[9]

- Rose Byrne as Cassie:

  The space vessel's pilot. Byrne was chosen by the director for her role in *Troy* (2004).[10] Byrne described Cassie as the most emotional member of the crew, "[wearing] her heart on her sleeve". Byrne considered Cassie's role among the crew was to possess an even temperament which helps her last the journey.[9]

- Michelle Yeoh as Corazon:

  The biologist who takes care of the ship's "oxygen garden". Boyle cast Yeoh based on her performance in *Tomorrow Never Dies* (1997),[9] and *Memoirs of a Geisha* (2005).[11] Yeoh described her character as more spiritual, explaining Corazon's background, as an "Asian influence or that she's always constantly surrounded by organic things – she's very grounded and more down-to-earth."[12]

- Cliff Curtis as Searle:

  The ship's doctor and psychological officer. He is obsessed with the Sun and how it looks like when staring at it without any type of protection. The role of Searle was originally written to be a "slightly stiff" British character.[9] Curtis was drawn to the role based on the script and also expressed interest in working with the director.[13] Boyle was familiar with Curtis from *Training Day* (2001) and *Whale Rider* (2002),[14] and Curtis's audition appealed to Boyle strongly enough to cast the actor as Searle.[9] Curtis initially foresaw an esoteric approach for his character, but he later pursued a military and scientific approach based on the seriousness of the mission. The actor also compared Searle to the character of Pinbacker, noting their similarities and differences: "[Searle] would sacrifice those beliefs and views, his life, for the greater good, whereas Pinbacker, who's come to a place he believes is right, would sacrifice the world for his beliefs. They're two sides of the same coin."[13]

- Troy Garity as Harvey:

  The communications officer and second-in-command. He is also the only crew member to be homesick. Garity's previous work was unknown to Boyle, but the director was impressed enough with the actor upon meeting him that he cast Garity. Garity described the character of Harvey as the only crew member who misses his family back home on Earth and attempts to hide the fact.[9]

- Hiroyuki Sanada as Kaneda:

  The ship's captain. The script originally had an American captain, but scientists and space experts persuaded Boyle to change the nationality to Japanese.[15] Boyle saw Sanada in *The Twilight Samurai* (2002), and director Wong Kar-wai recommended the actor to Boyle when the latter sought someone to cast as the Asian captain of the ship.[16] Sanada's character was originally called Kanada, but he asked Boyle to change the name to Kaneda, a more natural Japanese name. The character was Sanada's second English-language role in cinema, and Sanada learned different forms of English, depending on the circumstances. Sanada's base English language had a British dialect, and when the actor recited official statements as Kaneda, the dialect was official English. In communicating with other characters as Kaneda, Sanada spoke with an American English accent to reflect the fictional situation of the character training with the rest at NASA.[15]

- Benedict Wong as Trey:

  The navigator. Boyle saw Wong in *Dirty Pretty Things* (2002). Wong's character, Trey, was a child prodigy who created a computer virus that brought down one-sixth of the world's computers. As a result, Trey is recruited into the space program so his genius could be applied more beneficially.[9]

- Chipo Chung as the voice of Icarus:

  The on-board computer of the spacecraft *Icarus II* possesses a "natural-language" communication interface, allowing the crew to ask questions, give orders, and receive status updates and warnings verbally, as if they were talking to a human. Indeed, the ship itself is a major character in the movie. This was Chung's first named film role.[17]

- Mark Strong as Pinbacker:

The insane captain of *Icarus I*, the first ship that was sent to reignite the Sun. Pinbacker was inspired by the character of Sergeant Pinback from *Dark Star*.[18] The character's disfiguring burns were influenced by the injuries suffered by F1 driver Niki Lauda.[19] Boyle described the character of Pinbacker as a representation of fundamentalism.[20] The director also described the potentially unrealistic presence of Pinbacker as an example of something that breaks the pattern of realism, similar to his scene in *Trainspotting* (1996) in which Ewan McGregor's character dives into a toilet.[21]

Production

In March 2005, following the completion of *Millions* (2004),[22] director Danny Boyle was briefly attached to direct *3000 Degrees*, a Warner Bros. project about the 1999 Worcester Cold Storage Warehouse fire in Massachusetts, but due to opposition from surviving victims and firefighters, the project did not enter production. At the same time, Boyle received a script from screenwriter Alex Garland, who had paired with Boyle for *The Beach* (2000) and *28 Days Later* (2002). Producer Andrew Macdonald, working with Boyle and Garland, pitched the script to 20th Century Fox, who were reluctant to finance the film based on its similarities to the 2002 remake *Solaris*, which performed dismally for the studio. The project was instead financed by Fox's specialized film unit Fox Searchlight Pictures. Since the preliminary budget at US$40 million was too demanding for Fox Searchlight, Macdonald sought outside financing from British lottery funds, U.K. rebates, and outside investor Ingenious Film Partners.[19] With financing in place, Boyle entered pre-production work for *Sunshine*, for which he planned to commence production by the following July.[22] Since Boyle had previously worked with Fox Searchlight on *28 Days Later*, the existing relationship permitted the director with freedom in production, working in a small studio.[23]

Boyle and Garland worked on the script for a year, spent a second year preparing for production, filmed for three months, and spent a third full year editing and completing visual effects for *Sunshine*.[14] After completion of filming for *Sunshine*, Boyle said that he would not revisit the science fiction genre, citing production as a spiritually exhausting experience.[18] The director said making the film had conquered his fear of the difficulty encountered in producing a science fiction film, and that he would move on from the genre.[24]

Writing

"What interested me was the idea that it could get to a point when the entire planet's survival rests on the shoulders of one man, and what that would do to his head."

Screenwriter Alex Garland[25]

Screenwriter Alex Garland was inspired to write *Sunshine* based on scientific ideas about the heat death of the universe,[26] specifically "an article projecting the future of mankind from a physics-based, atheist perspective," according to Garland.[18] The article was from an American scientific periodical, and Garland had wondered about what would result from the Sun's death.[25] Garland brought the script to director Danny Boyle, who enthusiastically took up the project due to his long-time desire to direct a science fiction film in space.[27] Boyle and Garland worked on the script for a year, creating 35 drafts in their experimenting.[16]

The director (Danny Boyle) also considered the story of *Sunshine* as a counterintuitive approach for the contemporary issue of global warming, with the death of the Sun being a threat.[27] Originally, *Sunshine* was scripted to begin with a voiceover talking about how parents tell their children not to look into the Sun, but once told, the children would be compelled to look. Boyle described the Sun as a godly personality in the film, creating a psychological dimension for the astronauts due to its scale and power.[28] The director also described the film's villain as based on light, explaining, "That's quite a challenge because the way you generate fear in cinema is darkness." The director also sought to have the characters experience a psychological journey in which each person is worn mentally, physically, and existentially and is experiencing doubt in their faiths.[29] To capture the dangers of the voyage that the crew members went through, the director cited Bill Bryson's *A Short History of Nearly Everything* as influential in "articulating the universe's power".[30]

The story was also written in part to reflect the brilliance and "necessary arrogance" of real-life science when the world's scientists are presented with the crisis that threatens Earth.[31] The time period of the story, 50 years in the future, was chosen to enable the level of technology to advance to the ability to travel to the Sun, but to simultaneously keep a feel of familiarity for the audience. Scientific advisers, futurists, and people who developed products for the future were consulted to shape an idea of the future.[27]

To shape the science of the film, Boyle and Garland hired scientist advisers, including NASA employees and astrophysicists.[31] One physicist, Brian Cox of University of Manchester, was hired to advise the cast and crew after the director had seen Cox on the science TV series *Horizon*.[32] The physicist gave regular lectures to the film's cast members about solar physics. Cox also advised the filmmakers to scale down the nuclear device in the film from the mass of the Moon to the size of Manhattan. In the film's backstory, a Q-Ball enters the Earth's Sun and begins to eat it away. According to Cox, the Sun would not be dense enough in real life to stop a Q-ball, but filmmakers took creative licence in writing the backstory.[26]

Boyle originally included romantic subplots,[33] including a sex scene planned between the characters Capa (Murphy) and Cassie (Byrne) in the ship's oxygen garden.[34] However, the director considered the attempt for relationships in space too "embarrassing" and excluded the subplots.[33] Boyle further distanced the characters from possible relationships by ensuring that the cast members wore little to no make-up to avoid any romantic overtures.[35] The director also avoided including humor in the script with the exception of a few gags, believing that humor was a difficult fit for the story.[21] "You get intensity of experience in space movies but not joy. So there's not much room for comedy or sex - everything is waiting to destroy you," explained Boyle.[36]

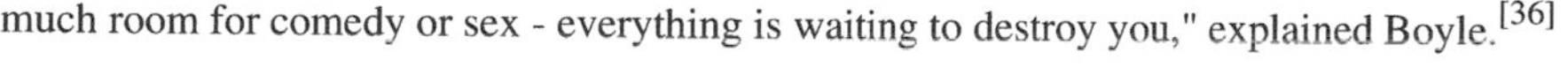

Casting

An ensemble cast of international actors was chosen for *Sunshine* to reflect both a democratic process and the international collaboration in saving the world

Director Danny Boyle chose to have an ensemble cast for *Sunshine* to encourage a more democratic process, similar to the ensemble cast in *Alien*. Boyle also chose to have the cast be international in order to reflect the mission's purpose "on behalf of all mankind".[31] The space crew in the film also consisted of American/Asian nationality because of the filmmakers' belief that the American and Chinese space programs would be the most developed and economically empowered 50 years in the future.[37] The director had also received advice that there would be advanced space programs with India and Brazil, but the advice was overlooked to avoid creating a cast that was too disparate.[38] According to producer Andrew Macdonald, the actors were required to speak with American accents to target the U.S. audience as much as international audiences due to the budget level of the project.[39]

To prepare the international actors for the film, Boyle had the cast undergo method acting.[35] At the beginning of the film, the characters had been together for sixteen months, so Boyle desired to capture a sense of togetherness among the actors by assigning them to live together. He also enrolled the cast members in space training and scuba diving, as well as watching films together,[27] such as *The Right Stuff* (1983) and the documentary *For All Mankind* (1989).[40] Boyle also took the cast on a tour of a nuclear submarine to comprehend claustrophobic living conditions. He also had the cast experience weightlessness in the zero G environment of an acrobatic plane.[27]

Cast members operated a Boeing 747 flight simulator and were introduced to futurologist Richard Seymour.[41] The book *Moondust* by Andrew Smith, a collection of accounts of the men who had walked on the moon, was required reading for cast members.[42] The book had been assigned by Boyle because it described the lasting psychological changes experienced by that particular group of astronauts. The director sought to manifest the effect by showing the Sun's awesome, radiant power influencing the psyches of the ship's crew.[43]

Filming

Filming for *Sunshine* took place at 3 Mills Studios in east London. An elaborate set was constructed, containing eight stages, 17 sets, and detailed models. The filmmakers employed three film units.[39] Filming began on 23 August 2005,[44] lasting for 15 weeks, with August and September being difficult months due to the heat and the cast's requirement to wear spacesuits for their roles.[6] Cinematographer Alwin H. Kuchler chose to film in anamorphic format to capture a physical sense of the light. "We shot certain sequences in a very dark environment, which you get used to, so when the Sun plays a role, we wanted the audience to have a physical reaction to it," Kuchler said.[45] Due to filming with the actors taking place on a stage, director Danny Boyle constructed live effects so the actors could realistically respond to computer-generated effects that were later implemented.[46]

To increase the feeling of claustrophobia in *Sunshine*, Boyle refused to cut back to scenes on Earth, a traditional technique in most films about the planet in jeopardy. The director also maintained an atmosphere of confinement in *Sunshine* by avoiding filming the primary ship, *Icarus II*, from the outside.[41] He also attempted to avoid filming star field backgrounds, keeping the ship's exterior pitch black, but he was ultimately compelled to show stars outside the spacecraft to help convey a sense of the ship's movement.[29]

A scene in a snow-covered park with three stone monoliths was a homage to a similar scene in *2001: A Space Odyssey*. The scene was filmed at a May Day memorial in Stockholm, Sweden.[47] The Sydney Opera House in Sydney, Australia was chosen by Boyle out of six monuments that he considered universally recognisable. The Opera House, according to the director, possessed a "heat-thing" quality that decided it as his choice for a final establishing shot on Earth.

The snowy territory of the final scene was shot in Stockholm, Sweden, and a composite shot was created combining Stockholm's background and the Sydney Opera House.[27] A slightly different ending was shot after the original but was not chosen as the director felt that it did not fit the film. The alternate ending became available on the DVD of *Sunshine*.[38]

Design

The presspack says that the claustrophobic environment in the film was inspired by Wolfgang Petersen's *Das Boot* (1981).[39] Boyle also cited inevitable visual influences from science fiction films in space by Andrei Tarkovsky (*Solaris* in 1972), Stanley Kubrick (*2001: A Space Odyssey* in 1968), and Ridley Scott (*Alien* in 1979).[48] Influences from other science fiction films also included Paul W. S. Anderson's *Event Horizon* (1997), John Carpenter's *Dark Star* (1974), and Douglas Trumbull's *Silent Running* (1971).[18]

Filmmakers consulted NASA in designing the scientific aspects of the film. Technical specifications for the ship were provided in order to make it more realistic. An oxygen garden was also recommended to provide oxygen for the ship and to enable the crew to grow their own food rather than rely completely on pre-packaged sustenance.[43] Boyle met with a department within NASA that was focused on the psychology of deep-space travel, and they advised the director that regular Earth routines like preparing one's own food, enjoying its consumption and cleaning up afterwards are activities crucial to an astronaut's sanity.[49]

The spacesuit's colour scheme was chosen to deflect heat and radiation in the film, and the helmet was purposely designed to be a claustrophobic experience for the actors.

The gold-leaf shielding in *Sunshine* was influenced by NASA satellite designs for deflecting heat and other forms of radiant energy. Director Danny Boyle designed the gold-colored space suits along these lines despite persistent encouragement to model them after the NASA template. The helmets were designed to have cameras mounted in them. This further enhanced a sense of claustrophobia useful to the actors in delivering more heartfelt performances.[27] The helmets were also limited to a horizontal slit for visibility instead of a full-face visor as further consideration toward protecting the characters from the ambient radiation of outer space.[29] According to Boyle, the funnel shape of the helmet was influenced by the character Kenny from *South Park*.[27]

Boyle included "Icarus" in the name of the ship to continue a theme of bleakness, opining that no American would give their craft such an ill-fated name. According to the director, "They'd call it *Spirit of Hope* or *Ship of Destiny*. They'd call it something optimistic... in America they would sacrifice all plausibility, because there would be hope."[50] The ship's exterior was designed to look like an oil tanker.[19] The ship's interior was influenced by the design of a nuclear submarine that filmmakers had visited in Scotland, though the space was larger due to NASA's advice that smaller quarters would adversely affect the crewmembers' sanity.[14] The corpses of burn victims in the film were modeled on the Pompeii victims from the Mount Vesuvius eruption.[19]

Visual effects

Cinematographer Alwin H. Kuchler provided an idea to render the interior of the ship in the colours of grey, blue, and green, with no reference to orange, red, or yellow. Scenes were intended to be shot inside the ship at long intervals, and when the shot changed to the outside, yellow-starved audiences would be "penetrated" by sunlight.[16] The visual effects of the sunlight were based on photographs from the Solar and Heliospheric Observatory project.[51] Boyle also sought to pursue inexpensive methods in filming sequences involving actors and visual effects. In a scene where Cillian Murphy's character dreams of falling into the sun, the actor was placed in a gantry around which 20 assistants rotated an assembly of bright lights.

In another scene in which a character dies from solar exposure among the ashes from cremated bodies, massive wind turbines propelled biodegradable dust at the actor in the director's attempt to have the computer-generated effects follow the actor instead of vice versa.[36] Boyle commented on his approach to using effects, "There is part of our brain where we admire the effect, but we put it in a side compartment of our experience because you know there's no way an actor can live through that, or be there in that moment."[2] During the post-production process, Boyle hired one visual effects company, London's Moving Picture Company, to work on the film's 750 visual effects. The assignment of a single company was contrary to the industry trend of hiring multiple vendors to work on a film's effects. Boyle chose one company for ease of quality control, though the decision resulted in a prolonged post-production process.[19]

Score

When the film was mostly complete, director Danny Boyle provided the footage to the band Underworld, who improvised a score.[35] Karl Hyde of Underworld was influenced by the music of avant garde composer György Ligeti which had been used in Stanley Kubrick's *2001: A Space Odyssey* (1968). *Lux Aeterna* by Ligeti particularly influenced Hyde.[18] When Underworld finished recording the band sent its work to composer John Murphy, who completed the score, resulting in a hybrid between Underworld and Murphy.[35] The band I Am Kloot also contributed to the score with the track "Avenue of Hope".[52]

Despite high praise for the score from fans of the film a soundtrack was significantly delayed. This was partly due to 'disputes' between the lawyers of Underworld and Fox Searchlight.[53] Although not available close to the film's debut, a soundtrack was still widely expected to be eventually released, until the film's producer Andrew Macdonald stated in a fansite interview that the soundtrack was "stuck" and that there were "no plans to release" it.[54]

The soundtrack was finally released on iTunes USA on November 25, 2008.

Release

Box office performance

Sunshine was originally slated for a theatrical release in October 2006, but the release was later changed to March 2007. The film was finally set to debut in April 2007.[55] *Sunshine* made its world premiere at Fantasy Filmfest in Bochum, Germany on 23 March 2007.[56] The film was released commercially in the home country of the United Kingdom on 6th April 2007, taking £1,021,063 in 407 cinemas for its opening weekend.[57]

The film also opened the same weekend in seven other markets, performing most strongly in Hong Kong (US$267,000), Taiwan (US$442,000) and Singapore (US$198,000).[58] On the weekend of 13 April 2007, *Sunshine* opened in 22 more markets, garnering US$5.3 million for the weekend. Its French debut was the strongest with US$1.2 million in 380 theatres, but the film only had average performance in New Zealand (US$120,149 from 36 theatres), Switzerland (US$60,285 from 11 theatres) and Finland (US$42,745 from 15 theatres).[59]

The following weekend of 20 April 2007, the film expanded to 44 markets, garnering US$5.9 million for a total of US$18.6 million thus far, considered a disappointing amount. *Sunshine* had poor debuts in Spain (US$1 million), Germany (US$638,549), and Italy (US$453,000).[60] By the end of April, *Sunshine* had opened to most markets, with the notable exception of the United States, for which a release date had yet to be established at the time.[58] The film's theatrical run in the UK lasted twelve weeks, totaling £3,175,911.[61]

The film was originally slated to be released in the United States in September 2007, but the release date was moved earlier to July 2007.[62] *Sunshine* was released in the United States and Canada at select locations in Los Angeles, New York City, Chicago, San Francisco, Boston, and Toronto on 20 July 2007.[63] *Sunshine* opened in 10 cinemas in the United States and took US$242,964 over the opening weekend.[3]

The film was released everywhere else in the two countries the following weekend of 27th July 2007.[63] In the film's first wide release weekend in the United States and Canada, *Sunshine* took US$1,262,996 in 461 theatres, ranking no. 13 at the weekend box office.[64] In its theatrical run, the film took US$3,675,753 in the United States and Canada and US$28,342,050 in other territories for a worldwide total of US$32,017,803;[3] the film's budget reportedly was US$40 million.[2]

Critical reception

The film currently holds a 74% positive rating out of 152 reviews at the movie review aggregator Rotten Tomatoes.[65] Among the "Cream of the Crop" reviews at Rotten Tomatoes, 61% of reviews were positive, with an average rating of 6.4/10.[66] On another aggregator, Metacritic, *Sunshine* received an average score of 64 out of 100 based on 34 reviews.[67]

Critically, the film was moderately well received in the UK.[68] [69] However, many found the last reels disappointing, with one critic suggesting the switch to 'slasher movie' mode might have been inserted to appease teenage audiences.[70]

Film critic Roger Ebert gave the film three stars out of four and said that "the [actors] are effective by trying not to be too effective; they almost all play professional astronaut/scientists, and not action-movie heroes," and also that the film "is strongest when it focuses on the sheer enormity of the mission and its consequences."[71]

Scientific accuracy

Professor Brian Cox served as the film's scientific advisor, though he noted in the DVD commentary that several inaccuracies were permitted to allow for plot. He also dismissed criticisms of the film by scientists: "*Sunshine* is not a documentary. It's trying to just, in an hour and forty minutes, get across a feeling of what it's like - not only to be a scientist, because obviously there's much more in it than that. So, I found it interesting to watch the kind of people that get upset because the gravity is wrong."[72]

Slow motion during weightlessness was inaccurately portrayed; the director had discovered this when riding the Vomit Comet, but he kept the slow motion to meet audiences' expectations. The film's premise of the sun dying out is also inaccurate, since the sun is estimated to die out in five billion years' time, after becoming a red giant and not by a gradual decline in brightness. Part of the film's back-story included the sun's death being caused by a Q-ball caught in the solar body, but realistically, the sun would not be dense enough to trap a Q-ball.[73] Another purposeful inaccuracy was the "whooshing" of the ship despite the vacuum - Cox later mentioned in the BBC's *Stargazing Live* programme in January 2011 that this was simply because without accompanying sound, the CGI shots seemed "cheap". Mercury's orbit was also pictured at many times its actual rate.

When the crew use the airlocks to move between ships without space suits, one of the crew members claims the temperature outside is −273 °C (0 K; −459 °F), which is absolute zero. Not only is this incorrect, as the temperature in outer space is slightly higher: −270 °C (3 K; −454 °F), but orbiting the planet of Mercury behind a heatshield as close as they are, the temperature would be higher than −173 °C (100 K; −279 °F).

The film's scientific content has been criticized by specialists with arguments often found contradicted by statements pertaining to the film.[74] For example, the science periodical *New Scientist* claimed that the nuclear device (stellar bomb) used by the crew would be woefully inadequate to reignite the dying sun (billions of such devices would be required).[75] The periodical found the film to be confusing and disappointing. Although some argue the 'stellar bomb' may have been an unknown type of advanced technology, the film specifically states it they have used 'all of Earth's fissile material' and the description of how the bomb works involved atoms 'becoming two' - i.e. fission. Similarly, solar physicist Anjana Ahuja, a columnist for *The Times*, commented on the lack of source of artificial gravity onboard the spacecraft, claiming "Danny Boyle could have achieved the same level of scientific fidelity in *Sunshine* by giving a calculator to a schoolboy". Ahuja was, however, more positive about the psychological aspect of the film, joking that "the psychology of extended space travel is covered well, although we could have done with a space bonk".[76]

Home media

The DVD for *Sunshine* was released in the United Kingdom on 27 August 2007. Extras include separate commentaries by Danny Boyle and Prof. Brian Cox, an alternative ending, 11 deleted scenes, web production diaries, and the short films *Dad's Dead* and *Mole Hills*.[77] A Blu-ray version was released in the UK in October of the same year. In the United States, *Sunshine* was released on high-definition Blu-ray Disc and standard definition DVD on 8 January 2008.[78] As of February 17, 2008, Sunshine has grossed $15.83 million in rental sales.[79]

Awards and nominations

Awards			
Award	**Category**	**Name**	**Outcome**
British Independent Film Awards	Best Technical Achievement	Mark Tildesley	Won
	Best Actor	Cillian Murphy	Nominated
Empire Awards	Best British Film		Nominated
	Best Sci-Fi/Fantasy		Nominated
Irish Film and Television Awards	Best Actor in a Lead Role in a Feature Film	Cillian Murphy	Nominated
London Critics Circle Film Awards	British Director of the Year	Danny Boyle	Nominated

Satellite Awards	Best Art Direction and Production Design	Mark Tildesley, Gary Freeman, Stephen Morahan, Denis Schnegg	Nominated
Saturn Awards	Best Science Fiction Film		Nominated

References

[1] John Hiscock (2007-03-16). "Another bright idea from Mr Sunshine" (http://www.telegraph.co.uk/arts/main.jhtml?xml=/arts/2007/03/16/bfboyle116.xml). London: Telegraph. . Retrieved 2007-04-05.

[2] Randee Dawn (2007-07-19). "Handmade VFX warms Boyle's 'Sunshine' pic" (http://web.archive.org/web/20070930210752/http://www.hollywoodreporter.com/hr/content_display/features/columns/film_reporter/e3i196c2593a031ddd0cf28807192ed8afd). The Hollywood Reporter. Archived from the original (http://www.hollywoodreporter.com/hr/content_display/features/columns/film_reporter/e3i196c2593a031ddd0cf28807192ed8afd) on 2007-09-30. . Retrieved 2007-09-21.

[3] "Sunshine (2007)" (http://www.boxofficemojo.com/movies/?id=sunshine06.htm). Box Office Mojo. . Retrieved 2007-08-19.

[4] Alistair Harkness (2007-03-31). "Starship trouper" (http://living.scotsman.com/ViewArticle.aspx?articleid=3358847). The Scotsman. . Retrieved 2007-07-20.

[5] Jon Keighren (2007-03-27). "Manchester scientist helps bring Sunshine to the big screen" (http://www.innovations-report.de/html/berichte/physik_astronomie/bericht-81640.html). Innovations Report. . Retrieved 2007-07-20.

[6] Rick Fulton (2007-03-30). "DANNY'S NEW GOLDEN BOY" (http://www.dailyrecord.co.uk/news/tm_headline=danny-s-new-golden-boy&method=full&objectid=18831455&siteid=66633-name_page.html). Daily Record. . Retrieved 2007-07-20.

[7] Sam Ashurst (2007-04-02). "Killing time with Cillian Murphy" (http://www.totalfilm.com/features/killing_time_with_cillian_murphy). Total Film. . Retrieved 2007-07-24.

[8] "Murphy Turns Atheist After Work on Sci-Fi Thriller" (http://www.hollywood.com/news/Murphy_Turns_Atheist_After_Work_on_Sci_Fi_Thriller/3673810). Hollywood News. 2007-03-27. . Retrieved 2007-05-15.

[9] "Sunshine Movie" (http://www.wildaboutmovies.com/movies/SunshineMovieDannyBoyledirector.php). Wild About Movies. . Retrieved 2007-07-24.

[10] Claire Sutherland (2007-04-12). "On the boyle" (http://www.news.com.au/heraldsun/story/0,21985,21544934-2902,00.html). Herald Sun. . Retrieved 2007-07-20.

[11] Ethan Sacks (2007-07-15). "Memoirs of a sensation" (http://www.nydailynews.com/entertainment/movies/2007/07/15/2007-07-15_memoirs_of_a_sensation.html). New York Daily News. . Retrieved 2007-07-24.

[12] Mumtaj Begum (2007-04-13). "To infinity and beyond" (http://www.star-ecentral.com/news/story.asp?file=/2007/4/13/movies/17398678&sec=movies). The Star. . Retrieved 2007-07-20.

[13] Chris Hewitt (2007-09-11). "Cliff Curtis takes a trip to see the *Sunshine* with *RT*" (http://www.rottentomatoes.com/m/sunshine/articles/1669882/). Rotten Tomatoes. . Retrieved 2007-09-21.

[14] Eric Alt. "Danny Boyle Basks in the 'Sunshine'" (http://www.premiere.com/features/3943/danny-boyle-basks-in-the-sunshine.html?print_page=y). Premiere. . Retrieved 2007-07-24.

[15] Noriko Nakamura (2007-04-22). "Hiroyuki Sanada Gets His Day in the Sun" (http://www.asahi.com/english/weekly/0422/01.html). Asahi Weekly. . Retrieved 2007-07-24.

[16] "The Danny Boyle Webchat Transcript" (http://www.empireonline.com/features/dannyboylewebchat/). Empire. . Retrieved 2007-07-20.

[17] Listed in the film's credits.

[18] Mark Kermode (2007-03-25). "2007: a scorching new space odyssey" (http://film.guardian.co.uk/features/featurepages/0,,2042102,00.html). London: The Observer. . Retrieved 2007-07-19.

[19] John Horn (2007-07-01). "Danny Boyle feels the heat with 'Sunshine'". Los Angeles Times.

[20] Benjamin Crossley-Marra (2007-07-19). "Interview: Danny Boyle" (http://www.ioncinema.com/news.php?nid=1192). . Retrieved 2007-07-24.

[21] Michael James Allen (2007-07-23). "An Interview with Danny Boyle" (http://www.luminomagazine.com/mw/content/view/2074/1). Lumino Magazine. . Retrieved 2007-09-21.

[22] Edward Douglas (2005-03-05). "In the Future With Danny Boyle" (http://www.comingsoon.net/news.php?id=8613). ComingSoon.net. . Retrieved 2007-01-13.

[23] Kurt Loder (2007-07-12). "Danny Boyle's Space Odyssey" (http://www.mtv.com/movies/news/articles/1564535/20070711/story.jhtml). MTV. . Retrieved 2007-07-24.

[24] Michelle Nichols (2007-07-18). "INTERVIEW - 'Sunshine' director Boyle vows no return to space" (http://in.reuters.com/articlePrint?articleId=INIndia-28528520070717). Reuters. . Retrieved 2007-07-24.

[25] Kevin Bourke (2007-03-27). "Flying into the sun" (http://www.manchestereveningnews.co.uk/entertainment/film_and_tv/s/1002/1002963_flying_into_the_sun.html). Manchester Evening News. . Retrieved 2007-07-20.

[26] Highfield, Roger (2007-03-13). "How to make science really shine" (http://www.telegraph.co.uk/connected/main.jhtml?xml=/connected/2007/03/13/nsunshine113.xml). London: The Daily Telegraph. . Retrieved 2007-07-19.

[27] Patrick Kolan (2007-03-14). "Interview: Danny Boyle" (http://movies.ign.com/articles/772/772907p1.html). IGN. . Retrieved 2007-07-19.

[28] Daniel Fienberg (2007-09-03). "A CONVERSATION WITH DIRECTOR DANNY BOYLE" (http://www.filter-mag.com/index.php?id=15281&c=2). Filter. . Retrieved 2007-09-21.

[29] Mark Salisbury (2007-03-29). "'Sunshine' set visit" (http://www.timeout.com/film/news/1795/). Time Out. . Retrieved 2007-07-20.

[30] Jacob Ward (June 2007). "The Terrifying Science Behind Danny Boyle's *Sunshine*" (http://www.popsci.com/environment/article/2007-06/terrifying-science-behind-danny-boyles-sunshine). Popular Science. . Retrieved 2007-09-21.

[31] Rosalie Higson (2007-03-28). "Space riders of the apocalypse" (http://www.theaustralian.news.com.au/story/0,20867,21457686-16947,00.html). The Australian. . Retrieved 2007-07-20.

[32] "Dr. Brian Cox" (http://web.archive.org/web/20071014015039/http://www.sci-fi-online.50megs.com/2006_Interviews/07-08-27_brian-cox.htm). Sci-Fi-Online.com. 2007-08-27. Archived from the original (http://www.sci-fi-online.50megs.com/2006_Interviews/07-08-27_brian-cox.htm) on 2007-10-14. . Retrieved 2007-10-10.

[33] Laura Heifetz (2007-06-28). "*Trainspotting* Director: No Sci-Fi Sex" (http://www.radaronline.com/exclusives/2007/06/director-danny-boyle-is-all.php). Radar. . Retrieved 2007-07-28.

[34] Charlotte O'Sullivan (2007-04-03). "A star is reborn" (http://www.thisislondon.co.uk/film/article 23391332-details/A star is reborn/article.do/). Evening Standard. . Retrieved 2007-07-24.

[35] Ben Rawson-Jones (2007-04-04). "'Sunshine' director Danny Boyle" (http://www.digitalspy.co.uk/movies/a44608/sunshine-director-danny-boyle.html). Digital Spy. . Retrieved 2007-07-20.

[36] Jennie Punter (2007-07-20). "Danny Boyle can't find room for love in outer space". Globe and Mail.

[37] "Sunshine Film" (http://www.sunshinedna.com/film). SunshineDNA.com. . Retrieved 2007-05-15.

[38] Sheila Roberts. "Danny Boyle Interview, Sunshine (2007)" (http://www.moviesonline.ca/movienews_12384.html). MoviesOnline.ca. . Retrieved 2007-07-28.

[39] Katja Hofmann (2005-11-27). "Scout's report: 3 pix poised for multiplexes" (http://www.variety.com/awardcentral_article/VR1117933535.html?nav=efan). Variety. . Retrieved 2007-07-19.

[40] Garry Maddox (2007-04-06). "Master of the cool change" (http://www.brisbanetimes.com.au/news/film/master-of-the-cool-change/2007/04/04/1175366329050.html). Brisbane Times. . Retrieved 2007-07-24.

[41] Barkham, Patrick (2007-03-23). "The sun is the star" (http://arts.guardian.co.uk/filmandmusic/story/0,,2040021,00.html). London: The Guardian. . Retrieved 2007-07-19.

[42] Andrew Mueller (2007-03-31). "Lost in space" (http://film.guardian.co.uk/features/featurepages/0,,2046781,00.html). London: The Guardian. . Retrieved 2007-07-30.

[43] Max Evry; Ryan Rotten (2007-07-16). "Exclusive: Danny Boyle on *Sunshine*!" (http://www.comingsoon.net/news/movienews.php?id=22029). ComingSoon.net. . Retrieved 2007-07-24.

[44] Fox Searchlight Pictures (2005-08-25). "Danny Boyle's *Sunshine* Begins Filming" (http://www.comingsoon.net/news.php?id=10915). ComingSoon.net. .

[45] Emanuel Levy. "Sunshine: Danny Boyle Fashions the Future" (http://www.emanuellevy.com/article.php?articleID=4921). EmanuelLevy.com. . Retrieved 2007-07-24.

[46] Jason Silverman (2007-07-17). "Q&A: Danny Boyle's *Sunshine* Makes Sci-Fi Smart Again" (http://www.wired.com/entertainment/hollywood/news/2007/07/sunshineQA). Wired News. . Retrieved 2007-07-24.

[47] Patrick Lee (2007-07-03). "*Sunshine* Contains Homages" (http://web.archive.org/web/20071011141651/http://scifi.com/scifiwire/index.php?id=42239). Sci Fi Wire. Archived from the original (http://www.scifi.com/scifiwire/index.php?id=42239) on 2007-10-11. . Retrieved 2007-07-24.

[48] "Interview : Danny Boyle" (http://web.archive.org/web/20070323133000/http://www.moviehole.net/interviews/20070319_interview_danny_boyle.html). Moviehole.net. 2007-03-19. Archived from the original (http://www.moviehole.net/interviews/20070319_interview_danny_boyle.html) on 2007-03-23. . Retrieved 2007-07-19.

[49] Reed Tucker (2007-07-15). "ROCKET MAN" (http://www.nypost.com/seven/07152007/entertainment/movies/rocket_man_movies_reed_tucker.htm). New York Post. . Retrieved 2007-07-24.

[50] James Luxford (2007-03-27). "Danny Boyle Discusses New Film Sunshine" (http://www.entertainmentwise.com/news?id=29814). Entertainmentwise. . Retrieved 2007-07-20.

[51] Dennis Lim (2007-07-10). "'Sunshine': Danny Boyle's latest visit to a vast new world" (http://www.iht.com/articles/2007/07/10/arts/boyle.php). International Herald Tribune. . Retrieved 2007-07-24.

[52] "SUNSHINE FILM NOW AT CINEMAS" (http://www.iamkloot.com/). I Am Kloot. . Retrieved 2007-07-31.

[53] "Sunshine Blog - Soundtrack Information" (http://www.sunshinedna.com/?p=261). . Retrieved 2008-01-19.

[54] "Sunshine Fan Online: Interview with Andrew Macdonald" (http://www.sunshinefan.com/events.php?interviewmac). . Retrieved 2008-01-19.

[55] John Horn (2007-07-01). "Danny Boyle feels the heat with 'Sunshine'". Los Angeles Times.

[56] "FREITAG 23. März" (http://web.archive.org/web/20070221013145/http://www.fantasyfilmfest.com/fantasy/fffnights/ffnights2007/stadt_Bo.html) (in German). Fantasy Filmfest. Archived from the original (http://www.fantasyfilmfest.com/fantasy/

fffnights/ffnights2007/stadt_Bo.html) on 2007-02-21. . Retrieved 2007-07-19.
[57] "Apr 06-Apr 08, 2007" (http://web.archive.org/web/20070927035516/http://www.ukfilmcouncil.org.uk/cinemagoing/archive/?p=D4A157780a0931BB27nUq33C2692&skip=). UK Film Council. Archived from the original (http://www.ukfilmcouncil.org.uk/cinemagoing/archive/?p=D4A157780a0931BB27nUq33C2692&skip=) on 2007-09-27. . Retrieved 2007-04-13.
[58] Conor Bresnan (2007-04-11). "Around the World Roundup: '300' Resurrected" (http://boxofficemojo.com/news/?id=2291&p=.htm). Box Office Mojo. . Retrieved 2007-07-19.
[59] Conor Bresnan (2007-04-16). "Around the World Roundup: 'Bean' Regains Lead" (http://boxofficemojo.com/news/?id=2295&p=.htm). Box Office Mojo. . Retrieved 2007-07-19.
[60] Conor Bresnan (2007-04-23). "Around the World Roundup: Comedies 'Hog' Business" (http://boxofficemojo.com/news/?id=2300&p=.htm). Box Office Mojo. . Retrieved 2007-07-19.
[61] "Jun 22-Jun 24, 2007" (http://web.archive.org/web/20070927035502/http://www.ukfilmcouncil.org.uk/cinemagoing/archive/?p=D4A157780f4f316CA8qMpSFC60B7&skip=). UK Film Council. Archived from the original (http://www.ukfilmcouncil.org.uk/cinemagoing/archive/?p=D4A157780f4f316CA8qMpSFC60B7&skip=) on 2007-09-27. . Retrieved 2007-07-19.
[62] "Danny Boyle's Sunshine North American Release Bumped Up to July" (http://www.filmjunk.com/2007/05/24/danny-boyles-sunshine-north-american-release-bumped-up-to-july/). 2007-05-24. . Retrieved 2007-07-24.
[63] "Sunshine Movie Information" (http://www.sunshinedna.com/?p=262). SunshineDNA.com. 2007-07-04. . Retrieved 2007-07-19.
[64] "Sunshine (2007) - Weekend Box Office" (http://www.boxofficemojo.com/movies/?page=weekend&id=sunshine06.htm). Box Office Mojo. . Retrieved 2007-07-31.
[65] "Sunshine" (http://www.rottentomatoes.com/m/sunshine/). Rotten Tomatoes. . Retrieved 2007-11-26.
[66] "Sunshine - Cream of the Crop" (http://www.rottentomatoes.com/m/sunshine/?critic=creamcrop). Rotten Tomatoes. . Retrieved 2010-09-30.
[67] "Sunshine (2007): Reviews" (http://www.metacritic.com/film/titles/sunshine2007). Metacritic. . Retrieved 2007-08-16.
[68] Prepare for a scorcher (http://www.telegraph.co.uk/arts/main.jhtml?view=DETAILS&grid=&xml=/arts/2007/04/06/bfsun06.xml), *Daily Telegraph*, accessed 27th April 2007
[69] Sunshine (http://www.timeout.com/film/reviews/83499/Sunshine.html), *Time Out*, accessed 27th April 2007
[70] Review: Sunshine (http://entertainment.timesonline.co.uk/tol/arts_and_entertainment/film/film_reviews/article1614026.ece), *The Times*, accessed 27th April 2007
[71] Roger Ebert (2007-07-20). ":: rogerebert.com :: Reviews :: Sunshine" (http://rogerebert.suntimes.com/apps/pbcs.dll/article?AID=/20070719/REVIEWS/70702003/1023). Chicago Sun-Times. . Retrieved 2007-09-03.
[72] Rea, Darren (27 August 2007). "Dr. Brian Cox (science consultant) - Sunshine - Interview" (http://www.sci-fi-online.com/2006_Interviews/07-08-27_brian-cox.htm). Sci-fi Online. . Retrieved 3 July 2010.
[73] Roger Highfield (2007-03-13). "How to make science really shine" (http://www.telegraph.co.uk/connected/main.jhtml;jsessionid=WSXFD4VEK2AMDQFIQMGCFGGAVCBQUIV0?xml=/connected/2007/03/13/nsunshine113.xml&page=1). London: The Daily Telegraph. . Retrieved 2008-03-24.
[74] Another View (http://film.guardian.co.uk/News_Story/Critic_Review/Guardian_review/0,,2060703,00.html), Dr. Chris Lintott, The Guardian, accessed 31 April 2007.
[75] Review: Sunshine (http://space.newscientist.com/article/mg19425981.700-review-isunshinei-directed-by-danny-boyle.html), New Scientist, 2007-04-07
[76] Ahuja, Anjana (2007-04-02). "Sunshine on my mind" (http://entertainment.timesonline.co.uk/tol/arts_and_entertainment/film/article1598953.ece). London: The Times. . Retrieved 2007-05-13.
[77] Gary Gray (2007-07-11). "Sunshine (2007) DVD News" (http://www.realmovienews.com/dvd/news/1231). Real Movie News. . Retrieved 2007-07-30.
[78] "Sunshine (2007)" (http://videoeta.com/movie.html?via=form&id=79062). VideoETA. . Retrieved 2007-10-04.
[79] "Box Office Mojo - DVD and home video sales." (http://www.boxofficemojo.com/movies/?page=homevideo&id=sunshine06.htm). . Retrieved 2008-07-09.

External links

- Official website (http://www.foxsearchlight.com/sunshine)
- Visual effects article (http://www.vfxworld.com/?sa=adv&code=319b255d&atype=articles&id=3352&page=1) at VFXWorld
- *Sunshine* (http://www.imdb.com/title/tt0448134/) at the Internet Movie Database
- *Sunshine* (http://www.allrovi.com/movies/movie/v328646) at AllRovi
- *Sunshine* (http://www.rottentomatoes.com/m/sunshine/) at Rotten Tomatoes
- *Sunshine* (http://www.metacritic.com/movie/sunshine2007) at Metacritic

Fantastic Four: Rise of the Silver Surfer

Fantastic Four: Rise of the Silver Surfer	
 Theatrical release poster	
Directed by	Tim Story
Produced by	Avi Arad Bernd Eichinger Ralph Winter
Screenplay by	Don Payne Mark Frost
Story by	John Turman Mark Frost
Based on	• *Fantastic Four* by • Stan Lee • Jack Kirby
Starring	Ioan Gruffudd Jessica Alba Chris Evans Michael Chiklis Doug Jones Julian McMahon
Music by	John Ottman
Cinematography	Larry Blanford
Editing by	William Hoy Peter S. Elliot
Studio	20th Century Fox Marvel Entertainment 1492 Pictures Constantin Film Ingenious Film Partners
Distributed by	20th Century Fox
Release date(s)	June 15, 2007
Running time	95 minutes
Country	United States
Language	English
Budget	$130 million[1]

Box office	$289,047,763

Fantastic Four: Rise of the Silver Surfer is a 2007 American superhero film, and the sequel to the 2005 film *Fantastic Four*. Both films are based on the *Fantastic Four* comic book and were directed by Tim Story. Ioan Gruffudd as Reed Richards, Jessica Alba as Sue Storm, Chris Evans as Johnny Storm, and Michael Chiklis as Ben Grimm are the film series' recurring protagonists, while Julian McMahon and Kerry Washington reprised their roles from the first film as, respectively, Victor Von Doom and Alicia Masters. Beau Garrett appears in the sequel as the Frankie Raye, along with Doug Jones as the Silver Surfer and Laurence Fishburne as the voice of the Silver Surfer. The plot follows the Fantastic Four as they confront, and later ally with, the Silver Surfer to save Earth from Galactus.

While the film was the highest-grossing film during the week that immediately followed its release on June 15, 2007 in North America and was the recipient of two out of fifteen awards nominations, it was received with unfavorable reviews by critics with critics noting an improvement on the first film, but continuing to criticize the film's flimsy direction and lack of humor. The film was released onto Blu-ray Disc, DVD, and VHS on October 2, 2007.

Plot

As Reed Richards (Ioan Gruffudd) and Sue Storm (Jessica Alba) prepare for their wedding, a silver object enters Earth's atmosphere, radiating cosmic energy that creates massive molecular fluctuations and causes deep craters at locations across the Earth. The US government approaches Richards to track and identify the movements of the object. He initially refuses, to appease Sue who feels he is again starting to neglect her after she catches him at a club with another woman, however, he surreptitiously builds a radar tracker which will locate the object, as the Army requests.

During the wedding, Reed's systems detect the phenomenon approaching the city, and as a result the city suffers a blackout, creating chaos and damage, which the Fantastic Four try to minimise. Johnny Storm (Chris Evans) pursues the object, discovering it to be a silvery humanoid riding a flying surfboard. The "Silver Surfer" drags him into the upper atmosphere then drops him back toward Earth. During his fall Johnny finds his abilities fluctuating, and barely manages to survive the fall, successfully flying at the last minute. Later, Sue and Johnny switch powers when they touch, prompting Reed to examine Johnny revealing that exposure to the Surfer has set Johnny's molecular structure in flux, allowing him to switch powers with his teammates through physical contact. Tracing the cosmic energy of the Surfer, Reed discovers that a series of planets the alien had visited have all been destroyed.

The Surfer has been creating deep artificial craters around the globe. Reed determines that the next crater will appear in London, and the team travel there. They arrive too late to stop the crater, and the river Thames drains into it. Afterwards, both Reed and Sue contemplate abandoning their lives as superheroes in order to provide a normal life to raise a family. The Surfer's movements around the globe bring him past Latveria, where the cosmic energy affects Victor von Doom (Julian McMahon), freeing him from two years as a metal statue. Doom, able to move again but scarred, traces the Surfer to the Russell Glacier and makes him an offer to join forces. When the Surfer rebuffs him, Doom attacks. The Surfer returns fire, blasting Doom through the ice. The cosmic energy of the Surfer's blast heals Doom's body.

Doom leverages his experience into a deal with the American military, who force the Fantastic Four to work with Doom. Deducing that the Surfer's board is the source of his power, Reed develops a pulse generator that will separate him from it, while Victor works on an unknown remote-like machine. In the Black Forest, Sue is confronted by the Surfer, during which he reveals he is merely a servant to the destroyer of worlds, and regrets the destruction he causes. The military opens fire on the Surfer, which distracts him and allows the four to fire the pulse, separating the Surfer from his board. The military imprisons the Surfer in Siberia, while they torture him for information. Sue uses her powers to sneak into his cell, where she learns more information from the Surfer. He tells her his master was known by the people of his world as Galactus, a massive cloud-like cosmic entity which feeds on life-bearing planets to survive, and that his board is a homing beacon which is summoning Galactus to the planet. The Silver Surfer has to serve Galactus who will otherwise destroy not only his loved ones but his planet.

Doom, using the device he created earlier, steals the board from the compound, killing the majority of the Army presence there at the same time. The Fantastic Four rescue the Surfer, and pursue Doom in the Fantasticar, confronting him in Shanghai. During the battle, Sue is mortally wounded. With the Surfer powerless, Johnny absorbs the combined powers of the entire team in order to battle the cosmic energy-empowered Doom. Johnny succeeds in breaking Doom's control over the Surfer's board, and Ben Grimm (Michael Chiklis) uses a nearby crane to knock Doom into the harbor, however, Galactus has already arrived, and Sue dies in Reed's arms. The Surfer regains the control of his board, and his power is restored. He revives Sue and chooses to defend Earth, flying into Galactus. The conflict results in a massive blast of energy that engulfs Galactus in a cosmic rift, and apparently kills the Surfer as well. Reed and Sue get married in Japan. The credits cut back to a shot of the Silver Surfer's seemingly lifeless body floating through space, but his eyes open and his board races towards him.

Cast

- Ioan Gruffudd as Dr. Reed Richards / Mr. Fantastic
- Jessica Alba as Susan Storm / Invisible Woman
- Chris Evans as Johnny Storm / Human Torch
- Michael Chiklis as Ben Grimm / The Thing
- Doug Jones as Norrin Radd / Silver Surfer
- Laurence Fishburne voices Norrin Radd / Silver Surfer
- Julian McMahon as Victor von Doom / Doctor Doom
- Kerry Washington as Alicia Masters
- Beau Garrett as Captain Frankie Raye
- Vanessa Minnillo as Julie Angel
- Andre Braugher as General Hager
- Stan Lee as Willie Lumpkin
- Brian Posehn as Wedding Minister

Production

With *Fantastic Four* grossing $330 million worldwide, 20th Century Fox hired director Tim Story and screenwriter Mark Frost in December 2005 to return for the superhero team's sequel.[2] Screenwriters Frost and Don Payne were hired to write the screenplay.[3] Payne has said the film is based upon "The Galactus Trilogy", in which Galactus also makes an appearance, as well as issues 57-60 in which Doom steals the Surfer's power. Payne has also said the film takes inspiration from the Ultimate Marvel limited series *Ultimate Extinction*.[4] As of March 2, 2007, Galactus' design was not yet done,[5] and by April 18, until hiring Laurence Fishburne to perform the voice, the filmmakers were unsure of whether the character would speak.[6]

Jessica Alba getting makeup placed on her face on the film set.

The film includes the Fantasti-Car,[7] a larger role for Kerry Washington's character Alicia Masters, and in June 2006, the Silver Surfer was announced to appear in the sequel as a "villain / hero".[8] The Silver Surfer has been created by combining the performance of actor Doug Jones, a grey-silver suit designed by Jose Fernandez and created by FX shop Spectral Motion which has then been enhanced by a new computer-generated system designed by WETA.

The sequel, whose working title was *Fantastic Four 2*, was officially titled *Fantastic Four: Rise of the Silver Surfer* in August 2006 with filming beginning on August 28 in Vancouver and set for a release date of June 15, 2007.[9] Michael Chiklis' prosthetics as The Thing were also redesigned to allow him to take it off in between takes[10] and for better ventilation.[11]

In August 2006, actor Andre Braugher dropped out of his supporting role in the TV series *ER* to be cast in *Rise of the Silver Surfer*.[12] Braugher was cast as General Hager, whom director Story described as "an old acquaintance of Reed Richards and one of the major additions to the movie".[13] In September, Jones was confirmed to portray the Silver Surfer in addition to Julian McMahon reprising his role as Doctor Doom.[14] The Baxter Building was also redesigned.[4]

Release

Promotion

The teaser trailer was initially exclusively attached to *Night at the Museum*. It was released to the general public online on December 26, 2006 on the film's official website. The theatrical trailer was scheduled to appear during the film *Disturbia* on April 13, 2007 but errors occurred and Tim Story announced that it would be released with *Spider-Man 3* on May 4, 2007. The theatrical trailer was finally released online on April 30, 2007 on Apple Trailer's website.[15] 20th Century Fox launched an outdoor advertising campaign at the end of February.[16] The cast also made an appearance at the Coca Cola 600 Nextel Cup NASCAR race in Charlotte over Memorial Day weekend.[17]

In late May 2007, 20th Century Fox struck a deal with the Franklin Mint to promote the movie by altering 40,000 U.S. quarters and releasing them into circulation.[18] All of the altered quarters were minted in 2005 and honor the state of California as part of the 50 State Quarters program created by the U.S. Mint. The altered quarters feature the Silver Surfer on the reverse along with a URL to the movie's official website. Once the U.S. Mint became aware of the promotion, it notified the studio and the Franklin Mint that it was breaking the law by turning government-issued currency into private advertising. The federal mint did not indicate whether a penalty would be effected.[18]

Home media

The film was released October 2, 2007 on DVD in two versions. The first was a single-disc Widescreen/Full Screen version. A two-disc "The Power Cosmic" Edition was also released that day.[19] and high-definition Blu-ray Disc.[20] The film was also released on HD DVD outside of the U.S.

Reception

Box office

On its opening weekend, the film was the highest-grossing movie at the U.S. box office, reaching approximately $58 million,[21] $2 million more than its predecessor.[22] By its second weekend, the film suffered a 66% drop and a 54% drop in its third weekend.[21] The film grossed $289 million worldwide, including a $131.9 million gross in the United States and in Canada.[1] The budget was $130 million.[1]

Critical response

Fantastic Four: Rise of the Silver Surfer received negative, but overall better, reviews than its predecessor. On the review aggregate site Rotten Tomatoes, 36% of critics gave the film positive reviews, based on 162 reviews.[23] On Metacritic, the film had a score of 45%, based on 45 reviews.[24] On Yahoo! Movies, the film is rated C+ by critics, based on 14 reviews.[25]

The New York Times critic Manohla Dargis called the film an "amalgam of recycled ideas, dead air, dumb quips, casual sexism and pseudoscientific mumbo jumbo".[26] Joe Morgenstern of *The Wall Street Journal* said the film was "good fun - more fun than in the original - punctuated by some lines of admirable awfulness" but "fails to sustain its modest running time of 87 minutes."[27] James Berardinelli of ReelViews.com called the film "so lackluster it makes *Spider-Man 3* feel like a masterpiece by comparison".[28]

Kevin Maher of *The Times* liked the film's light tone, saying "the film is everything you'd expect from a movie that began in the pages of a 1960s comic book – garish, giddy, emotionally simplistic, boldly idiotic and mercifully short".[29] *New York Daily News* liked the movie: "It's almost a surprise that the sequel is actually better — much better — than the original."[30]

Awards and nominations

Rise of the Silver Surfer was nominated for fifteen awards, winning two: the 2008 Golden Trailer Award for "Best Teaser Poster",[31] and star Jessica Alba winning the 2008 "Favorite Female Movie Star" Kids' Choice Award.[32] *Rise of the Silver Surfer* was nominated for five additional Kids' Choice awards.

Reboot

IGN has confirmed that a reboot of the franchise will start in 2014.[33]

References

[1] "Fantastic Four: Rise of the Silver Surfer (2007)" (http://www.boxofficemojo.com/movies/?id=fantasticfour2.htm). *Box Office Mojo*. Amazon.com. 2007. . Retrieved 2008-11-01.

[2] Michael Fleming (2005-12-04). "Story booked solid with Fox" (http://www.variety.com/article/VR1117933976.html?categoryid=13&cs=1&nid=2562). Variety. . Retrieved 2006-12-09.

[3] Michael Fleming; Dave McNary (2006-05-03). "Inside Move: Surfer may board *Four*" (http://www.variety.com/article/VR1117942541.html?categoryid=1350&cs=1&query=silver+and+surfer&display=silver+surfer). Variety. . Retrieved 2006-12-09.

[4] Ben Morse; Brian Warmoth (2007-01-15). "2007 Preview: *Fantastic Four: Rise of the Silver Surfer*" (http://web.archive.org/web/20071211045159/http://www.wizarduniverse.com/movies/fantasticfour2/003014399.cfm). Wizard. Archived from the original (http://www.wizarduniverse.com/movies/fantasticfour2/003014399.cfm) on 2007-12-11. . Retrieved 2010-06-13.

[5] Tim Story (2007-03-02). "Fantastic Four 2 Set Footage & Story Comments" (http://www.superherohype.com/news/topnews.php?id=5276). Superherohype.com. . Retrieved 2007-03-02.

[6] Pamela McClintock (2007-04-18). "Fishburne voices Surfer" (http://www.variety.com/article/VR1117963368.html?categoryid=13&cs=1). Variety. . Retrieved 2007-04-19.

[7] Bowles, Scott (2006-11-30). "First look: Fantasticar flows onto film" (http://www.usatoday.com/life/movies/news/2006-11-29-fantasticar_x.htm). USA Today. . Retrieved 2006-11-30.

[8] William Keck (2006-06-01). "Jessica Alba plans a fantastic summer" (http://www.usatoday.com/life/people/2006-05-31-alba_x.htm?csp=34). USA Today. . Retrieved 2006-12-09.

[9] Stax (2006-08-17). "Fantastic New Title" (http://movies.ign.com/articles/726/726218p1.html). IGN. . Retrieved 2006-12-09.

[10] Ftopel (2007-03-12). "Washington Waits for "Fantastic Four" Final Cut" (http://uk.rottentomatoes.com/news/1648425/washington_waits_for_andquotfantastic_fourandquot_final_cut). Rotten Tomatoes. . Retrieved 2010-06-13.

[11] Director Tim Story's DVD commentary

[12] Stax (2006-08-24). "Braugher Joins *Fantastic* Sequel" (http://movies.ign.com/articles/727/727902p1.html). IGN. . Retrieved 2006-12-09.

[13] Stax (2006-09-05). "*Fantastic Four* Sequel Under Way" (http://movies.ign.com/articles/730/730409p1.html). IGN. . Retrieved 2006-12-09.

[14] Stax (2006-09-25). "Weta Surfs to *Fantastic Four*" (http://movies.ign.com/articles/734/734987p1.html). IGN. . Retrieved 2006-09-25.

[15] "Apple.com - Trailers - *Fantastic Four: Rise of the Silver Surfer*" (http://www.apple.com/trailers/fox/fantasticfourriseofthesilversurfer/). Apple, Inc.. . Retrieved 2008-11-03.

[16] "Fox Set To Launch Outdoor RISE Campaign" (http://web.archive.org/web/20080218114208/http://www.f4movies.com/news/0459.shtml). F4movies.com. 2007-02-14. Archived from the original (http://www.f4movies.com/news/0459.shtml) on 2008-02-18. . Retrieved 2010-06-13.

[17] "Jessica Alba mothers her co-stars, attends NASCAR Coca Colar race in North Carolina" (http://www.celebrity-gossip.net/celebrities/hollywood/jessica-alba-mothers-her-co-stars-does-nascar-200863/). Celebrity-Gossip. May 28, 2007. . Retrieved 2008-11-01.

[18] "U.S. Mint: *Silver Surfer* Coin is Breaking the Law" (http://www.foxnews.com/story/0,2933,275655,00.html). Fox News Network. May 26, 2007. . Retrieved 2008-11-01.

[19] "Fantastic Four: Rise of the Silver Surfer (2007) DVD/Home Video Rentals" (http://www.boxofficemojo.com/movies/?page=homevideo&id=fantasticfour2.htm). *Box Office Mojo*. Amazon.com. 2007. . Retrieved 2008-11-01.

[20] "Fantastic Four: Rise of the Silver Surfer (Blu-Ray)" (http://www.blu-ray.com/movies/movies.php?id=376). Blu-Ray.com. 2007. . Retrieved 2008-11-01.

[21] "Fantastic Four: Rise of the Silver Surfer (2007) - Weekend Box Office" (http://www.boxofficemojo.com/movies/?page=weekend&id=fantasticfour2.htm). Box Office Mojo. . Retrieved 2007-09-09.

[22] "Fantastic Four (2005)" (http://www.boxofficemojo.com/movies/?id=fantasticfour.htm). Box Office Mojo. . Retrieved 2007-09-09.

[23] "The Fantastic Four: Rise of the Silver Surfer" (http://www.rottentomatoes.com/m/fantastic_four_2_rise_of_the_silver_surfer/). *Rotten Tomatoes*. Flixster. . Retrieved 2010-06-13.

[24] "Fantastic Four: Rise of the Silver Surfer (2007)" (http://www.metacritic.com/film/titles/fantasticfourriseofthesilversurfer). *Metacritic*. . Retrieved 2007-09-09.

[25] "Fantastic Four: Rise of the Silver Surfer (2007)" (http://movies.yahoo.com/shop;_ylt=An4fTbxZPwnWNV7Yd7pVtENfVXcA?d=hv&cf=info&id=1809699127). *Yahoo! Movies*. Yahoo!. . Retrieved 2007-09-09.

[26] Dargis, Manohla (2007-06-14). "Armageddon Comes Knocking" (http://www.nytimes.com/2007/06/14/movies/15fant.html). The New York Times. . Retrieved 2007-06-17.

[27] Joe Morgenstern (2007-06-15). "Film Review - WSJ.com" (http://online.wsj.com/article/SB118186395464336075.html). The Wall Street Journal. . Retrieved 2007-09-09.

[28] James Berardinelli. "Fantastic Four: Rise of the Silver Surfer" (http://web.archive.org/web/20070926223951/http://www.reelviews.net/movies). ReelViews. Archived from the original (http://www.reelviews.net/movies/f/fantastic_four2.html) on 2007-09-26. . Retrieved 2007-06-19.

[29] Kevin Maher (2007-06-14). "Fantastic Four: Rise of the Silver Surfer review" (http://entertainment.timesonline.co.uk/tol/arts_and_entertainment/film/film_reviews/article1927003.ece). *The Times* (London). . Retrieved 2007-09-09.

[30] Mathews, Jack (June 15, 2007). "Second time's the charm: Team strikes gold with Silver Surfer" (http://www.movietome.com/pages/tracking/index.php?tid=0&ref_id=357144). *New York Daily News*. . Retrieved 2008-11-01.

[31] "9th Annual Golden Trailer Award Winner and Nominees" (http://www.goldentrailer.com/awards.gta9.php). Golden Trailer Awards. . Retrieved 2010-06-13.

[32] "Cyrus dominates Kids Choice Awards" (http://www.upi.com/Entertainment_News/2008/03/30/Cyrus-dominates-Kids-Choice-Awards/UPI-22901206900342/). UPI. March 30, 2008. . Retrieved 2010-06-13.

[33] Vejvoda, Jim. "Fantastic Four Reboot Confirmed" (http://uk.movies.ign.com/articles/102/1020293p1.html). September 1, 2009. .

External links

- Official website (http://www.fantasticfourmovie.com)
- *Fantastic Four: Rise of the Silver Surfer* (http://www.imdb.com/title/tt0486576/) at the Internet Movie Database
- *Fantastic Four: Rise of the Silver Surfer* (http://www.allrovi.com/movies/movie/v346942) at AllRovi
- *Fantastic Four: Rise of the Silver Surfer* (http://www.rottentomatoes.com/m/fantastic_four_2_rise_of_the_silver_surfer/) at Rotten Tomatoes
- *Fantastic Four: Rise of the Silver Surfer* Production Notes (http://madeinatlantis.com/movies_central/2007/fantastic_four.htm)

The Nanny Diaries (film)

The Nanny Diaries	
Directed by	Shari Springer Berman Robert Pulcini
Produced by	Richard N. Gladstein
Written by	Shari Springer Berman Robert Pulcini **Novel:** Emma McLaughlin Nicola Kraus
Starring	Scarlett Johansson Chris Evans Laura Linney Paul Giamatti Nicholas Art Donna Murphy Alicia Keys
Music by	Mark Suozzo
Cinematography	Terry Stacey
Editing by	Robert Pulcini
Distributed by	The Weinstein Company Metro-Goldwyn-Mayer FilmColony
Release date(s)	August 24, 2007
Running time	106 min.
Country	United States
Language	English
Budget	$20,000,000
Box office	$44,638,886

The Nanny Diaries is a 2007 American comedy-drama film, based on the novel of the same name by Emma McLaughlin and Nicola Kraus. Written and directed by Shari Springer Berman and Robert Pulcini, it stars Scarlett Johansson, Alicia Keys, Paul Giamatti, and Laura Linney; and was produced by Richard N. Gladstein.

Plot

21-year-old Annie Braddock (Scarlett Johansson) has just graduated from Montclair State University. Annie has no idea what or who she wants to be. While sitting in the park, Annie sees a young boy in a uniform almost getting run over. Annie saves him and then the boy's mother, Mrs. Alexandra X (Laura Linney), mistakes Annie for a nanny. She gives her a card. Annie lies to her mother about taking a job at a bank and, in reality, moves in with the X's to be the nanny for Grayer, the boy she saved. Life with the incredibly privileged X's isn't all she thought it would be, and her life is complicated further when she falls for "Harvard Hottie" (Chris Evans), who lives in the building.

Cast

- Scarlett Johansson as Annie 'Nanny' Braddock
- Chris Evans as Hayden "Harvard Hottie"
- Laura Linney as Mrs. Alexandra X
- Paul Giamatti as Mr. Stan X
- Nicholas Art as Grayer Addison X
- Donna Murphy as Judy Braddock
- Alicia Keys as Lynette
- Nina Garbiras as Miss Chicago
- Brande Roderick as Tanya
- Heather Simms as Murnel
- Julie White as Jane Gould
- Judith Roberts as Milicent

Reception

As of September 1, 2007, the film had an average score of 46 out of 100 on Metacritic based on 33 reviews.[1] On Rotten Tomatoes, 33% of critics gave the film positive reviews based on 126 reviews.[2]

The film opened at #6 at the U.S. box office and earned $7.4 million in 2,629 theaters in its opening weekend. As of November 23, 2007, the film had grossed $25,918,399 domestically and $9,451,716 overseas for a total worldwide gross of $35,370,115 against a $20 million budget.[3]

References

[1] Nanny Diaries, The (2007): Reviews (http://www.metacritic.com/film/titles/nannydiaries). Metacritic. Retrieved 2007-09-01
[2] The Nanny Diaries - Rotten Tomatoes (http://www.rottentomatoes.com/m/nanny_diaries/). Rotten Tomatoes. Retrieved 2007-09-01
[3] The Nanny Diaries (2007) - Weekend Box Office (http://www.boxofficemojo.com/movies/?page=weekend&id=nannydiaries.htm). Box Office Mojo.

External links

- Official website (http://www.thenannydiariesmovie.com/)
- *The Nanny Diaries* (http://www.imdb.com/title/tt0489237/) at the Internet Movie Database
- *The Nanny Diaries* (http://www.allrovi.com/movies/movie/v347615) at AllRovi
- *The Nanny Diaries* (http://www.boxofficemojo.com/movies/?id=nannydiaries.htm) at Box Office Mojo
- *The Nanny Diaries* (http://www.rottentomatoes.com/m/nanny_diaries/) at Rotten Tomatoes
- *The Nanny Diaries* (http://www.metacritic.com/movie/nannydiaries) at Metacritic

Battle for Terra

Battle for Terra	
Theatrical release poster	
Directed by	Aristomenis Tsirbas
Produced by	Ryan Colucci Keith Calder Dane Allan Smith Jessica Wu
Screenplay by	Evan Spiliotopoulos
Story by	Aristomenis Tsirbas
Starring	Evan Rachel Wood Brian Cox James Garner Chris Evans Danny Glover Amanda Peet David Cross Justin Long Dennis Quaid Luke Wilson
Music by	Abel Korzeniowski
Cinematography	Aristomenis Tsirbas
Editing by	J. Kathleen Gibson
Studio	MeniThings Productions Snoot Entertainment
Distributed by	Lionsgate Roadside Attractions
Release date(s)	August 8, 2007 (TIFF) May 1, 2009
Running time	90 minutes
Country	United States
Language	English
Box office	$6,101,046[1]

Battle for Terra, originally screened as ***Terra***, is a 2007 computer animated science fiction film, based on a short film of the same name about a peaceful alien planet which faces destruction from colonization by the displaced remainder of the human race. The film was directed by Aristomenis Tsirbas who conceived it as a hard-edged live action feature with photo-real Computer-Generated Imagery (CGI) environments. The close collaboration with producing partner and investor Snoot Entertainment redirected the project to become fully animated and appeal to younger audiences. The film features the voices of Evan Rachel Wood, Brian Cox, Luke Wilson, Amanda Peet, Dennis Quaid and Justin Long among others.

It premiered on September 8, 2007 at the Toronto International Film Festival. It was widely released in the United States on May 1, 2009.[2] The film was originally shot in 2D but was made so that a second camera could be added to the film.[3] After the film was shown at festivals and distributors showed an interest in it a small team was hired to render the entire film again from the perspective of the second camera for a true 3D effect.[3]

It won the Grand Prize for Best Animated Feature at the 2008 Ottawa International Animation Festival.[4]

Plot

Mala (Evan Rachel Wood) and Senn (Justin Long) are young alien creatures who live on Terra, a planet from a solar system in the Milky Way. Terra is a peaceful planet of small alien creatures who have a rich semi-advanced culture.

One day a Large Mysterious object blocks the Terrian sun, piquing the Terrians' interest. However, since the Terrian culture bans the development of new technologies, such as telescopes, without the approval of the ruling council, none of the inhabitants are able to get a closer look at the huge object in their sky.

Mala, who is inventive and headstrong, goes against the rules of her community and creates a telescope, which she takes out into the dark empty area outside the Terrian city and uses to view the object and witnesses smaller objects coming from the large object that turn out to be incoming scout spaceships. She returns to the city to find that the scout spaceships have already started abducting Terrians (who willingly offer themselves to their new "gods"). After Mala's own father is abducted she goads a ship into tailing her and lures it into a trap, which causes it to crash. Afterward, she saves the life of the pilot, revealed to be a human, an officer named Lieutenant Jim Stanton (Luke Wilson). After his personal robot assistant warns Mala that Stanton will die without a supply of oxygen, (The Terran atmosphere contains none) she creates an oxygen generator and fills a tent with air so that he can breathe. The Robot informs Mala that the mysterious object is a generation ship called The Ark, containing humans from Earth. Centuries beforehand, Both Mars and Venus were terraformed by humans and colonized. But 200 years later, demanded Independence, and the resulting war left all three planets uninhabitable. The Ark, containing the remnants of the human race, traveled for several generations looking for a new home. When Stanton awakes the robot informs Stanton and Mala that a crucial part of the ship was damaged in the crash, Mala offers to make a replacement part herself. When Stanton, Mala, and the robot return to the crash site, they discover that the ship has been moved.

The trio track the ship to a huge underground military facility which was built by a previous, warlike generation of the Terrians. The trio realizes that despite the current peaceful nature of the Terrian city, the elders have secretly retained the military technology from the dark days of war. After infiltrating the facility, fixing the ship and flying back to the Ark, Jim orders Mala to stay and goes to be debriefed.

Mala ventures off and finds her father, but before she can rescue him, the human guards are alerted to her presence. While trying to save Mala, her father kills himself and two men after breaching the hull, and she is captured, but Stanton helps her to escape back to Terra. The commander of the military wing of the Ark, General Hemmer (Brian Cox), takes power over the civilian leaders in a coup, and declares war on Terra, citing the deteriorating condition of the Ark. His goal is to annihilate the Terrians so that the humans can turn Terra into the new Earth. He plans to drop a huge machine onto the planet's surface--called the Terraformer--which will create an Earthlike atmosphere. Stanton is sent to be in the first group of spacefighters designated to defend the Terraformer, while General Hemmer will go down to the planet's surface in the Terraformer to personally supervise the terraforming process.

After the humans drop the Terraformer machine onto the surface, it begins to replace the native gases with oxygen and nitrogen, which will asphixiate the aliens. The alien elders bring out all of the secretly-hidden military technologies from their secret base, and huge waves of alien glider-fighters attack the Terraformer machine. The human spacefighter ships begin a huge and bloody battle against the relatively low-tech alien glider-fighters, and the sky is filled with laser cannon fire and explosions.

Finally, as the Terraformer is close to the completion of its goal of turning the Terrian atmosphere into an Earth atmosphere, Lieutenant Stanton realizes that annihilating all of the inhabitants is morally wrong. He turns his ship towards the Terraformer machine, and, with his laser cannons blazing, attacks it. As his ship is raked with anti-aircraft defensive fire, Stanton fires his air-to-air missiles at the Terraformer's command module, destroying it, General Hemmer and himself in a ball of flame.

An epilogue shows what happens in Terra some time later. The Terrians and the humans have decided to live in peace. With the Terraformer machine destroyed, the Terrian atmosphere becomes safe once again for the aliens. The aliens create a huge domed city for the human colonists to live in, with an Earth-like atmosphere. In the human domed city, a large statue of Lieutenant Stanton is erected, in honor of his memory and sacrifice.

Cast

- Evan Rachel Wood as Mala
- Brian Cox as General Hemmer
- Luke Wilson as Jim Stanton
- David Cross as Giddy
- Justin Long as Senn
- Amanda Peet as Maria Montez
- Dennis Quaid as Roven
- Chris Evans as Stewart Stanton
- James Garner as Doron
- Danny Glover as President Chen
- Mark Hamill as Elder Orin
- Tiffany Brevard as Singer Soloist

Release

Roadside Attractions handled theatrical marketing in North America and used its business relationship with Lionsgate to open the film wide in the United States. *Battle for Terra* received uncharacteristically little marketing for a wide release film. The television campaign consisted of a small number of television spots on Cartoon Network and a handful of network television ads in select markets. Awareness for the film on its opening weekend was subsequently little to non-existent. This strategy of having a disproportionately small advertising campaign for a wide release was employed only one other time a year earlier with the film *Delgo*. The results for that film were disastrous as the $40 million *Delgo* grossed a mere $694,782 on 2,160 screens. The lower costing *Battle for Terra* fared considerably better by taking in more than twice as much revenue ($1,647,083) on roughly half as many screens (1,159) and continued on to gross $6 million internationally. *Battle For Terra* opened May 1 in the United States against 2 other wide releases: *X-Men Origins: Wolverine* (4,099 screens) and *Ghosts of Girlfriends Past* (3,175).

Reception

Critical reaction

The film has received average reviews from critics. Based on 93 reviews collected by Rotten Tomatoes, the film has an average rating of 5.5/10, and a score of 48% from all critics, with 52% from Top Critics.[5] Another review aggretator, Metacritic, which assigns a normalized rating out of 100 top reviews from mainstream critics, the film has received an average score of 54%, based on 19 reviews.[6]

Box office

The film opened at #12 in the United States grossing $1,082,064 in 1,159 theaters with an average of $934 per theater. The film's international box office began May 14, 2009 in Russia with a 5th place opening of $332,634 at 83 screens. "Battle for Terra's" current worldwide total is $6,101,046.

Home media release

Battle for Terra was released on DVD and Blu-ray Disc September 22, 2009 by Lionsgate Home Entertainment.[7]

Battle for Terra was released in France in French and English version by Rézo Films on DVD and Blu-ray Disc October 20, 2010 and include a 3D version of the movie with 4 3D glasses. [8] It uses the TriOviz Inficolor 3D technology, a patent pending stereoscopic system, first demonstrated at the International Broadcasting Convention in 2007 and deployed in 2010. It works with traditional 2D flat screens and HDTV sets and uses glasses with complex color filters and dedicated image processing that allow natural color perception with a pleasant 3D experience. When observed without glasses, some slight doubling can be noticed in the background of the action which allows watching the movie in 2D without the glasses. This is not possible with traditional brute force anaglyphic systems.[9]

A Region B Blu-ray 3D was released in Germany.[10]

References

[1] "Battle for Terra" (http://www.boxofficemojo.com/movies/?page=main&id=battleforterra.htm). Box Office Mojo. . Retrieved 2009-07-08.

[2] Welcome to MeniThings.com (http://www.menithings.com/main.php?action=movies&movie_id=23)

[3] "Battle for Terra: About the film: Production notes" (http://www.battleforterra.com/site/index.html). . Retrieved 2009-04-22.

[4] Ottawa 08 International Animation Festival - History (http://ottawa.awn.com/archives/OIAF08Archive/index.php?option=com_content&task=blogcategory&id=163&Itemid=806)

[5] "Battle for Terra Movie Reviews, Pictures" (http://www.rottentomatoes.com/m/10009859-terra/). *IGN Entertainment*. Rotten Tomatoes. . Retrieved 2009-05-03.

[6] "Battle for Terra (2009): Reviews" (http://www.metacritic.com/film/titles/battleforterra). Metacritic. . Retrieved 2009-05-03.

[7] "Lionsgate Announces 'Battle for Terra' Blu-ray" (http://www.highdefdigest.com/news/show/Lionsgate/Disc_Announcements/Lionsgate_Announces_Battle_for_Terra_Blu-ray/2970). High-Def Digest. . Retrieved 2009-07-08.

[8] "Battle for Terra 3D (Blu-ray): The test (Google Translation: French to English)" (http://translate.google.fr/translate?js=n&prev=_t&hl=fr&ie=UTF-8&layout=2&eotf=1&sl=fr&tl=en&u=http://www.unificationfrance.com/spip.php?article12085). Unification France. . Retrieved 2010-10-04.

[9] www.digitalcinemareport.com: The Games We Play, by Michael Karagosian (http://www.digitalcinemareport.com/Darkworks-Trioviz-3D)

[10] Terra Blu-ray

External links

- Battle for Terra (http://www.battleforterra.com)
- *Battle for Terra* (http://www.imdb.com/title/tt0858486/) at the Internet Movie Database
- *Battle for Terra* (http://www.rottentomatoes.com/m/10009859-terra/) at Rotten Tomatoes
- Battle for Terra 3D with INFICOLOR 3D technology (http://www.trioviz.com/en/consumer)

Street Kings

Street Kings	
Promotional poster	
Directed by	David Ayer
Produced by	Lucas Foster Alexandra Milchan Erwin Stoff
Written by	James Ellroy Kurt Wimmer Jamie Moss
Starring	Keanu Reeves Forest Whitaker Hugh Laurie Chris Evans Common The Game Naomie Harris Terry Crews Jay Mohr Martha Higareda
Studio	Regency Enterprises
Distributed by	Fox Searchlight Pictures
Release date(s)	April 11, 2008
Running time	109 minutes
Country	United States
Language	English
Budget	$20 million
Box office	$65,572,887

Street Kings is a 2008 action-crime film, directed by David Ayer, and starring Keanu Reeves, Hugh Laurie, Forest Whitaker and Chris Evans. It was released in theaters on April 11, 2008.

The initial screenplay drafts were written by James Ellroy in the late 1990s under the title *The Night Watchman.*

Plot

A disillusioned LAPD detective, Detective II Tom Ludlow (Keanu Reeves), rarely plays by the rules and is haunted by the death of his wife. All of the cops in Ludlow's unit, including the unit's commander, Captain III Jack Wander (Forest Whitaker), bend and break the rules of conduct on a regular basis.

The movie starts with Tom Ludlow waking up, having been drinking the night before. Working undercover, he meets with Korean gangsters (whom he believes have kidnapped two Korean schoolgirls) in a parking lot, who are looking to buy a machine gun from him. After a vicious beatdown, the Koreans then proceed to steal Tom's car. Tom however planned on this and has the cops locate the vehicle via GPS. Upon arrival at their hideout, Tom storms in and kills the four inside, and then locates the missing children. Using a pair of rubber gloves, he then proceeds to cover up what really happened. While the other officers in his unit congratulate him, he is confronted by his former partner, Detective II Terrence Washington (Terry Crews). Washington no longer approves of the corruption and deception and has gone straight, reporting the problems to Captain II James Biggs (Hugh Laurie), of internal affairs, who starts an investigation against Ludlow.

Upset at Washington for "snitching", Ludlow follows him to a convenience store to confront him. However, Washington is executed in the store in an apparent robbery, with Ludlow present. Though Ludlow is innocent, the circumstances can heavily implicate him in the murder. The DNA of two criminals known as Fremont and Coates is found at the scene, as well as a large amount of cash in Washington's possession. It is assumed that Washington himself was corrupt, despite his seemingly changed attitude, and that he had been stealing drugs from the department's evidence room and selling them to Fremont and Coates. Ludlow teams up with Detective I Paul "Disco" Diskant (Chris Evans), who has been assigned to the case to join him in his personal investigation. Their search for the two involves some tough interrogation of other criminals, which eventually leads them to a house in the hills where they discover the bodies of the real Fremont and Coates buried in a shallow grave. The condition of the bodies makes it apparent that they were killed well before Washington's murder.

Ludlow and Disco, posing as cops who are willing to take over Washington's supposed activity of stealing and selling drugs, are able to set up a meeting with the two criminals masquerading as Fremont and Coates. The meeting goes bad when Disco recognizes the two; he is shot and killed. Ludlow manages to kill both men and escapes back to his girlfriend's house, where a news report reveals the criminals were Sheriff's deputies.

Shortly afterward, Ludlow is subdued at his girlfriend's house by Detective I Cosmo Santos (Amaury Nolasco) and Detective I Dante Demille (John Corbett), two fellow officers from his unit who admit that they planted Fremont and Coates' DNA and the drugs at the scene of Washington's murder. The two cops take Ludlow out to the house where the two bodies were found earlier, for execution. However, Ludlow manages to kill both of them. He then heads to Washington's house to take care of their supervisor, Sergeant II Mike Clady (Jay Mohr), whom he later captures and places in the trunk of his car. Ludlow eventually learns that he has been a pawn in a plan masterminded by Captain III Wander. Ludlow shows up at Wander's house intending to kill him, when Wander reveals that he has incriminating evidence on just about everybody in the department, as well as judges, councilmen and politicians. With so many people in Wander's pocket, he has been able to quickly move up the department's ranks as well as bury his unit's corruptions. Wander tries to convince Ludlow that he is his friend and best officer, and tries to bribe him with a large amount of stolen money and incriminating documents hidden in a wall of his home. However, Ludlow shoots and kills Wander.

Captain II Biggs and Sergeant I Green, who were "investigating" Ludlow, arrive at the scene and reveal that they used Ludlow to bring down Wander and get access to his files by opening Ludlow's eyes to the real corruption going on within his unit. As he leaves, Biggs tells Ludlow that the department does indeed need men like him; officers who are willing to bend the rules, but are ultimately honest at heart.

Cast

- Keanu Reeves as Detective II Tom Ludlow
- Forest Whitaker as Captain III Jack Wander
- Hugh Laurie as Captain II James Biggs
- Chris Evans as Detective I Paul Diskant
- Jay Mohr as Sergeant II Mike Clady
- Terry Crews as Detective II Terrence Washington
- Naomie Harris as Linda Washington
- Martha Higareda as Grace Garcia
- John Corbett as Detective I Dante Demille
- Amaury Nolasco as Detective I Cosmo Santos
- Clifton Powell as Sergeant I Green
- Cedric the Entertainer (as Cedric 'The Entertainer' Kyles) as Winston "Scribble"
- Common as a Deputy Sheriff impersonating "Coates"
- Cle Shaheed Sloan (as Cle Sloan) as a Deputy Sheriff impersonating "Fremont"
- Noel Gugliemi (as Noel G.) as Quicks
- Game (rapper) as Grill
- Daryl Gates (as Daryl F. Gates) as Chief Gates
- Angela Sun as Julie Fukashima
- Michael Monks as Pathologist
- Kenneth Choi as Boss Kim
- Walter Wong as Thug Kim

Production

In 2004, it was announced that Spike Lee would be directing the film for a 2005 release.[1] In 2005, it was announced that Oliver Stone was in talks to direct the film.[2] However, Stone later denied this.[3] *Training Day* screenwriter David Ayer took over the project.

On February 5, 2008, it was announced that Fox Searchlight Pictures changed the film's title from *The Night Watchman* to *Street Kings*.[4]

Critical reception

Street Kings received mixed reviews from critics. Metacritic reported the film had an average score of 55 out of 100, based on 28 reviews.[5] Many viewers praised the film for its numerous plot twists. On the other hand, Rotten Tomatoes's Tomatometer gave a 37% for the film, with their consensus saying, "Street Kings contains formulaic violence but no shred of intelligence."

Box office

In its opening weekend, the film grossed an estimated $12 million in 2,467 theaters in the United States and Canada, ranking 2 at the box office. The movie as of August 1, 2008 has made $26,418,667 domestically and $35,347,445 in foreign box offices totaling $62,973,667 in total worldwide sales, making it a moderate financial success.[6]

DVD release

The DVD was released on August 19, 2008, as a single disc offering with director commentary, and 2-disc special-edition set with numerous documentaries, interviews and a digital copy of the film. It is also available on Blu-ray disc with all the special features of the 2-disc DVD version.

Sequel

- Street Kings: Motor City

References

[1] The Night Watchman Movie - Keanu Reeves to Star in The Night Watchman (Street Kings) (http://movies.about.com/od/reeveskeanu/a/watchman111604.htm)
[2] The Night Watchman Movie - Oliver Stone May Direct The Night Watchman (Street Kings) (http://movies.about.com/od/moviesinproduction/a/watchman042805.htm)
[3] IGN: Stone Denies Night Watchman (http://filmforce.ign.com/articles/613/613388p1.html)
[4] The Night Watchman Retitled to Street Kings - ComingSoon.net (http://www.comingsoon.net/news/movienews.php?id=41661)
[5] "Street Kings (2008): Reviews" (http://www.metacritic.com/film/titles/streetkings). Metacritic. . Retrieved 2008-04-11.
[6] "Street Kings (2008) - Weekend Box Office Results" (http://www.boxofficemojo.com/movies/?page=weekend&id=streetkings.htm). Box Office Mojo. . Retrieved 2008-08-01.

External links

- Official website (http://foxsearchlight.com/streetkings/)
- Korean Herald, English edition, Weekly/People (http://www.koreaherald.co.kr/)
- *Street Kings* (http://www.imdb.com/title/tt0421073/) at the Internet Movie Database
- *Street Kings* (http://www.allrovi.com/movies/movie/v321760) at AllRovi
- *Street Kings* (http://www.rottentomatoes.com/m/street_kings/) at Rotten Tomatoes
- *Street Kings* (http://www.metacritic.com/movie/streetkings) at Metacritic
- *Street Kings* (http://www.boxofficemojo.com/movies/?id=streetkings.htm) at Box Office Mojo
- Hollywood Street King (http://diaryofahollywoodstreetking.com)

The Loss of a Teardrop Diamond

The Loss of a Teardrop Diamond	
Theatrical release poster	
Directed by	Jodie Markell
Produced by	Brad Michael Gilbert Robbie Kass Brad Stokes Roxanna Raanan
Written by	Tennessee Williams (Screenplay)
Starring	Bryce Dallas Howard Chris Evans Ellen Burstyn Ann-Margret Jennifer Sipes
Cinematography	Giles Nuttgens
Release date(s)	December 30, 2009
Country	United States
Language	English

The Loss of a Teardrop Diamond is a 2009 film by director Jodie Markell. The film is based on Tennessee Williams's long-forgotten 1957 screenplay. The film stars Bryce Dallas Howard in the leading role of Fisher Willow.

Plot

The film tells the story of heiress Fisher Willow (Bryce Dallas Howard). Fisher returns home from overseas to find that her father has become a hated man in Memphis as he had intentionally blown up the southern half of his levee earlier that year, resulting in the deaths of two people and enormous property damage for anyone downstream. Fisher is to come out to society this season, but because of her father's reputation - and her inappropriate/wild behavior - she is unable to find a man willing to be her escort. She asks Jimmy (Chris Evans) to be her escort for the season.

Jimmy is not her social equal, but she was always taken with him. His father works on Fisher's land though he is a heavy drinker and is at risk of losing his job, and his mother was committed to an insane asylum and no longer recognizes her son. Jimmy agrees to be her escort as she is willing to pay him and he could use the money to help his parents. Fisher arranges for him to be outfitted properly and promises that there are better places for Jimmy's mother.

For the season Fisher borrows $10,000 teardrop diamond earrings from her aunt. Fisher and Jimmy attend the first society party together where she causes a scene when she has the band play controversial music and dances in "flapper" fashion. Soon the entire party views her as a joke and laughs at her, insulting her father and the fact that she had to pay a man to be her escort. In response, Jimmy yells at everyone to shut up and helps Fisher to the car.

Because of her behavior at the previous party, the only other social gathering that Fisher is invited to is a Halloween party in northern Memphis where no one knows of her father's previous actions. As he waits for Fisher to pick him up for the next party, Jimmy mentions to his father that Fisher seemed to be sending him the message that she wanted to become more intimate. Jimmy suggests that if he were to agree to be more than her escort, then it would certainly lead to marriage which meant a permanent job for his father and better care for his mother.

On the way to the Halloween gathering, Fisher asks Jimmy to stop up at the levee so she can look at the water. She rests her head on his shoulder before moving to kiss him. Jimmy, in spite of what he said to his father earlier, pulls back instead, causing Fisher to be hurt and embarrassed. When they arrive at the party, Fisher is so angry with Jimmy that she gets out of the car before it fully stops. When she straightens out her clothes she realizes that one of her teardrop earrings has fallen off. Becoming frantic and somewhat hysterical - especially when Jimmy recognizes a girl outside, Vinnie, an old romantic interest of his - Fisher believes that the earring fell off when she walked away from the car and begins searching the ground for it. When she is unsuccessful she remembers that she had rested her head on Jimmy's shoulder earlier and asks him to check his pockets to see if the earring was there. Jimmy misunderstands and thinks that Fisher is accusing him of stealing the jewelry. He becomes furious, as his father was fired from a job once for stealing, and demands that she search his jacket. Fisher, confused as to why he is so angry, refuses causing Jimmy to go into the party and demand that he be searched down to the skin in order to clear his good name.

Fisher, needing to get away from all the commotion, goes upstairs where she meets Aunt Addie who is bedridden and unable to move her limbs due to a series of severe strokes. Addie says that she senses a kindred spirit in her, the same character that will not bend to the rules of society, and tells Fisher of a drug she used to use Opium before she was sick. She points to a bottle on the shelf and says it contains the last of her stash. She asks Fisher to give her all of the pills (since she is unable to move herself) so she can die and stop the pain. Fisher agrees but before she can go through with it she is interrupted by Vinnie telling her that Jimmy was searched and the earring was not on him. Fisher puts the bottle back on the counter and places her remaining earring next to it, promising Addie that she would be back to get her earring and would give her the rest of the opiates then.

Fisher goes back downstairs to find everyone suspects her of "losing" her diamond on purpose so that she could blame Jimmy and not have to pay him for being her escort. Jimmy is still angry at Fisher for her accusation of theft and leaves her alone to go be with Vinnie. Soon, the people begin to play Post Office, a kissing game. Jules, the hostess and friend of Fisher, gives her the highest card so that she can call Jimmy away from the other girl and kiss him herself. Fisher, growing increasingly distant, hides in the bathroom. She finds a bottle of Addie's "medicine" which contains a small amount of Opium and drains it. Drifting through the party in a dreamy haze she reveals to everyone that, while overseas, she was actually at a mental institution. Still in a daze, Fisher misses when Jules asks who has the highest card and so Jimmy, who had the next highest, calls Vinnie to go out on the porch with him instead of Fisher. When she realizes that he chose Vinnie over herself, Fisher goes to the piano and plays a beautiful song, crying the whole time.

In the meantime, Jimmy and Vinnie have sex in a car outside. Vinnie tells Jimmy that she had an offer of marriage from a respectable man, but turned him down because she wasn't attracted to him like she was to Jimmy. Claiming that she didn't want any secrets between them, she brings him over to the back garden and digs in the ground to unearth the missing teardrop diamond. She had seen it on the ground while Fisher searched for it and had taken it herself. Vinnie says she knows where the other one is (she saw Fisher put it next to the bottle on the shelf upstairs) and that she and Jimmy could run away with the jewelry and start a life together. Jimmy refuses, telling her that just because they are poor, it doesn't mean they are without honor, and she should return the earring to Fisher. Vinnie, angry, runs away with the earring.

Jimmy goes to look for Fisher and finds her in the car. She says she wants to go home, but Jimmy won't let her leave (he wants to find Vinnie and get the earring back). Jimmy pulls Fisher out of the car and there is a brief moment where they are close and Fisher looks longingly at him, before they are interrupted by Vinnie. She came back to return the earring to Fisher. Jimmy yells that they can leave now that she has her damn earring back, but before they go Fisher remembers her promise to Addie and runs back inside. After she leaves Jimmy thanks Vinnie for doing the right thing. Vinnie says that they will probably never see each other again as her only option now is to go marry the gentleman who made her an offer earlier. They embrace, and Jimmy returns to the car to wait for Fisher. Fisher retrieves her other teardrop diamond and fulfills her promise to Addie, giving her the entire contents of the bottle and bidding her farewell. Addie tells her to go with God. Fisher replies that she is: she's leaving with Jimmy.

On the way home Fisher asks Jimmy to stop at the same levee they went to before the party so she can see the moon on the water. They stand on the levee together and Fisher tells him that she intends to fix her father's mistake and that she can't run away anymore. She makes an offer to Jimmy: that his mother will be taken care of, his father will always have a job, and while she knows that no one could ever love her, he could get used to her. She reaches up to touch his face, but he pulls away again. Heartbroken, Fisher turns to walk away, only to find that Jimmy had grabbed her hand - a silent agreement to her proposal. She turns back to him and once again rests her head on his shoulder.

Production

In November 2006, it was announced that Lindsay Lohan was going to play the lead role, but in March 2007, Bryce Dallas Howard was under negotiations for Lohan's role and went on to be cast.[1] Shooting for the film began on August 13, 2007 in Baton Rouge, Louisiana.

Cast

- Bryce Dallas Howard as Fisher Willow
- Chris Evans as Jimmy Dobyne
- Ellen Burstyn as Miss Addie
- Ann-Margret as Aunt Cornelia
- Mamie Gummer as Julie
- Will Patton as Old Man Dobyne
- Jessica Collins as Vinnie

Reception

The film has received generally negative reviews. Review aggregate Rotten Tomatoes reports that 26% of critics have given the film a positive review based on 38 reviews, with an average score of 4.4/10.[2] Metacritic, however, gave it an overall 51 out of 100 rating. [3]

References

[1] Bryce Dallas Howard on 'The Loss of a Teardrop Diamond' (http://movies.radiofree.com/interviews/thelosso_bryce_dallas_howard.shtml)

[2] "Rotten Tomatoes" (http://www.rottentomatoes.com/m/loss_of_a_teardrop_diamond/). . Retrieved 2010-09-05.

[3] http://www.metacritic.com/movie/the-loss-of-a-teardrop-diamond/critic-reviews

External links

- *The Loss of a Teardrop Diamond* (http://www.imdb.com/title/tt0896031/) at the Internet Movie Database

Push (2009 film)

Push	
Theatrical release poster	
Directed by	Paul McGuigan
Produced by	Bruce Davey William Vince Glenn Williamson
Written by	David Bourla
Narrated by	Dakota Fanning
Starring	Chris Evans Dakota Fanning Camilla Belle Djimon Hounsou Li Xiaolu Cliff Curtis Neil Jackson Ming-Na Maggie Siff
Music by	Neil Davidge
Cinematography	Peter Sova
Editing by	Nicolas Trembasiewicz
Studio	Icon Productions
Distributed by	Summit Entertainment (USA) Icon Film Distribution (UK)
Release date(s)	February 6, 2009
Running time	111 minutes
Country	United States
Language	English
Budget	$38 million[1]
Box office	$48,808,215[1]

Push is a 2009 American science fiction thriller film directed by Paul McGuigan. The film stars Chris Evans, Dakota Fanning, Camilla Belle, Cliff Curtis and Djimon Hounsou. The film centers on a group of people born with various superhuman abilities who band together in order to take down a government agency that is using a dangerous drug to enhance their powers in hopes of creating an army of super soldiers.

Plot

A narrator describes how people with psychic abilities have been involved with the United States government since 1945. Two "Movers", Nick Gant and his father, are on the run from the "Division". Realizing that escape is impossible, Nick's father tells him of a vision he received from a "Watcher"; a girl will give him a flower and he is to help her in order to help all the people with powers. Nick's father throws Nick into an air vent as Agent Henry Carver of the Division arrives. Nick's father is killed.

A decade later, the American Division tests a power boosting drug on a "Pusher" (someone who can implant thoughts in others' minds), named Kira. Hundreds of subjects died from the drug before her; she is the first to survive. Rendering the doctor unconscious, Kira steals his security clearance card and an augmentation drug-filled syringe and escapes. In Hong Kong, Nick is hiding from the Division as an expatriate. He attempts to use his ability to make a living, but his poor skills at "moving" at a dice game leave him indebted to a local Triad controlled by "Bleeders", bred by the now-defunct Chinese Division. A young girl named Cassie Holmes arrives at Nick's apartment, explaining that she is a "Watcher" and that they are going to find a case containing 6 million dollars. They are attacked by Triad Bleeders but escape.

Nick and Cassie go to a nightclub on a hint from Cassie's predictions. Nick sees an old friend, "Hook" Waters, who is a "Shifter". He uses his abilities to make a replica of the clue in Cassie's drawing and tells them to go to Emily Hu, a "Sniff" who can help them find Kira. Nick and Cassie find Kira, who had a romantic relationship with Nick. They recruit a "Shadow" named "Pinky" Stein to hide Kira from the "Sniffs". Cassie finds the key to a locker in which Kira hid a case. With the aid of Cassie's visions, they piece together the events that led them to meet; Cassie's mother used her visions to set a complex plan in motion that will destroy Division. Nick devises a plan that involves seven envelopes in which he places instructions; each person in the group is entrusted with one red envelope, and none are to be opened until the right time. While Kira and Pinky leave, Nick and Cassie share a goodbye. Cassie tells him to "take an umbrella, it's going to rain", he replies with "you be careful too".

Nick uses a "Wiper" to erase his memories of the plan, ensuring that Watchers from both Division and the Triads will not be able to interfere. Hook retrieves the case, which has the syringe Kira stole, and brings it to Cassie. He shifts another case to match the case with the syringe. Cassie takes the shifted case to Nick's apartment and waits. Nick regains consciousness: he has no memory of the envelopes or his plan. He opens his envelope, which tells him to return home. He finds the case in his room but Carver introduces himself to Kira as a friend, stating that her memories are false; she is a Division agent who volunteered to take the augmentation injection and suffered amnesia as a side-effect. Carver shows Kira her badge.

Nick goes to retrieve the augmentation drug and confronts Carver and Kira. Carver tells Kira and Nick that their relationship never happened; it was a "push" memory. Kira reveals she has been using Nick and Nick takes the three to the building that contains the lockers and the case. They are ambushed by the Triads. In the midst of the fight, Carver injures Nick. Nick grabs the case and jams the syringe into his arm, which "kills" him. After the fights ends, Nick wakes up. Cassie appears with an umbrella and smiles at him. "I told you to bring an umbrella" she tells him, revealing it was part of the plan. Cassie retrieves the true case, revealing that Nick injected himself with soy sauce, as they planned. Asked whether they will see Kira again, Cassie tells Nick that they will see "Miss Trouble soon enough".

Flying back to America with a sleeping Agent Carver, Kira opens her purse, finding her red envelope. She remembers Nick telling her to open it when "she started doubting the truth" and opens it. She finds a photograph of herself and Nick obviously in a relationship, and a message written on the photograph that says "KILL HIM" on the upper left corner and "See U soon, Nick" on the lower right. Kira "pushes" Carver, commanding him to put his gun in his mouth and pull the trigger. The screen fades to black, followed by the sound of a gunshot.

Types of Superhumans

Watchers

Watchers have the ability to foresee the future to varying degrees. As knowledge of the future invariably causes that future to change, Watchers' visions of the future in their direct sphere of influence are subject to frequent shifting.

Movers

Movers are powerful telekinetics who are trained to identify the specific atomic frequency of a given material and alter the gravitational field around it, usually causing the nearby air to appear warped. This allows them to move both animate and inanimate objects. Advanced Movers can work at the molecular level, creating protective force fields in the air around them or to reinforce punches and other strikes to make them stronger.

Pushers

Pushers have the ability to implant memories, thoughts and emotions into the minds of other people in order to manipulate them. The skill level of the Pusher determines how many people the Pusher is able to control at one time, and how vivid the implanted memories are. A powerful Pusher can push a large group of people at the same time, basically creating a personal army. A Pusher is able to make a person do anything the Pusher desires, even commit suicide. A Pusher's eyes indicate how powerful they are: their pupils will dilate to certain degrees depending on how powerful the push is (for example, Henry Carver's eyes are rendered completely black, signifying that he is an extremely able and effective Pusher).

Bleeders

Bleeders have the ability to emit high-pitched sonic vibrations that cause ruptures in a target's blood vessels. While using this ability, their pupils turn into vertical slits, like a snake's, because of synthetic materials implanted in them to protect the blood vessels from the effects of their own ability. They are also sometimes known as Screechers or Screamers.

Sniffs

Sniffs are highly developed psychometrics who can track the location of people or objects over varying distances. Like bloodhounds, their ability is increased if they have tactile access to an object that has been in direct contact with the subject. Sniffs receive information in the form of images, which is why identifiable landmarks help increase their effectiveness.

Shifters

Shifters can temporarily alter the appearance of an object by manipulating the patterns of light interacting with it. Once the illusion is established, it remains with the object for a short period of time. For example, a Shifter could touch a one dollar bill and alter it to appear as a one hundred dollar bill until the effect expires. The object shifted must have roughly the same dimensions as the object it is shifted into. The length of time that the effect will last is based on the Shifter's experience and ability.

Wipers

Wipers are skilled at either temporarily or permanently erasing memory, an invaluable asset in espionage. Experience will dictate the accuracy of their wipes, though there is always the danger that they will eliminate a desired memory.

Shadows

Shadows are trained to block the vision of other clairvoyants such as Sniffs, making any subject within their target radius appear "dark". Experience will enhance the size of the area they can shadow and the intensity of their shielding effect. Shadows need to be awake to manifest their ability, so it is common for a detail of two Shadows to operate in shifts while protecting a person or object for extended periods. Most Shadows are effective only against Sniffs, but some extremely powerful Shadows are able to block even Watchers.

Stitches

Stitches are psychic surgeons trained to quickly reconstruct cells to their previous or healthy state. Using only their hands, they can heal and even "unheal" whatever they have done. For more detailed work, Stitches use a silver based cream on their hands which acts as a conductor for their ability.

Phasers

Phasers Are able to alter their body density and can pass through any and all solid objects. They are also able to phase others and objects through solid objects as well but they have to be holding on to that certain person/object. Phasers can only stay phased for how ever long they are able to hold their breath for.

Jumpers

Jumpers are skilled teleporters, they can teleport from one place to another in a split second.

Changers

Changers the ability to shapeshift into anyone person they desire.

Readers

Readers have the ability to read the minds and thoughts of others.

Stoppers

Stoppers have the ability to stop time. They can only freeze the objects/people in the rooms they are in. Some stoppers have been noted to be able to freeze entire households. They are able to selectively freeze at will. (Meaning if there is a big group of people they can freeze how ever many people they desire and freeze and unfreeze certain body parts of others) but this has been noted to take a great more deal of concentration for them. When outside they can only freeze within the area they are in.

Shockers

Shockers have the ability to absorb and create electricity through the palms and fingertips of their hands, because of their ability to absorb electric they can with stand being shocked on a greater scale then the average human being but they are more prone to tempers and fits.

Stealths

Stealths Have the ability to absorb light and are able to bend the light around themselves to make them invisible to the naked eye, which gives them a stealth-like ability. By touching others, they are able to make them invisible alike. Stealths can be seen by infra-red goggles or animals that hunt by sensing body heat. They are only able to stay in invisible for a certain period of time because eventually the light they absorbed to bend the light around their bodies will dissipate and they will have to absorb more light. Also because of their ability to absorb light and shield it around them, bright shiny lights like the sun or LED lights have no effect on their eyes.

Whisperers

Whisperers are skilled telepaths. Experience will increase the amount of people a Whisperer can connect with. As the number of people they connect with increases, the harder it is to stay connected. They can also connect with strong emotions in the form of a psychic blast that gives the receiver an extreme headache; if the Whisperer focuses hard enough they can immobilize the receiver.

Cast

- Chris Evans as Nick Gant, a Mover living in Hong Kong in order to stay hidden from Division, whose father was killed by Carver. He was born in America and once had a relationship with Kira. One form of income - although not always successful - is to manipulate betting games involving dice using his ability.
  - Colin Ford as a young Nick Gant.
- Joel Gretsch as Nick's father Jonah, an advanced Mover whose refusal to join the Division cost him his life. It is implied the he and Hook once worked in Division together.
- Dakota Fanning as Cassie Holmes, the daughter of the greatest Watcher Division has ever encountered, and a Watcher in her own right. Like all abilities, hers is not fully developed as this happens through training. She is sometimes confused by what she draws in her premonitions.
  - Cassie's mother Elisabeth is uncredited; a powerful Watcher who was captured by Division to prevent her use of powers against them. It is through her that most of the events occur as she helped Kira escape Division HQ, paid Wo to erase Kira's memories, as well as get Teresa in the right place to heal Nick and told Nick's father to tell his son to follow the one who gave him a flower. Though this alone shows the strength of her Watcher abilities, as she saw this all happen at least a decade ago where most can only see a few hours or days into the future.
- Camilla Belle as Kira Hudson/Hollis, a high-level Pusher, a recent escapee of Division, and the only Division patient to have survived experimentation.
- Djimon Hounsou as Agent Henry Carver, a Division agent and a powerful Pusher that killed Nick's father. He is sent to recapture Kira.
- Ming-Na as Emily Hu, a Sniffer who helps Nick & Cassie find Kira. She works as a fortune teller in Hong Kong.
- Cliff Curtis as "Hook" Waters, a Shifter. He used to be in Division and after getting out, his wife died in a "car accident," and he knew Division was involved. Since he moved to Hong Kong he has begun hanging out in high class escort bars where he uses his shifting ability to pay his way. He implies that Nick's father had a similar past and it is confirmed in the Comics that both use to work for Division. He has a habit of saying "that won't last long" after he uses his abilities.
- Nate Mooney as "Pinky" Stein, a Shadow who hid Kira from the Sniffs. His nickname is derived from Division's removal of his right "pinky" finger.
- Corey Stoll as Agent Mack, a Sniffer agent.
- Scott Michael Campbell as Agent Holden, a Sniffer agent.
- Neil Jackson as Victor Budarin, an advanced Mover and Carver's right hand man.
- Maggie Siff as Teresa Stowe, a Stitch who helps heal Nick after an encounter with the bleeders, as requested by Cassie's mother, who told her to be in a certain place at a certain time and help whomever was there. She is, however, not seen as altruistic, but, instead, out for personal gain, rather than helping Cassie and Nick overthrow Division.
- Paul Car as Wo Chiang, a Wiper who lives on a house boat in Hong Kong Harbour.
- Xiao Lu Li as Pop Girl, a Chinese Triad Watcher who tries to find Nick and Cassie throughout Hong Kong. Like Cassie, she draws her visions. Her visions are based on others' intentions and decisions.
- Kwan Fung Chi and Jacky Heung as Pop Boys, the two Triad Bleeders.
- Haruhiko Yamanouchi as Pop Father, Triad Bleeder and father to the three 'Pop' siblings.

Reception

Push was generally poorly received by critics.[2] Rotten Tomatoes reported that 21% of critics had given the film positive reviews, based upon a sample of 106.[3] At Metacritic, which assigns a normalized rating out of 100 to reviews from mainstream critics, the film has received an average score of 36, based on 21 reviews.[2]

On its opening weekend, the film opened #6 grossing $10,079,109 in 2,313 theaters with a $4,358 average.[4] As of Nov 2010, the film has grossed $48,858,618 worldwide, and $16,285,488 in DVD sales in the US alone making $65,157,106 (not including worldwide DVD sales) surpassing its budget cost of $38,000,000 by over $27 million.[1]

Variety: "A confused jumble of parts in search of a whole, Push plays like a mix-tape sample of scenes from *Heroes*, *Fringe*, *Alias* and *The X-Files* as it follows good guys gifted with paranormal powers trying to stave off bad guys with the same..."

The Hollywood Reporter: "While the concept of corralling assorted Movers (those with telekinetic talents), Watchers (clairvoyants) and, of course, Pushers (mind controllers with the ability to alter one's memories) and placing them against a stylish Asian backdrop is intriguing, the picture seldom rises to the occasion. ...monotonous..."

Screen Daily: "The most compelling thing about *Push* is its setting. The film was shot entirely on location, which affords it a fresh look and feel, be it in a chase through a local fish market or the juxtaposition of modern skyscrapers and bamboo scaffolding...[The screenplay] is a jumbled mess of narrative clichés."

Comic

Wildstorm, an imprint of DC Comics, published a comic book mini-series that acts as a prequel to the film. It was written by Marc Bernardin and Adam Freeman (who write *The Highwaymen* for Wildstorm) and Bruno Redondo supplied the art.[5] Issues were published between November 2008 and February 2009, and a softcover collection (ISBN 978-1401224929) was published in September, 2009.

Home release

Push was released on DVD and Blu-ray on July 7, 2009. The DVD included deleted scenes, a commentary, and a 'making of' featurette. Wal-Mart released the film as a double-feature DVD with *Knowing*.

Television series

On January 19, 2010, Summit Entertainment, E1 Entertainment, and Icon Productions announced that they were developing a television series based on the film. David Hayter will write the pilot and will executive produce with Dark Hero Studios partner Benedict Carver. It is unknown if the actors and actresses from the original film will reprise their roles.[6]

Soundtrack and score

No official soundtrack has been released, although the full score is available to stream online on the official Neil Davidge website.

Artist	Title
The Kills	What New York Used to Be
Yin Xiangjie	The Love Of Boat Trackers
Radio Citizen and Bajka	The Hop
Working for a Nuclear Free City	Rocket
Neil Davidge	Original music for *Push*
UNKLE	Glow
Daniele Benatie and Fernando Paterlini	Everybody Ciao
South Rakkas Crew	Elevator China
The Notwist	Consequence
South Rakkas Crew	China Funk
The Old Ceremony	Bao Qian
Jiang Xianwei	A Visit to Suzhou

References

[1] "Push (2009)" (http://boxofficemojo.com/movies/?id=push09.htm). Box Office Mojo. . Retrieved 2009-05-06.
[2] "Push (2009): Reviews" (http://www.metacritic.com/film/titles/push). *Metacritic*. CNET Networks, Inc. . Retrieved 2009-02-06.
[3] "Push Movie Reviews, Pictures" (http://www.rottentomatoes.com/m/10010066-push/). *Rotten Tomatoes*. IGN Entertainment, Inc. . Retrieved 2009-05-06.
[4] "Weekend Box Office Results for February 6–8, 2009" (http://www.boxofficemojo.com/weekend/chart/?yr=2009&wknd=006&p=.htm). Box Office Mojo. 2009-02-08. . Retrieved 2009-02-10.
[5] SDCC 08: Wildstorm Snares Push License (http://uk.comics.ign.com/articles/892/892803p1.html), IGN, July 22, 2008
[6] 2010 Press Releases & News (http://www.summit-ent.com/news.php?news_id=132), Summit Entertainment, February 24, 2010

External links

- Official website (http://www.push-themovie.com)
- *Push* (http://www.imdb.com/title/tt0465580/) at the Internet Movie Database
- *Push* (http://www.allrovi.com/movies/movie/v413360) at AllRovi
- *Push* (http://www.rottentomatoes.com/m/10010066-push/) at Rotten Tomatoes
- *Push* (http://www.metacritic.com/movie/push) at Metacritic
- *Push* (http://www.boxofficemojo.com/movies/?id=push09.htm) at Box Office Mojo
- *Push* (http://www.reelsoundtrack.com/index.php?act=movie_details&id=53617) at ReelSoundtrack

The Losers (film)

The Losers	
Theatrical release poster	
Directed by	Sylvain White
Produced by	• Joel Silver • Akiva Goldsman • Kerry Foster
Screenplay by	• Peter Berg • James Vanderbilt
Based on	• *The Losers* by • Andy Diggle
Starring	• Jeffrey Dean Morgan • Zoe Saldana • Chris Evans • Idris Elba • Columbus Short • Óscar Jaenada • Jason Patric • Holt McCallany • Peter Macdissi
Music by	John Ottman
Cinematography	Scott Kevan
Editing by	David Checel
Studio	• DC Entertainment • Dark Castle Entertainment • Weed Road Pictures
Distributed by	Warner Bros. Pictures
Release date(s)	April 23, 2010
Running time	97 minutes
Country	United States
Language	English
Budget	$25 million[1] [2] [3]
Box office	$29,379,723[1] [2]

The Losers is a 2010 American action based on the adaptation of the Vertigo comic book series of the same name by Andy Diggle. Directed by Sylvain White, the film features an ensemble cast that includes Jeffrey Dean Morgan, Zoe

Saldana and Chris Evans.

The film received negative reviews from critics and drew comparisons to *The A-Team*, a remake of which was released shortly after *The Losers* premiered.

Plot

The Losers are an elite black-ops team of United States Special Forces operatives, led by Clay (Jeffrey Dean Morgan) and formed by Roque (Idris Elba), Pooch (Columbus Short), Jensen (Chris Evans) and Cougar (Óscar Jaenada), who are sent to Bolivia in a search-and-destroy mission on a compound run by a drug lord. While painting a target for an upcoming air strike, the Losers spot slave children in the compound and try to call off the attack, but their superior, codenamed "Max" (Jason Patric), ignores their pleas.

With no other option, the Losers enter the compound, successfully rescue the children and kill the drug lord in the process. As a helicopter arrives to pick them up, Max, convinced that they know too much, orders it to be destroyed, unaware that they decided to rescue the children first. The Losers watch as a missile destroys the helicopter and kills 25 innocents. Knowing that the attack was meant to kill them, they fake their deaths and become stranded in Bolivia, determined to get revenge on the mysterious Max.

Four months later, Clay is approached by Aisha (Zoe Saldana), a mysterious woman who offers him the chance to kill Max, against whom she wants revenge. Clay accepts and Aisha arranges for the Losers to return to the United States, where they proceed to attack a convoy supposedly carrying Max, only to discover that they were tricked by Aisha into stealing a hard drive with Max's secrets.

Unable to access the files, Jensen infiltrates the company that made the drive and steals an algorithm that allows him to crack the code, discovering that the drive contains credits for a $400 million transfer in Max's name, which he received for selling "Snukes" - eco-friendly bombs with the potency of a nuclear warhead, but no fall-out - to international terrorists. Tracing the money flow to the Los Angeles International Port Of Entry, which the Losers deduce is Max's base, a plan is formed to attack it and kill Max.

While studying the drive, Jensen discovers that their mission in Bolivia was a cover so Max could steal the drug lord's money, and that Aisha is the man's daughter, seeking to reclaim what Max stole from her. After her cover is blown, Aisha shoots Jensen and escapes. Believing that she might betray them, the Losers decide to speed up their attack on Max's base, only to be betrayed by Roque and captured by Max and his right-hand man and chief of security, Wade (Holt McCallany).

As the Losers are lined up to be executed, Aisha returns and ambushes Max's team. In the ensuing fight, Clay confirms that he killed Aisha's father. Roque attempts to steal Max's plane, loaded with his money, and tries to escape. As Roque's jet heads down the runway, Wade takes a motorcycle and goes after him to retrieve Max's money. Cougar shoots the engine of a pursuing Wade's motorcycle, causing Wade to be hurled into the jet's engine and the flaming motorcycle to be hurled into the cockpit of the plane, which explodes, killing Roque.

As Jensen, Cougar and Aisha help Pooch, who has been shot in both legs by one of Max's security guards, Clay pursues Max to a crane, where Max says that he has activated a Snuke that'll destroy Los Angeles, and Clay will have to choose between de-activating it or killing Max. Clay choses the former and Max escapes, but Clay affirms that he now knows what Max looks like and will soon find him.

Shortly thereafter, the Losers help Pooch reach the hospital where his pregnant wife is giving birth to their son and attend Jensen's 8-year-old niece's soccer game.

Cast

- Jeffrey Dean Morgan as Colonel Franklin Clay
- Idris Elba as William Roque
- Zoe Saldana as Aisha al-Fadhil
- Chris Evans as Jake Jensen
- Columbus Short as Linwood "Pooch" Porteous
- Óscar Jaenada as Carlos "Cougar" Alvarez
- Jason Patric as Max
- Holt McCallany as Wade
- Peter Macdissi as Vikram

Production

Development

In 2007 it was announced that a movie adaptation is in development with a screenplay by Peter Berg and James Vanderbilt, to be directed by Tim Story for Warner Bros.[4] In October 2008 *Variety* reported that Sylvain White had now taken the director's chair, with Dark Castle Entertainment acting as the financiers.[5]

In February 2009, it was reported that Jeffrey Dean Morgan would headline the upcoming adaptation playing Clay. In March 2009, it was confirmed that Columbus Short will play Pooch, Idris Elba will play Roque and Zoe Saldana will play Aisha, Chris Evans playing Jensen, and Óscar Jaenada playing Cougar. In August 2009, it was announced that Jason Patric will play Max.[6]

White explained how he worked closely with the creators of the comic book to recreate the visual tone of the story.[7] The film adapts the first two volumes of the comic book, "Ante Up"[8] and "Double Down"[9] and tells the story in a more linear way than in the comic books. Elements of the story have been left out instead of trying to squeeze the whole story into one film and the director would like to tell the rest of the story if the film does well at the box office.[10]

Filming

Jeffrey Dean Morgan took the role of leader very seriously and was on set every day, even if he was not in the scene.[11]

Filming for *The Losers* began in Miami, Florida and Puerto Rico in July 2009.[12]

Many of the movie's scenes were filmed in many of Miami's neighborhoods such as Brickell, Downtown Miami, Midtown Miami and South Beach. City scenes were shot in the Downtown Miami area, with driving scenes in the city filmed along Brickell Avenue and near the Adrienne Arsht Center for the Performing Arts.

Filming in Puerto Rico included scenes at the Arecibo Observatory, Port of San Juan and the Milla de Oro area of Hato Rey, Puerto Rico.

Marketing

Promotional artwork for the film was released at Comic Con, the poster was drawn in the style of the comic book by series artist Jock, and was later recreated photographically with the cast from the film and used as the theatrical release poster.[13]

A four minute preview of the film was shown at WonderCon.[14]

A special "double volume" collected edition graphic novel was released to tie in with the film adaptation collecting including the volumes *Ante Up* and *Double Down*. A second book to collect the rest of the series was also released.[15]

Release

In June 2009, Warner Bros. set a tentative release date of April 9, 2010 for the film.[16] The release date was then pushed back to June 4, 2010, to avoid going up against *Clash of the Titans* also from Warner Bros.[17] The trailer for the film was released online January 29, 2010, and was shown in theaters with *Edge of Darkness*.[18] An official photo for the film was released online.[19] The release date was subsequently moved up to April 23, 2010.[20] [21]

Reception

Critical response

The film has received mixed to negative reviews. It holds an approval rating of only 48% on Rotten Tomatoes based on 152 reviews, with a consensus stating *The Losers* is loud, fast, and unrelentingly violent.

Review aggregation website Metacritic assigned the film a weighted average score of 44% based on 32 reviews from selected critics.[22]

Peter Debruge of *Variety* criticized the film as "the sort of pyro-heavy exercise parodied in *Tropic Thunder*. He notes that casting against type helps make the team more memorable but complains that despite the polished production the film offers only a hollow junk-food high.[23] John Anderson describes the film as a good idea pushed to excess, and with all the freshness of last week's salad bar.[24] Scott Tobias of The AV Club complains about the lack of humility or self-deprecation in the heroes despite their title. He notes how the film tries so strenuously to be cool and describes the film as nothing more than style for its own sake.[25] Kyle Smith of the *New York Post* lambasts the film giving it half a star out of 4. He describes Zoe Saldana as a femme banale, saying actors Jeffrey Dean Morgan, Idris Elba, deserved better and Chris Evans deserved worse. He dismisses the film as G.I. Joke, The D-Team, and says that even though the film tries to do so little, it still falls so short.[26]

Phelim O'Neill of *The Guardian* newspaper gave the film 3 stars out of 5. He notes similarities to the A-Team and criticises the film for being full of action movie cliches. He praises the film for the lighter comedic touches, and overall describes it as big dumb fun.[27] His colleague Philip French of *The Observer* described the film as being in "A-Team territory" with the action sequences being well enough put together but that it was all done far better in Walter Hill's *Extreme Prejudice*.[28]

Box office

The film played in 2,936 theaters and earned $9,406,348 on its opening weekend at the box office at #4.[29] [3] The film went on to earn $23.5 million in the United States and more than $5 million internationally for a worldwide total of over $29 million. Added to this, it made over $8.2 million on DVD sales in the USA alone, giving it a minimum earning of $37.6 million - a profit of over $12.6 million before worldwide DVD sales.[1]

Home media

In the United States, the DVD release date for the film was July 20, 2010.[30]

References

[1] "The Losers (2010)" (http://www.boxofficemojo.com/movies/?id=losers.htm). *Box Office Mojo*. Amazon.com. . Retrieved 2010-08-14.

[2] "The Losers" (http://www.the-numbers.com/movies/2010/LOSRS.php). *The Numbers*. . Retrieved 2010-05-20.

[3] Horn, John (April 22, 2010). "Movie Projector: 'Dragon' will breathe fire again" (http://latimesblogs.latimes.com/entertainmentnewsbuzz/2010/04/box-office-back-up-plan-train-your-dragon-kick-ass.html). *Los Angeles Times* (Tribune Company). . Retrieved May 9, 2010.

[4] McClintock, Pamela; Fleming, Michael (June 8, 2007). "Tim Story to direct 'Losers'" (http://www.variety.com/article/VR1117966583.html). *Variety*. . Retrieved 2007-06-08.

[5] Fleming, Michael (November 6, 2008). "Sylvain White to direct 'The Losers'" (http://www.variety.com/article/VR1117995421.html). *Variety*. . Retrieved 2008-11-06.

[6] Michael Fleming (2009-07-13). "Jason Patric joins 'Losers'" (http://www.variety.com/article/VR1118007244.html). *Variety*. . Retrieved 2009-07-15.

[7] Rick Marshall (2010-03-24). "'The Losers' Director On Creator Collaboration, Scheduling, And His Favorite Scenes" (http://splashpage.mtv.com/2010/03/24/the-losers-creator-collaboration-scheduling-favorite-scenes). *MTV Splashpage*. Viacom. .

[8] *Ante Up* (collects #1-6, 158 pages, 2004 ISBN 1-40120-198-9)

[9] *Double Down* (with Shawn Martinbrough, collects #7-12, 144 pages, 2004 ISBN 1-40120-348-5)

[10] Rick Marshall (2010-04-23). ""the Losers" director on where the movie and comics Connect, revealing the Villain, and potential sequels!" (http://splashpage.mtv.com/2010/04/23/the-losers-director-on-where-the-movie-and-comics-connect-revealing-the-villain-and-potential-sequels). *MTV Splashpage*. Viacom. .

[11] Ian Caddell (April 22, 2010). "Jeffrey Dean Morgan gambles on The Losers" (http://www.straight.com/article-318920/vancouver/morgan-gambles-losers). .

[12] "The Losers" (http://www.hollywoodreporter.com/hr/content_display/news/e3i7c23ccda60974aa212e4b64a53d2e876). Hollywood Reporter. . **(subscription required)**

[13] Peter Sciretta (2010-01-30). "New Promo Photo for The Losers Recreates Comic Con Teaser Poster" (http://www.slashfilm.com/2010/01/30/new-promo-photo-for-the-losers-recreates-comic-con-teaser-poster). */Film*. .

[14] Rocco Passafuime (April 22, 2010). "Jeffrey Dean Morgan interview for The Losers" (http://www.thecinemasource.com/blog/interviews/jeffrey-dean-morgan-interview-for-the-losers/#page3). *The Cinema Source*. p. 3. . Retrieved 2011-02-14.

[15] *Book 1* (collects #1-12, 304 pages, ISBN 1-4012-2733-3). *Book 2* (collects #13-32, 480 pages, ISBN 1-4012-2923-9)

[16] "The Losers" (http://www.comingsoon.net/films.php?id=50350). ComingSoon.net. . Retrieved 2009-06-25.

[17] Ian Mason (February 14, 2010). "'The Losers' release date put back" (http://www.digitalspy.co.uk/movies/news/a203145/the-losers-release-date-put-back.html). .

[18] The Losers Trailer (2010) (http://www.youtube.com/watch?v=o_K6y8ihyi8) on YouTube Retrieved on 2010-05-20.

[19] Promotion photograph of cast (http://omelete.uol.com.br/images/galerias/thelosers/05.jpg)

[20] BrentJS (2010-02-17). "The Losers Release Date Moved (Again)" (http://www.reelz.com/movie-news/5867/the-losers-release-date-moved-again/). . Retrieved 2011-10-22. "It's likely that Warner is looking to avoid a box-office shootout with The A-Team, which opens on June 11th."

[21] Ronnita Miller (February 16, 2010). "THE LOSERS' release date moved again" (http://gordonandthewhale.com/the-losers-release-date-moved-again). .

[22] "The Losers Reviews, Ratings, Credits" (http://www.metacritic.com/movie/the-losers). *Metacritic*. CBS. . Retrieved 2010-06-03.

[23] Peter Debruge (April 21, 2010). "The Losers Review" (http://www.variety.com/review/VE1117942597.html). *Variety*. .

[24] John Anderson (April 23, 2010). "Only Action Clichés Win in 'Losers'" (http://online.wsj.com/article/SB10001424052748703876404575199903883041696.html). *Wall Street Journal*. .

[25] Scott Tobias (April 22, 2010). "The Losers" (http://www.avclub.com/articles/the-losers,40403/). *The AV Club*. The Onion. .

[26] Kyle Smith (April 23, 2010). "'The Losers' is a no-win situation" (http://www.nypost.com/p/entertainment/movies/no_win_situation_ck3uSWcYtuS0ZnsazoFIAJ). *New York Post*. . 0.5/4 stars

[27] Phelim O'Neill (May 27, 2010). "The Losers" (http://www.guardian.co.uk/film/2010/may/27/the-losers-film-review). *The Guardian* (London). . 3/5 stars ★

[28] Philip French (May 30, 2010). "The Losers" (http://www.guardian.co.uk/film/2010/may/30/philip-french-the-losers-film-review). *The Observer* (London: The Guardian). .

[29] "The Losers (2010) - Weekend Box Office Results" (http://www.boxofficemojo.com/movies/?page=weekend&id=losers.htm). *Box Office Mojo*. Amazon.com. . Retrieved 2010-05-20.

[30] "The Losers (2010)" (http://www.amazon.com/Losers-Zoe-Saldana/dp/B002ZG99G8). Amazon.com. . Retrieved 2011-01-31.

External links

- Official website (http://www.the-losers.com)
- *The Losers* (http://www.imdb.com/title/tt0480255/) at the Internet Movie Database
- *The Losers* (http://www.rottentomatoes.com/m/1226860/) at Rotten Tomatoes
- *The Losers* (http://www.metacritic.com/movie/losers) at Metacritic
- *The Losers* (http://www.boxofficemojo.com/movies/?id=losers.htm) at Box Office Mojo

Scott Pilgrim vs. the World

Scott Pilgrim vs. the World	
Official international poster	
Directed by	Edgar Wright
Produced by	Edgar Wright Marc Platt Eric Gitter Nira Park
Screenplay by	Edgar Wright Michael Bacall
Based on	*Scott Pilgrim* by Bryan Lee O'Malley
Narrated by	Bill Hader
Starring	Michael Cera Mary Elizabeth Winstead Kieran Culkin Chris Evans Anna Kendrick Alison Pill Brandon Routh Jason Schwartzman
Music by	Nigel Godrich
Cinematography	Bill Pope
Editing by	Jonathan Amos Paul Machliss
Studio	Big Talk Films Relativity Media
Distributed by	Universal Studios
Release date(s)	July 27, 2010 (Fantasia Festival) August 13, 2010 (United States)
Running time	112 minutes[1]
Country	United States United Kingdom
Language	English
Budget	$85–90 million[2] [3] [4] $60 million after tax rebates[5]

Box office	$47,664,559[2] [5]

Scott Pilgrim vs. the World is a 2010 comedy film directed by Edgar Wright, based on the graphic novel series *Scott Pilgrim* by Bryan Lee O'Malley. The film is about Scott Pilgrim (Michael Cera), a young Canadian musician, meeting the girl of his dreams, Ramona Flowers (Mary Elizabeth Winstead), an American delivery girl. In order to win Ramona, Scott learns that he must defeat Ramona's "seven evil exes", who are coming to kill him.

Scott Pilgrim vs. the World was planned as a film after the first volume of the comic was released. Wright became attached to the project and filming began in March 2009 in Toronto. *Scott Pilgrim vs. the World* premiered after a panel discussion at the San Diego Comic-Con International on July 22, 2010. It received a wide release in North America on August 13, 2010 in 2,818 theaters.[5] [6] The film finished fifth on its first weekend of release with a total of $10.5 million.[5] [7] The film received generally positive reviews by critics and fans of the graphic novel, but it failed to recoup its production budget during its release in theaters, grossing $31.5 million in North America and $16 million overseas.[5] [8] However, the film has fared better on home video, becoming the top-selling Blu-ray on Amazon.com during the first day it was available.[9]

Plot

In Toronto, Scott Pilgrim (Michael Cera), the bass guitarist for the band "Sex Bob-omb", begins dating high schooler Knives Chau (Ellen Wong) much to the disapproval of his friends. Scott meets an American girl, Ramona Flowers (Mary Elizabeth Winstead), who has been appearing in his dreams, and becomes obsessed with her - losing interest in Knives. While playing in a battle of the bands, Scott is attacked by Matthew Patel (Satya Bhabha), who introduces himself as the first of Ramona's "evil exes." Scott defeats Patel and learns from Ramona that, in order for them to date, he must defeat all seven of her evil exes.

Her second evil ex, popular actor and skateboarder Lucas Lee (Chris Evans), comes to Toronto to film a movie. Scott breaks up with Knives; still in love, Knives attempts to win him back from Ramona. Scott defeats Lee by tricking him into performing a dangerous skateboard grind which he fails to complete. Scott later encounters the third evil ex, Todd Ingram (Brandon Routh), who is dating Scott's ex-girlfriend, Natalie "Envy" Adams (Brie Larson). Todd initially overpowers Scott using his psychic vegan abilities, but is stripped of his powers by the Vegan Police (Thomas Jane and Clifton Collins, Jr.) after Scott tricks him into having coffee with half and half milk, allowing Scott to defeat him.

Scott begins to grow upset with Ramona over her dating history by the defeat of the fourth ex, Roxy Richter (Mae Whitman), as he is afraid of fighting girls. During the second round of the battle of the bands, Sex Bob-omb faces off against the fifth and sixth evil exes, twin Katayanagi brothers Kyle (Keita Saito) and Ken (Shota Saito), earning Scott an extra life upon their defeat. During the battle, Scott sees Ramona together with her seventh evil ex, Gideon Graves (Jason Schwartzman), who turns out to be Sex Bob-omb's sponsor, G-Man. Gideon offers the members of Sex Bob-omb a record deal and a chance to perform at his newly opened Chaos Theatre. While the rest of the band signs the contract, Scott refuses to accept the offer and leaves the band. Shortly after, Ramona breaks up with Scott. Scott returns home to get a phone call from Gideon, inviting him to the Chaos Theatre to show there are no hard feelings.

Scott enters the Chaos Theatre and challenges Gideon to a fight, and professes his love for Ramona, gaining the "Power of Love" sword which he uses to fight Gideon. Gideon strikes Scott in mid-air, making him lose the sword. Knives also crashes the scene (and blocks another attack), to fight Ramona over Scott. Not able to take it any more, Scott goes to break up the girls' fight, and admits that he cheated on them with each other. He is killed by Gideon before he can apologize.

In Limbo, Scott and Ramona discuss the reasons for each other's actions. Ramona tells Scott that she broke up with Gideon because he ignored her during their relationship. While they were together however, Gideon had a mind control device planted on the back of her neck. Scott realizes he still has an extra life, which he uses to escape limbo and returns to life at the moment in time where Gideon calls him. Scott re-enters the Chaos Theatre.

Scott challenges Gideon again, stating he is fighting for himself and gaining the "Power of Self-Respect" sword. The mid-air strike is repeated, and Scott strikes Gideon. With Gideon unconscious, Scott blocks Knives' attack on Ramona, and apologizes to both girls. Gideon rises to fight Scott again and knocks down Ramona, who betrayed him, but is defeated when Knives and Scott team up to destroy him. Shortly afterwards, Nega Scott (a shadow-like alter ego of Scott) appears, but instead of fighting, the two get along quite well. Free from Gideon's control, Ramona prepares to leave. Knives accepts that her relationship with Scott is over, and encourages him to chase after Ramona. He does, and the two start their relationship anew.

Cast

Main characters

- Michael Cera as Scott Pilgrim, a 22-year-old Canadian, who falls in love with Ramona Flowers. He is the bass guitarist of the band Sex Bob-omb.
- Mary Elizabeth Winstead as Ramona Victoria Flowers, a mysterious American delivery girl with a dating history that drives the plot of the film.
- Kieran Culkin as Wallace Wells, Scott's 25-year-old gay roommate and close friend.
- Ellen Wong as Knives Chau, a 17-year-old high school girl whom Scott dates before meeting Ramona.[10]
- Alison Pill as Kim Pine, the 23-year-old drummer of Sex Bob-omb and one of Scott's ex-girlfriends.
- Mark Webber as Stephen Stills, the 22-year-old lead singer and "talent" of Sex Bob-omb.
- Johnny Simmons as "Young" Neil Nordegraf, a 20-year-old fan of Sex Bob-omb and Scott's replacement after he leaves the band.
- Anna Kendrick as Stacey Pilgrim, Scott's 18-year-old sister.
- Brie Larson as Natalie V. "Envy" Adams, one of Scott's ex-girlfriends who went on to become the singer of the successful band The Clash at Demonhead.[10]
- Aubrey Plaza as Julie Powers, Stephen's ex-girlfriend, who has issues.

The League of Evil Exes, in numerical order

1. Satya Bhabha as Matthew Patel, who has mystical powers, such as fireballs and levitation
2. Chris Evans as Lucas Lee, a "pretty good" skateboarder turned "pretty good" action movie star.
3. Brandon Routh as Todd Ingram, the bassist for The Clash at Demonhead who possesses telekinetic powers as a result of his veganism; he is the boyfriend of Scott's ex-girlfriend Envy Adams.
4. Mae Whitman as Roxanne "Roxy" Richter, a self-conscious lesbian half-ninja.
5. Shota Saito as Kyle Katayanagi
6. Keita Saito as Ken Katayanagi, twins and popular Japanese musicians.
7. Jason Schwartzman as Gideon Gordon Graves, manager of the Chaos Theatre, Sex Bob-Omb's sponsor and the mastermind behind the League of Evil Exes.

Other characters

- Kjartan Hewitt as Jimmy, Stacey's boyfriend; Wallace stole him and the two kiss as Ramona leaves the first round of the Battle of the Bands at the "Rockit"; from Stacey's reaction, it is implied that Wallace has done this before
- Ben Lewis as Other Scott, another one of Wallace's boyfriends
- Nelson Franklin as Comeau, one of Scott's friends who "knows everybody" "including you"
- Christine Watson as Matthew Patel's Demon Hipster Chicks
- Chantelle Chung as Tamara Chen, Knives' best friend
- Don McKellar as Director, the director of the Lucas Lee film
- Emily Kassie as Winifred Hailey, a 16-year-old actress who was due to star in a movie with Lucas Lee before he was defeated by Scott; she briefly appears on the film set at the Casa Loma
- John Patrick Amedori as the Chaos Theatre's bouncer

- Erik Knudsen as Luke "Crash" Wilson, singer and guitarist of the band Crash and the Boys who competes in the battle of the bands.
- Tennessee Thomas as Lynette Guycott, drummer for The Clash at Demonhead.
- Maurie W. Kaufmann as Joel, a member of Crash and the Boys
- Abigail Chu as Trisha "Trasha" Ha, the 8-year-old drummer of Crash and the Boys
- Kristina Pesic and Ingrid Haas as Sandra and Monique, two popular girls at Julie's party

Thomas Jane and Clifton Collins, Jr. appear uncredited as the Vegan Policemen. The author, Bryan Lee O'Malley, and his wife, Hope Larson, also appear uncredited as Lee's Palace bar patrons. Reuben Langdon (known for being the voices of Ken in Street Fighter IV, and Dante in the Devil May Cry series) has a cameo as one of Lucas Lee's stunt doubles.

Production

Development

After artist Bryan Lee O'Malley completed the first volume of *Scott Pilgrim*, his publisher Oni Press contacted producer Marc Platt with the proposition for a film version.[11] Universal Studios contracted Edgar Wright who had just finished his last film, *Shaun of the Dead*, to adapt the *Scott Pilgrim* comics.[11] [12] O'Malley originally had mixed feelings about a film adaptation, stating that he "expected them to turn it into a full-on action comedy with some actor that I hated" [but ultimately] "didn't even care. I was a starving artist, and I was like, 'Please, just give me some money.'"[13]

In May 2005, the studio signed Michael Bacall to write the screenplay adaptation.[12] Bacall said that he wanted to write the *Scott Pilgrim* film because he "felt strongly" about the story and "empathized" with *Scott Pilgrim*'s characters.[14] By January 2009, filmmakers rounded out its cast for the film, now titled *Scott Pilgrim vs. the World*.[15] Edgar Wright noted that O'Malley was "very involved" with the script of the film from the start, and even contributed lines to and "polished" certain scenes in the film. Likewise due to the long development process several lines from the various scripts written by Wright and Bacall ended up in books four and five as well.[16]

O'Malley confirmed that no material from *Scott Pilgrim's Finest Hour*, the sixth Scott Pilgrim volume, would appear in the film, as production had already begun. While he had given ideas and suggestions for the final act of the film, he admitted to that some of those plans might change throughout the writing process and ultimately stated that "Their ending is their ending".[17] O'Malley gave Wright and Bacall his notes for the sixth book while filming took place.[18]

Casting of the principal characters began in June 2008.[19] Principal photography began in March 2009 in Toronto[20] [21] and wrapped as scheduled in August.[19] [22] In the film's original ending, written before the release of the final *Scott Pilgrim* book, Scott ultimately gets back together with Knives. After the final book in the series was released, in which Scott and Ramona get back together, and negative audience reaction to the ending during testing, a new ending was filmed to match the books, with Scott and Ramona getting back together.[23]

The film was given a production budget of $85–90 million, an amount offset by tax rebates that resulted in a final cost around $60 million.[5] Universal fronted $60 million of the pre-rebate budget.[24]

Casting

Director Wright felt confident with his casting in the film. Wright stated that "Like with *Hot Fuzz* how we had great people in every single tiny part, it's the same with this. What's great with this is that there's people you know, like with Michael [Cera] and Jason [Schwartzman], and then we have people who are up and coming, like Anna Kendrick, Aubrey Plaza and Brie Larson, and then there's complete unknowns as well".[25] There was no studio interference with casting more unknowns, as Wright stated that "Universal never really gave me any problems about casting bigger people, because in a way Michael [Cera] has starred in two $100 million-plus movies, and also a lot of the other people, though they're not the biggest names, people certainly know who they are."[25] Wright planned on casting Cera while writing *Hot Fuzz* after watching episodes of *Arrested Development*.[25] Wright said he needed an actor that "audiences will still follow even when the character is being a bit of an ass."[26] Edgar Wright ran all his casting decisions by O'Malley during the casting session.[18] Mary Elizabeth Winstead was Wright's choice for Ramona Flowers two years before filming had started, because "she has a very sunny disposition as a person, so it was interesting to get her to play a version of herself that was broken inside. She's great in the film because she causes a lot of chaos but remains supernaturally grounded."[10] Ellen Wong, a Toronto actress known mostly from a role in *This Is Wonderland*,[19] auditioned for the part of Knives Chau three times. On her second audition, Wright learned that Wong has a green belt in tae kwon do, and says he found himself intrigued by this "sweet-faced young lady being a secret badass".[10]

Music

Radiohead producer Nigel Godrich, Beck, Metric, Broken Social Scene, Cornelius, Dan the Automator, Kid Koala, and David Campbell all contributed to the film's soundtrack.[27] [28] [29] [30] [31] Beck wrote and composed the music played by Sex Bob-omb in the film, and two unreleased songs can also be heard in the teaser trailer.[32] Cast members Mark Webber, Alison Pill and Johnny Simmons all had to learn to play their respective instruments, and spent time rehearsing as a band with Michael Cera (who already played bass) and Beck before filming began.[33] The actors also perform on the movie soundtrack.[34] Brendan Canning and Kevin Drew of Broken Social Scene wrote all the songs for Crash and the Boys. The tracks were sung by actor Erik Knudsen, who plays Crash in the film. Drew stated that the reason behind this was that "[he] knew that [Knudsen] didn't need to be a singer to pull [it] off" because the songs were "so quick and punk and fast" and "it needed to be the character's voice."[35] Metric is the inspiration for the film's fictional band, the Clash at Demonhead, and contributed the song "Black Sheep" to the film. The clothing of Metric's lead singer, Emily Haines, is also the basis for the clothing of the lead singer of Clash at Demonhead.[36] Brie Larson provides the vocals for "Black Sheep" in the film, while the soundtrack features a version of the song with Haines as lead singer.[37] Chris Murphy of the band Sloan was the guitar coach for the actors in the film.[25] Music from *The Legend of Zelda* video game series is used in a dream sequence in the film. To get permission to use the music, Edgar Wright sent a clip of the film and wrote a letter to Nintendo that described the music as "like nursery rhymes to a generation."[26]

Release

A *Scott Pilgrim vs. the World* panel featured at the San Diego Comic-Con International held on July 22, 2010. After the panel Edgar Wright invited selected members of the audience for a screening of the film which was followed by a performance by Metric.[39] *Scott Pilgrim vs. the World* was also shown at the Fantasia Festival in Montreal, Quebec, Canada on July 27, 2010 and was also featured at the Movie-Con III in London, England on August 15, 2010.[40] [41]

The film premiered in Japan during the Yubari International Fantastic Film Festival on February 26, 2011 as an official selection. It was released to the rest of the country on April 29, 2011.[42] [43]

Michael Cera dressed up as Captain America at the *Scott Pilgrim* panel at the San Diego Comic-Con.[38]

Marketing

On March 25, 2010, the first teaser trailer for the film was released.[44] A second trailer featuring music by The Ting Tings, LCD Soundsystem, Be Your Own Pet, Cornelius, Blood Red Shoes, and The Prodigy was released May 31, 2010.[45]

At the 2010 MTV Movie Awards, the first clip from the film was released featuring Scott Pilgrim facing Lucas Lee in battle. The actors playing Lucas Lee's stunt doubles are the actual stunt doubles for Chris Evans.[46] Alison Pill who plays Kim Pine in the film stated that her character's past relationship with Scott will be explored in other media stating that "There will be a little something-something that will air on Adult Swim".[47] The animated short, *Scott Pilgrim vs. the Animation*, produced by Titmouse Inc., adapts the opening prologue of the second *Scott Pilgrim* book and was aired on Adult Swim on August 12, 2010, later being released on their website.[48] Michael Cera stated that he felt the film was "a tricky one to sell. I don't know how you convey that movie in a marketing campaign. I can see it being something that people are slow to discover. In honesty, I was slow to find *Shaun of the Dead*".[49]

Video game

A video game was produced based on the series. It was released for PlayStation Network on August 10, 2010 and on Xbox Live Arcade on August 25, being met with mostly positive reviews.[50] [51] The game is published by Ubisoft and developed by Ubisoft Montreal and Ubisoft Chengdu, featuring animation by Paul Robertson and original music by Anamanaguchi.[52] [53]

Home media

Scott Pilgrim vs. the World was released on DVD and Blu-ray in North America on November 9, 2010[54] and in the United Kingdom on December 27, 2010.[55]

The DVD features include four audio commentaries: (director Edgar Wright, co-writer Michael Bacall, and author Bryan Lee O'Malley; Wright and director of photography Bill Pope; Michael Cera, Jason Schwartzman, Mary Elizabeth Winstead, Ellen Wong, and Brandon Routh; and Anna Kendrick, Aubrey Plaza, Kieran Culkin, and Mark Webber), 21 deleted, extended, and alternate scenes with commentary, bloopers, photo galleries, and a trivia track.

The Blu-ray release includes all DVD features, plus alternate footage, six featurettes, production blogs, Scott Pilgrim vs. the Animation, trailers and TV spots, storyboard picture-in-picture, a DVD copy, and a digital copy. The "Ultimate Japan Version" Blu-ray includes a commentary track that features Wright and Shinya Arino. It also includes footage of Wright and Michael Cera's publicity tour through Japan and a roundtable discussion with Japanese film critic Tomohiro Machiyama. It was released on September 2, 2011[56] .

In its first week of release, the DVD sold 190,217 copies, earning $3,422,004 in revenue.[57] It reached the top of the UK Blu-ray charts in its first week of release.[58]

Reception

Box office

The film was widely released in North America on August 13, 2010, opening in 2,818 theaters.[5] [6] The film finished fifth on its first weekend of release with a total of $10.5 million,[5] [7] [24] and by its second weekend of release had dropped to the bottom of the top ten.[59] *The Wall Street Journal* described this as "disappointing"[7] while Ben Fritz of the *Los Angeles Times* noted that the film appeared to be a "major financial disappointment".[3] Universal acknowledged their disappointment at the opening weekend, saying they had "been aware of the challenges of broadening this film to a mainstream audience"; regardless, the studio's spokeman said Universal was "proud of this film and our relationship with the visionary and creative filmmaker Edgar Wright.... Edgar has created a truly unique film that is both envelope pushing and genre bending and when examined down the road will be identified as an important piece of filmmaking."[24]

In the UK, the film opened in 408 cinemas, finishing second on its opening weekend with £1.6 million,[60] dropping to fifth place by the next weekend.

Critical response

Response to the film post-premiere has been very positive. Review aggregation website Rotten Tomatoes gives the film a score of 81% based on 217 reviews, with an average score of 7.5 out of 10. Rotten Tomatoes' consensus is that "its script may not be as dazzling as its eye-popping visuals, but *Scott Pilgrim vs. the World* is fast, funny, and inventive".[61]

Metacritic has assigned an average score of 69, based on 38 reviews, which indicates generally favorable reviews.[62] David Edelstein of *New York* magazine wrote that "The film is repetitive, top-heavy: Wright blows his wad too early. But a different lead might have kept you laughing and engaged. Cera doesn't come alive in the fight scenes the way Stephen Chow does in the best (and most Tashlin-like) of all the surreal martial-arts comedies, *Kung Fu Hustle*."[63]

At a test screening, director Kevin Smith was impressed by the film saying "That movie is great. It's spellbinding and nobody is going to understand what the fuck just hit them. I would be hard pressed to say, 'he's bringing a comic book to life!' but he is bringing a comic book to life." Smith also said that fellow directors Quentin Tarantino and Jason Reitman were "really into it".[64] Singer for the band Sister and writer for *Now*, Carla Gillis, also commented on the film.[65] Gillis was the singer of the now-disbanded Canadian group Plumtree, and their single "Scott Pilgrim" that inspired O'Malley to create the character and the series.[65] In an interview describing the film and the song that inspired it, Gillis felt the film carried the same positive yet bittersweet tone of the song.[65]

After premiere screenings at the San Diego Comic-Con International, the film received positive reviews. *Variety* gave the film a mixed review, referring to the film as "An example of attention-deficit filmmaking at both its finest and its most frustrating" and that "anyone over 25 is likely to find director Edgar Wright's adaptation of the cult graphic novel exhausting, like playing chaperone at a party full of oversexed college kids."[1] *The Hollywood Reporter* wrote a negative review, stating that "What's disappointing is that this is all so juvenile. Nothing makes any real sense...[Michael] Cera doesn't give a performance that anchors the nonsense." and "Universal should have a youth hit in the domestic market when the film opens next month. A wider audience among older or international viewers seems unlikely."[66]

IGN gave the film a positive rating of 8/10 calling the film "funny and offbeat" as well as noting that the film is "best suited for the wired generation and those of us who grew up on Nintendo and MTV. Its kinetic nature and quirky sensibilities might be a turnoff for some."[67]

Nick Schager of *Slant Magazine* gave the film a positive review of three and a half stars out of four, calling Edgar Wright an "inspired mash-up artist, and Scott Pilgrim vs. the World may be his finest hybridization to date".[68] A. O. Scott made the film his "critics pick", stating "There are some movies about youth that just make you feel old, even if you aren't...*Scott Pilgrim vs. the World* has the opposite effect. Its speedy, funny, happy-sad spirit is so infectious that the movie makes you feel at home in its world even if the landscape is, at first glance, unfamiliar."[69]

After its premiere in Japan, several notable video game, film and anime industry personalities have praised *Scott Pilgrim vs. the World*, among them Hironobu Sakaguchi, Goichi Suda, Miki Mizuno, Tomohiko Itō, Rintaro Watanabe and Takao Nakano.[70]

Top ten lists

The film appeared on several critics' top ten lists of the best films of 2010.[71]

- 1st — Armond White, *indieWIRE*[72]
- 1st — Harry Knowles, *Ain't It Cool News*
- 3rd — Drew McWeeny, *HitFix*
- 3rd — Tasha Robinson, *The Onion A.V. Club*
- 5th — Jeremy Jahns, YouTube
- 6th — Amy Nicholson, *Boxoffice Magazine*
- 6th — *Empire*
- 6th — Neil Miller, *Film School Rejects*
- 6th — Mike Russell, *The Oregonian*
- 6th — *Slant Magazine*
- 6th — *Collider*
- 8th — Steve Ramos, *Boxoffice Magazine*
- 10th — Glenn Kenny, *MSN Movies*
- 10th — Nathan Rabin, *The Onion A.V. Club*
- 10th — Kimberley Jones, *Austin Chronicle*
- 10th — *NOW Magazine (Toronto)*
- 10th — Josh Tyler, *Cinemablend*

The film also appeared, unranked, on the following critics' top ten lists.

- Wesley Morris, *The Boston Globe*
- Carrie Rickey, *The Philadelphia Inquirer*

Accolades

The film received four nominations at the 2010 Satellite Awards held on the 19th of December at the Intercontinental Hotel in Century City. It won in two categories; Best film - Comedy or Musical and Best Actor - Musical or Comedy for Michael Cera. The film also made the final short list for a nomination for Best Visual Effects at the Academy Awards but did not receive a nomination.

Awards			
Award	**Category**	**Name**	**Outcome**
Artios Awards	Outstanding Achievement in Casting - Big Budget Feature - Comedy	Robin D. Cook and Jennifer Euston	Nominated
Austin Film Critics Association Awards	Best film		Nominated
Central Ohio Film Critics Association	Best Picture		Nominated
	Best Overlooked Film		Nominated
Detroit Film Critics Society Awards	Best Director	Edgar Wright	Nominated
	Best Ensemble	Overall casting	Nominated

Award	Category	Recipient	Result
Empire Awards	Best Film		Nominated
	Best Sci-Fi/Fantasy		Nominated
	Best Director	Edgar Wright	Won
GLAAD Media Awards	Outstanding Film - Wide Release		Nominated
Hugo Awards	Best Dramatic Presentation - Long Form	Michael Bacall and Edgar Wright	Nominated
Sierra Awards	Best Art Direction		Nominated
	Best Costume Design	Laura Jean Shannon	Nominated
	Best Song	Beck for "We Are Sex Bob-Omb"	Nominated
	Best Visual Effects		Nominated
Online Film Critics Society Awards	Best Editing	Jonathan Amos and Paul Machliss	Nominated
	Best Adapted Screenplay	Michael Bacall and Edgar Wright	Nominated
SFX Awards	Best Film Director	Edgar Wright	Won
San Diego Film Critics Society Awards	Best Editing	Jonathan Amos and Paul Machliss	Won
	Best Adapted Screenplay	Michael Bacall and Edgar Wright	Nominated
Satellite Awards[73]	Best Film - Musical or Comedy		Won
	Best Actor - Motion Picture Musical or Comedy	Michael Cera	Won
	Best Art Direction and Production Design	Nigel Churcher and Marcus Rowland	Nominated
	Best Adapted Screenplay	Michael Bacall and Edgar Wright	Nominated
Saturn Awards	Best Fantasy Film		Nominated

Scream Awards	The Ultimate Scream		Nominated
	Best Director	Edgar Wright	Nominated
	Best Scream-Play		Nominated
	Best Villain	Satya Bhabha, Chris Evans, Brandon Routh, Mae Whitman, Shota Saito, Keita Saito and Jason Schwartzman as The League of Evil Exes	Nominated
	Best Supporting Actress	Ellen Wong	Nominated
	Best Supporting Actor	Kieran Culkin	Nominated
	Fight Scene of the Year	Final Battle: Scott Pilgrim and Knives vs. Gideon Graves	Won
	Best Comic Book Movie		Won
Teen Choice Awards	Choice Movie: Action Actor	Michael Cera	Nominated
	Choice Movie: Action Actress	Mary Elizabeth Winstead	Nominated
	Choice Movie: Action		Nominated
Utah Film Critics Association Awards	Best Director	Edgar Wright	Nominated
	Best Screenplay	Michael Bacall and Edgar Wright	Nominated

References

[1] Debruge, Peter (July 23, 2010). "Scott Pilgrim vs. the World" (http://www.variety.com/review/VE1117943219.html). *Variety*. . Retrieved July 23, 2010.

[2] "Scott Pilgrim vs. The World - Box Office Data" (http://www.the-numbers.com/movies/2010/SPILG.php). *The Numbers*. . Retrieved April 12, 2011.

[3] Fritz, Ben (2010-08-15). "Box office: 'Expendables' blows up, 'Scott Pilgrim' out of tune, 'Eat Pray Love' has decent first bite" (http://latimesblogs.latimes.com/entertainmentnewsbuzz/2010/08/box-office-expendables-on-target-scott-pilgrim-out-of-tune-eat-pray-love-has-decent-first-bite-.html). *Los Angeles Times*. . Retrieved 2010-08-21. "Universal spent about $85 million to make the picture, along with a small investment by Relativity Media"

[4] Kit, Borys; Masters, Kim (August 13, 2010). "The $200 million gamble on 'Battleship' film" (http://www.hollywoodreporter.com/hr/content_display/news/e3i38fc3a9296f214d3ab7258a05995da36). *The Hollywood Reporter*. . Retrieved August 13, 2010. "Universal's "Scott Pilgrim vs. the World," opening Friday, cost $80 million-$90 million"

[5] *Scott Pilgrim vs. the World* (http://www.boxofficemojo.com/movies/?id=scottpilgrim.htm) at Box Office Mojo

[6] "Scott Pilgrim vs. the World" (http://www.scottpilgrimthemovie.com/). . Retrieved 2010-08-21.

[7] "'The Expendables' Tops Weekend Box Office" (http://blogs.wsj.com/speakeasy/2010/08/15/the-expendables-tops-weekend-box-office/). *The Wall Street Journal*. 15 August 2010. . Retrieved 2010-08-18.

[8] Szklarski, Cassandra. " Scott Pilgrim vs. the disappointing box office (http://www.thestar.com/entertainment/movies/article/886087--scott-pilgrim-vs-the-disappointing-box-office)." *The Canadian Press* at *The Toronto Star*. November 4, 2010. Retrieved on November 12, 2010.

[9] "Blu-ray Review: Scott Pilgrim vs. The World" (http://wtf-film.com/site/2010/11/12/scott-pilgrim-vs-the-world/). Wtf-Film.com. . Retrieved 2011-05-01.

[10] Swerdloff, Alexis (July 16, 2010). "The Girls of Summer" (http://www.papermag.com/arts_and_style/2010/07/the-girls-of-summer.php). *Paper*. . Retrieved July 18, 2010.

[11] "Q&A: Scott Pilgrim creator Bryan Lee O'Malley" (http://www.totalfilm.com/news/q-a-scott-pilgrim-creator-bryan-lee-o-malley/page:3). *Total Film*. June 2, 2010. . Retrieved June 3, 2010.

[12] Snyder, Gabriel (May 24, 2005). "'Pilgrim's' progresses" (http://www.variety.com/article/VR1117923467.html). *Variety*. . Retrieved April 11, 2009.

[13] Martens, Todd (July 15, 2010). "Hero Complex for your Inner Fanboy" (http://latimesblogs.latimes.com/herocomplex/2010/07/comiccon-2010-scott-pilgrim-is-ready-to-put-up-a-fight.html). *Los Angeles Times*. . Retrieved July 16, 2010.

[14] " 'Scott Pilgrim' Gets a New Life on DVD (http://www.youtube.com/watch?v=Nt1aQKwRHZU&feature=fvsr)." *Associated Press*. Retrieved on December 5, 2010.

[15] Kit, Borys (January 20, 2009). "Exes mark spots in 'Pilgrim'". *The Hollywood Reporter*.

[16] Dan (August 16, 2010). "Geekadelphia: An EPIC Conversation with Edgar Wright & Michael Cera of Scott Pilgrim Vs. The World" (http://geekadelphia.com/2010/08/16/an-epic-conversation-with-edgar-wright-michael-cera-of-scott-pilgrim-vs-the-world/). .

[17] Sciretta, Peter. "Scott Pilgrim vs. The World Will End Differently Than The Graphic Novels" (http://www.slashfilm.com/2009/05/22/scott-pilgrim-vs-the-world-will-end-differently-than-the-graphic-novels/). . Retrieved January 13, 2010.

[18] "Q&A: Scott Pilgrim creator Bryan Lee O'Malley" (http://www.totalfilm.com/news/q-a-scott-pilgrim-creator-bryan-lee-o-malley/page:4). *Total Film*. June 2, 2010. . Retrieved June 3, 2010.

[19] Villeneuve, Nicole (April 8, 2009). "Scott Pilgrim vs. the World (Just Not Toronto)" (http://torontoist.com/2009/04/scott_pilgrim_vs_toronto.php). *Torontoist*. Gothamist. . Retrieved 2011-06-08.

[20] "Edgar Wright's photoblog" (http://scottpilgrim.ning.com/xn/detail/972072:Comment:44811). *Bryan Lee O'Malley*. . Retrieved January 21, 2009.

[21] "Blog One - Introduction - Scott Pilgrim Vs. The World" (http://www.vimeo.com/3993590). *Scott Pilgrim The Movie*. . Retrieved April 13, 2009.

[22] "August 28th, 2009 21:40 (EDT) Wrap!" (http://edgarwrighthere.com/2009/08/august-28th-2009-2140-edt-wrap/). *Edgar Wright Here*. August 28, 2009. . Retrieved August 30, 2009.

[23] Lussier, Germain (August 7, 2010.). "Mary Elizabeth Winstead and Ellen Wong Interview Scott Pilgrim VS. THE WORLD; Plus Info on THE THING Prequel, DIE HARD 5, and the Alternate Ending" (http://www.collider.com/2010/08/07/scott-pilgrim-interview-mary-elizabeth-winstead-ellen-wong-scott-pilgrim-vs-the-world-interview-the-thing-prequel-die-hard-5-alternate-ending/). *Collider.com*. . Retrieved 2010-08-18.

[24] Corliss, Richard (2010-08-15). "Box Office: Sly Preys on Julia, World Beats Pilgrim" (http://www.time.com/time/arts/article/0,8599,2010830,00.html). *Time* (Time Inc.). . Retrieved 2010-08-18.

[25] "Edgar Wright, Michael Cera, Jason Schwartzman Interview Scott Pilgrim vs. the World" (http://www.collider.com/2010/05/25/scott-pilgrim-vs-world-interview-edgar-wright-michael-cera-jason-schwartzman/). *Collider*. May 25, 2010. . Retrieved June 1, 2010.

[26] Miller, Nancy (June 22, 2010). "Director Edgar Wright, Actor Michael Cera Crack Wise About Scott Pilgrim" (http://www.wired.com/magazine/2010/06/ff_cerawright/all/1). *Wired*. . Retrieved June 23, 2010.

[27] Hasty, Katie (March 31, 2010). "Preview new Beck songs in 'Scott Pilgrim' trailer" (http://www.hitfix.com/blogs/immaculate-noise/posts/preview-new-beck-songs-in-scott-pilgrim-trailer). *HitFix*. . Retrieved March 31, 2010.

[28] Martens, Todd (March 25, 2010). "Rock 'n' roll: 'Scott Pilgrim' launches with Beck-scored trailer" (http://latimesblogs.latimes.com/music_blog/2010/03/rock-n-roll-scott-pilgrim-launches-with-beckscored-trailer.html). *Los Angeles Times*. . Retrieved March 31, 2010.

[29] Carlick, Stephen (July 20, 2010). "Scott Pilgrim vs. The World Soundtrack Adds Beck Bonus Tracks with Deluxe Edition" (http://www.exclaim.ca/articles/generalarticlesynopsfullart.aspx?csid1=145&csid2=844&fid1=48249). *Exclaim!*. . Retrieved July 21, 2010.

[30] "Scott Pilgrim Vs. The World" (http://www.edgarwrighthere.com/2010/08/09/scott-pilgrim-vs-the-world-original-score-digital-release-10th-august-2010/). *Edgar Wright Here*. August 10, 2010. . Retrieved August 12, 2010.

[31] "Music from Scott Pilgrim vs. the World" (http://musicfromfilm.com/movies/scottpilgrimvstheworld.php). MusicfromFilm.com. . Retrieved 2010-11-15.

[32] "Edgar Wright Talks Scott Pilgrim Trailer" (http://www.empireonline.com/features/edgar-wright-talks-scott-pilgrim-teaser-trailer/3.asp). *Empire*. . Retrieved June 1, 2010.

[33] Scott Pilgrim vs. The World DVD extra Music documentary

[34] Scott Pilgrim Vs. The World Soundtrack credits

[35] Warner, Andrea (July 21, 2010). "Bryan Lee O'Malley, Edgar Wright and Kevin Drew Talk the Music of Scott Pilgrim" (http://exclaim.ca/articles/generalarticlesynopsfullart.aspx?csid1=145&csid2=844&fid1=48261). *Exclaim!*. . Retrieved July 21, 2010.

[36] Rayner, Ben (August 8, 2009). "Toronto finally gets to play itself" (http://www.thestar.com/news/insight/article/678159). *Toronto Star*. . Retrieved June 1, 2010.

[37] Scott Pilgrim Vs. The World Film and soundtrack album credits

[38] Lee Joyce (July 23, 2010). "Scott Pilgrim vs. the World" Director Treats Comic-Con Attendees to Free Screening of Film" (http://www.cbsnews.com/8301-31749_162-20011511-10391698.html). *CBS News*. . Retrieved August 18, 2010.

[39] Lang, Derrik J. (July 23, 2010). "'Scott Pilgrim' creates Comic-Con pandemonium" (http://www.washingtontimes.com/news/2010/jul/23/scott-pilgrim-creates-comic-con-pandemonium/). *The Washington Times*. . Retrieved July 23, 2010.

[40] "Movie-Con III Is Coming! Scott Pilgrim Screening Announced!" (http://www.empireonline.com/movie-con/). *Empire*. . Retrieved July 5, 2010.

[41] "Films & Schedules: Scott Pilgrim Vs. the World" (http://www.fantasiafestival.com/2010/en/films/film_detail.php?id=420). *Fantasia Festival*. . Retrieved July 5, 2010.
[42] "Yubari International Fantastic Film Festival 2011" (http://yubarifanta.com/index_pc.php?ct=films.php&langue=21002). *Yubari International Fantastic Film Festival*. 2011. . Retrieved March 9, 2011.
[43] "Release dates for Scott Pilgrim vs the World" (http://www.imdb.com/title/tt0446029/releaseinfo/). *Internet Movie Database (IMDb)*. 2011. . Retrieved March 8, 2011.
[44] Wright, Edgar (March 25, 2010). "It's here... The Official Scott Pilgrim Vs. The World Teaser Trailer" (http://www.edgarwrighthere.com/2010/03/its-here-the-official-scott-pilgrim-vs-the-world-teaser-trailer/). *Edgar Wright Here*. . Retrieved June 10, 2010.
[45] Wright, Edgar. "The New Scott Pilgrim Vs. The World Trailer!" (http://www.edgarwrighthere.com/2010/05/the-new-scott-pilgrim-vs-the-world-trailer/). *Edgar Wright Here*. . Retrieved June 1, 2010.
[46] Marshall, Rick. "First 'Scott Pilgrim Vs. The World' Clip Featuring Chris Evans as Lucas Lee" (http://www.mtv.com/news/articles/1641192/20100609/story.jhtml). *MTV*. . Retrieved June 10, 2010.
[47] Amaya, Erik (July 24, 2010). "CCI: Cast & Crew React to "Scott Pilgrim" screening" (http://www.comicbookresources.com/?page=article&id=27432). *Comic Book Resources*. . Retrieved July 29, 2010.
[48] Fischer, Russ (August 3, 2010). "Exclusive: First Video From the Scott Pilgrim Animated Short Produced by Adult Swim" (http://www.slashfilm.com/2010/08/03/exclusive-video-scott-pilgrim-animated-short-adult-swim/). *SlashFilm*. . Retrieved August 4, 2010.
[49] Calhoun, Dave. "Michael Cera: Hollywood's go-to-geek" (http://www.timeout.com/film/features/show-feature/10517/michael-cera-hollywoods-go-to-geek.html). *Time Out London*. . Retrieved August 31, 2010.
[50] Goldstein, Hilary; Hatfield, Daemon; Miller, Greg (July 19, 2010). "SDCC 10: Scott Pilgrim vs. The World - Clash at Demonhead. The world doesn't stand a chance." (http://xboxlive.ign.com/articles/110/1107047p1.html). *IGN*. News Corporation. . Retrieved 2010-08-26.
[51] "Scott Pilgrim vs. the World Critic Reviews for PlayStation 3 at" (http://www.metacritic.com/game/playstation-3/scott-pilgrim-vs-the-world/critic-reviews). *Metacritic*. CBS Interactive. 2010-08-10. . Retrieved 2010-08-16.
[52] "Ubisoft and Universal Pictures Partner on Scott Pilgrim VS. The World Video Game" (http://www.ubisoftgroup.com/index.php?p=59&art_id=60&vars=Y29tX2lkPTY5NSZzZW5kZXI9SE9NRSZzZW5kZXJfdXJsPW1uZGV4LnBocCUzRnNpdF9pZCUzRDImZmlsdGVyX3R5cGU9JmZpbHRlcl9tb250aD0nPHPSESSID=8a70ae8932d3bd1531393174fb25aa26). *Ubisoft*. . Retrieved August 23, 2009.
[53] Vore, Bryan (June 8, 2010). "Scott Pilgrim Game First Hands On" (http://gameinformer.com/games/scott_pilgrim_vs_the_world/b/ps3/archive/2010/06/08/scott-pilgrim-game-first-hands-on.aspx?PostPageIndex=1). *Game Informer*. . Retrieved June 8, 2010.
[54] "Scott Pilgrim vs. The World (US - DVD R1" (http://www.dvdactive.com/news/releases/scott-pilgrim-vs-the-world.html). . Retrieved September 22, 2010.
[55] "/FILM - 'Scott Pilgrim vs. The World' Hits DVD and Blu-Ray November 9" (http://www.slashfilm.com/2010/09/20/scott-pilgrim-vs-the-world-hits-dvd-and-blu-ray-november-9/). . Retrieved September 20, 2010.
[56] Gifford, Kevin (August 24, 2011). "Check Out the Retro Game Master Guy's Commentary Track on Scott Pilgrim vs. The World" (http://www.1up.com/news/check-retro-game-master-guy?PostPageIndex=1). *1UP.com*. . Retrieved September 23, 2011.
[57] The Numbers http://www.the-numbers.com/dvd/charts/weekly/thisweek.php
[58] "Video Archive Chart" (http://www.theofficialcharts.com/video-archive-chart/_/26/2011-01-08/). Theofficialcharts.com. 2011-01-08. . Retrieved 2011-05-01.
[59] "Weekend Box Office Results for August 20–22, 2010" (http://boxofficemojo.com/weekend/chart/?yr=2010&wknd=34&p=.htm). Box Office Mojo.. .
[60] "UK Box Office 27–29 August 2010" (http://www.ukfilmcouncil.org.uk/article/16967/UK-Box-Office-27---29-August-2010). UK Film Council. .
[61] *Scott Pilgrim vs. the World* (http://www.rottentomatoes.com/m/scott_pilgrims_vs_the_world/) at Rotten Tomatoes
[62] "Scott Pilgrim vs. the World (2010): Reviews" (http://www.metacritic.com/movie/scott-pilgrim-vs-the-world). *Metacritic*. CBS Interactive. . Retrieved August 29, 2010.
[63] Edelstein, David (August 1, 2010). "A Not So Super Hero" (http://nymag.com/movies/reviews/67400/). *New York*. . Retrieved August 3, 2010.
[64] "Kevin Smith Talks Scott Pilgrim" (http://thefilmstage.com/2010/03/03/exclusive-kevin-smith-talks-scott-pilgrim-vs-the-world/). *The Film Stage* (http://www.thefilmstage.com). March 3, 2010. . Retrieved June 3, 2010.
[65] Kaplan, Ben (11 August 2010). "Scott Pilgrim marches to the beat of a Plumtree (oh, and Metric, too)" (http://www.nationalpost.com/arts/Scott+Pilgrim+marches+beat+Plumtree+Metric/3387032/story.html). National Post. . Retrieved 3 December 2010.
[66] Honeycutt, Kirk (July 23, 2010). "Scott Pilgrim vs. the World -- Film Review" (http://www.hollywoodreporter.com/review/scott-pilgrim-vs-world-film-29836). . Retrieved July 23, 2010. "What's disappointing is that this is all so juvenile. Nothing makes any real sense. The "duels" change their rules on a whim, and no one takes the games very seriously, including the exes, who, when defeated, explode into coins the winner may collect.
Certainly Cera doesn't give a performance that anchors the nonsense. His character sort of drifts, not really attached to any idea or goal other than winning the heart of an apparently heartless woman while dissing a girlfriend who, despite her "youth," seems ideally suited to his slacker personality."
[67] White, Cindy (August 12, 2010). "Scott Pilgrim Vs. the World Review. Edgar Wright's take on the videogame-inspired comic series is full of win." (http://movies.ign.com/articles/110/1108240p1.html). *IGN*. News Corporation. . Retrieved 2010-08-21.

[68] Schager, Nick (August 1, 2010). "Scott Pilgrim vs. the World" (http://www.slantmagazine.com/film/review/scott-pilgrim-vs-the-world/4927). *Slant Magazine*. . Retrieved August 3, 2010.
[69] Scott, A.O. (August 12, 2010). "This Girl Has a Lot of Baggage, and He Must Shoulder the Load" (http://movies.nytimes.com/2010/08/13/movies/13scott.html). *The New York Times*. . Retrieved August 18, 2010.
[70] Wright, Edgar (March 1, 2011). "Scott Pilgrim Vs. The World – Notable Japanese Personalities Tributes to the film" (http://www.edgarwrighthere.com/2011/03/01/scott-pilgrim-vs-the-world-notable-japanese-personalities-tributes-to-the-film/). *Edgar Wright Here*. . Retrieved March 9, 2011.
[71] "2010 Film Critic Top Ten Lists" (http://features.metacritic.com/features/2010/film-critic-top-ten-lists/?tag=supplementary-nav;article;3). *Metacritic*. . Retrieved January 6, 2011.
[72] "Annual Critics Survey 2010 - indieWIRE" (http://www.indiewire.com/critic/armond_white/#). .
[73] Child, Ben (December 20, 2010). "Take that! Twice. Scott Pilgrim Vs the World wins two Satellite awards" (http://www.guardian.co.uk/film/2010/dec/20/scott-pilgrim-world-satellite-awards). *The Guardian*. Guardian News and Media Limited. . Retrieved 2010-12-28.

External links

- Official website (http://www.scottpilgrimthemovie.com/)
- *Scott Pilgrim* film diary (http://www.vimeo.com/scottpilgrim) on Vimeo
- Edgar's Photo A Day 2009 (http://www.flickr.com/photos/edgarwright/sets/72157612796619700/) from Flickr, with numerous photographs related to the film
- *Scott Pilgrim vs. the World* (http://www.imdb.com/title/tt0446029/) at the Internet Movie Database
- *Scott Pilgrim vs. the World* (http://www.allrovi.com/movies/movie/v1:446336) at AllRovi
- *Scott Pilgrim vs. the World* (http://www.boxofficemojo.com/movies/?id=scottpilgrim.htm) at Box Office Mojo
- *Scott Pilgrim vs. the World* (http://www.rottentomatoes.com/m/scott_pilgrims_vs_the_world/) at Rotten Tomatoes
- *Scott Pilgrim vs. the World* (http://www.metacritic.com/movie/scott-pilgrim-vs-the-world) at Metacritic

Puncture (film)

Puncture	
Theatrical release poster	
Directed by	Adam Kassen Mark Kassen
Produced by	Adam Kassen Mark Kassen Jordan Foley
Written by	Chris Lopata
Story by	Ela Thier Paul Danziger
Starring	Chris Evans Mark Kassen Vinessa Shaw Brett Cullen Michael Biehn Marshall Bell
Music by	Ryan Ross Smith
Cinematography	Helge Gerull
Editing by	Chip Smith
Release date(s)	April 21, 2011 (Tribeca)
Running time	99 minutes
Country	United States
Language	English

Puncture is an independent feature film starring Chris Evans, directed by Adam Kassen and Mark Kassen. It was chosen as one of the spotlight films for the 2011 Tribeca Film Festival, premiering on April 21, 2011 in New York City.[1]

Cast

- Chris Evans as Mike Weiss
- Mark Kassen as Paul Danziger
- Marshall Bell as Jeffrey Dancort
- Michael Biehn as Red
- Vinessa Shaw as Vicky
- Jesse L. Martin as Daryl King
- Brett Cullen as Nathaniel Price
- Kate Burton as Senator O'Reilly
- Roxanna Hope as Sylvia
- Jennifer Blanc as Stephany
- Mark Lanier as Mark Lanier

Plot

Based on a true story, Mike Weiss (Chris Evans) is a young Houston lawyer and a drug addict. Paul Danziger (co-director Mark Kassen), is his longtime friend and straight-laced law partner. Their personal injury law firm is getting by, but things really get interesting when they decide to take on a case involving Vicky (Vinessa Shaw), a local ER nurse, who is pricked by a contaminated needle. As Weiss and Danziger dig deeper into the case, a health care and pharmaceutical conspiracy teeters on exposure and heavyweight attorneys move in on the defense. Out of their league but invested in their own gain, the mounting pressure of the case pushes the two underdog lawyers and their business to the breaking point.[2]

Underlying Issues

The story is based on two young lawyers and a syringe manufacturer who had invented a safety syringe that he was unable to sell. The safety syringe manufacturer filed an antitrust lawsuit against the two largest hospital group purchasing organizations and a large syringe manufacturer claiming he was being shut out of the market.[3] The case was settled before trial for $150 million dollars.[4]

In addition the film brings to light several issues affecting American health care:

1. Accidental needle sticks cause thousands of US nurses to be infected by HIV, Hepatitis C and other infectious diseases every year. [5]
2. Needle reuse in Africa and Asia directly cause 1.3 million deaths annually, 23 million hepatitis infections annually and 260,000 HIV/AIDS infections annually. [6]

A passing reference in the movie also touches on whether AIDS in Africa is spread by sex or needle reuse. Research has found needle reuse, rather than sex, may have been the main cause of the rapid spread of AIDS in Africa. [7] Fearing that if this comes to light Africans will refuse needle immunization and other important treatments, some health care professionals allege that the UN and WHO have moved to suppress this information. [8] .

Development

Paul Danziger drafted the first version of the script which was rewritten by Ela Thier. After filmmakers Mark and Adam Kassen agreed to take on the project they brought in Chris Lopata to rewrite. Filming began on February 10, 2010 in Texas.[9] The film was directed by Adam Kassen and Mark Kassen. Adam Kassen was quoted as saying "From the moment we heard about this story, we connected to what it says about the current state of our medical industry and the flawed hero that tries to fix it."[10] The film was selected by the 2011 Tribeca Film Festival to serve as one of the spotlight premiere features in the program's lineup. Millennium Films acquired the distribution rights with the movie premiering in New York on September 11 and opening in selected cities September 23, 2011.

References

[1] http://www.tribecafilm.com/filmguide/puncture-film36410.html
[2] "Evans gets a Puncture" (http://www.killerfilm.com/articles/read/evans-gets-a-puncture-27973). *KillerFilm.com*. 2010-03-17. . Retrieved 2010-08-26.
[3] "2 Big Hospital Buying Groups Settle Lawsuit by Needle Maker" (http://www.nytimes.com/2003/05/08/business/08BUYE.html?scp=23&sq=Retractable Technologies Inc.&st=cse). *The New York Times*. 2003-05-08. .
[4] "Syringe Manufacturer Settles Claim of Market Manipulation" (http://www.nytimes.com/2004/07/03/business/03buyer.html?scp=16&sq=Retractable Technologies Inc&st=cse). *The New York Times*. 2004-07-03. .
[5] Susan Wilburn, MPH, RN. *Occupational Health and Safety* (http://www.wsna.org/Topics/Workplace-Environment-You/Workplace-Hazards/Needlestick/). .
[6] http://ijsa.rsmjournals.com/cgi/content/abstract/15/1/7
[7] David D. Brewer, Stuart Brody, Ernest Drucker, David Gisselquist, Stephen F. Minkin, John J. Potterat, Richard B. Rothernberg, and Francois Vachon, "Mounting Anomalies in the Epidemiology of HIV in Africa: Cry the Beloved Paradigm," Int. J. of STD & AIDS 2003; 14:144-147. David Gisselquist, John J. Potterat, Stuart Brody, and Francois Vachon, "Let it be Sexual: how Health Care Transmission of AIDS in Africa was Ignored," Int. J. of STD & AIDS 2003; 14:148-161. David Gisselquist and John J. Potterat, "Heterosexual Transmission of HIV in Africa: An Empiric Estimate," Int. J. of STD & AIDS 2003; 14:162-173. http://sites.google.com/site/davidgisselquist/chapter9
[8] http://www.pop.org/content/are-africans-promiscuous-unto-death-560?old=452
[9] http://www.imdb.com/title/tt1582248/business
[10] By (2010-03-16). "Chris Evans joins 'Puncture'" (http://www.variety.com/article/VR1118016545.html?categoryid=13&cs=1). *Variety*. . Retrieved 2010 08 26.

External links

- *Puncture* (http://www.imdb.com/title/tt1582248/) at the Internet Movie Database
- 2011 Premier at the Tribeca Film Festival in NYC (http://www.tribecafilm.com/filmguide/puncture-film36410.html)
- Official website (http://www.puncture-the-movie.com)
- Unofficial Website (http://www.puncturemovie.com)
- Safe Needle Usage (http://www.safeneedle.org)

Captain America: The First Avenger

Captain America: The First Avenger	
Domestic release poster	
Directed by	Joe Johnston
Produced by	Kevin Feige
Screenplay by	Christopher Markus Stephen McFeely
Based on	Captain America by Joe Simon Jack Kirby
Starring	Chris Evans Tommy Lee Jones Hugo Weaving Hayley Atwell Sebastian Stan Dominic Cooper Neal McDonough Derek Luke Stanley Tucci
Music by	Alan Silvestri
Cinematography	Shelly Johnson
Editing by	Robert Dalva Jeffrey Ford
Studio	Marvel Studios
Distributed by	Paramount Pictures
Release date(s)	July 19, 2011 (world premiere) July 22, 2011 (United States)
Running time	124 minutes[1]
Country	United States
Language	English
Budget	$140 million[2]
Box office	$367,457,035[3]

Captain America: The First Avenger is a 2011 American superhero film based on the Marvel Comics character Captain America. It is the fifth installment of the Marvel Cinematic Universe. The film was directed by Joe Johnston, written by Christopher Markus and Stephen McFeely, and stars Chris Evans, Tommy Lee Jones, Hugo Weaving, Hayley Atwell, Sebastian Stan, Dominic Cooper, Neal McDonough, Derek Luke, and Stanley Tucci. The film tells the story of Steve Rogers, a sickly man from Brooklyn who is transformed into super soldier Captain America to aid in the war effort. Captain America must stop Red Skull, Adolf Hitler's ruthless head of weaponry, and the leader of a mysterious organization that intends to use a device called a tesseract as an energy-source for world domination.

Captain America: The First Avenger began as a concept in 1997, and was scheduled to be distributed by Artisan Entertainment. However, a lawsuit, not settled until September 2003, disrupted the project. After Marvel Studios received a grant from Merrill Lynch, the project was set up at Paramount Pictures. Directors Jon Favreau and Louis Leterrier were interested in directing the project before Johnston was approached in 2008. The principal characters were cast between March and June 2010. Production of *Captain America: The First Avenger* began in June 2010, and filming took place in London, Manchester and Liverpool in the United Kingdom, and Los Angeles in the United States. The film was converted to 3D in post-production.

Captain America: The First Avenger premiered in Hollywood on July 19, 2011, and was released in the United States on July 22, 2011. The film became a critical success and has grossed $367.4 million worldwide as of October 2011. The Blu-ray and DVD were released on October 25, 2011.

Plot

In the present day, scientists in the Arctic uncover a circular object with a red, white and blue motif.

In March 1942, Nazi officer Johann Schmidt (Hugo Weaving) and his men invade Tønsberg, Norway, to steal a mysterious tesseract possessing untold powers. In New York City, Steve Rogers (Chris Evans) is rejected for World War II military duty due to various health and physical issues. While attending an exhibition of future technologies with his friend Bucky Barnes (Sebastian Stan), Rogers again attempts to enlist. Having overheard Rogers' conversation with Barnes about wanting to help in the war, Dr. Abraham Erskine (Stanley Tucci) allows Rogers to enlist. He is recruited as part of a "super-soldier" experiment under Erskine, Colonel Chester Phillips (Tommy Lee Jones), and British agent Peggy Carter (Hayley Atwell). Phillips is unconvinced of Erskine's claims that Rogers is the right person for the procedure but relents after seeing Rogers commit an act of self-sacrificing bravery. The night before the treatment, Erskine reveals to Rogers that Schmidt underwent an imperfect version of the treatment, and suffered side-effects.

In Europe, Schmidt and Dr. Arnim Zola (Toby Jones) successfully harness the energies of the tesseract, intending to use the power to fuel Zola's inventions. Schmidt, having discovered Erskine's location, dispatches an assassin to kill him. In America, Erskine subjects Rogers to the super-soldier treatment, injecting him with a special serum and dosing him with "vita-rays". After Rogers emerges from the experiment taller and muscular, one of the attendees kills Erskine, revealing himself as Schmidt's assassin, Heinz Kruger (Richard Armitage). Rogers pursues and captures Kruger but the assassin commits suicide via cyanide capsule before he can be interrogated.

With Erskine dead and the super-soldier formula lost, U.S. Senator Brandt (Michael Brandon) has Rogers tour the nation in a colorful costume as "Captain America" to promote war bonds rather than allow scientists to study him and attempt to rediscover Erskine's formula. In Italy 1943, while on tour performing for active servicemen, Rogers learns that Barnes' unit was lost in battle against Schmidt's forces. Refusing to believe that Barnes is dead, Rogers mounts a solo rescue attempt with Carter and Howard Stark (Dominic Cooper) flying him behind enemy lines. Rogers infiltrates the fortress belonging to Schmidt's HYDRA organization, freeing Barnes and the other captured soldiers. Rogers confronts Schmidt who reveals his face to be a mask, removing it to display the red, skull-like face that earned him the sobriquet, the Red Skull. Schmidt escapes and Rogers returns to base with the freed soldiers.

Rogers recruits Barnes, Dum Dum Dugan (Neal McDonough), Gabe Jones (Derek Luke), Jim Morita (Kenneth Choi), James Montgomery Falsworth (J. J. Feild), and Jacques Dernier (Bruno Ricci) to attack the other known HYDRA bases. Stark outfits Rogers with advanced equipment, in particular a circular shield made of vibranium, a rare, nigh-indestructible metal. Rogers and his team successfully sabotage various HYDRA operations. The team later assaults a train carrying Zola. Zola is captured, but Barnes falls off the train to his apparent death. Using information extracted from Zola, the final HYDRA stronghold is located and Rogers leads an attack to stop Schmidt from using WMDs on American cities. Rogers clambers aboard Schmidt's aircraft as it takes off. During the subsequent fight, the tesseract's container is damaged. Schmidt physically handles the tesseract, causing him to dissolve in a bright light. The tesseract falls to the floor, burning through the plane and falling to Earth. Seeing no way to safely land the plane without risking its weapons detonating, Rogers crashes it in the Arctic. Stark later recovers the tesseract from the ocean floor, but is unable to locate Rogers or the aircraft.

Rogers awakens in a 1940s-style hospital room. Deducing that something is wrong due to an anachronistic radio broadcast, he flees outside into what is revealed to be present-day Times Square. There Nick Fury (Samuel L. Jackson) informs him he has been "asleep" for nearly 70 years.

In a post-credits scene, Fury approaches Rogers, proposing a mission with worldwide ramifications.

Cast

- Chris Evans as Steve Rogers / Captain America:

  A frail, sickly young man who is enhanced to the peak of human perfection by an experimental serum in order to aid the United States war effort.[4] Evans, who previously worked with Marvel as the Human Torch in the *Fantastic Four* film series, said he declined the part three times before signing a six-picture deal with Marvel, explaining that, "At the time, I remember telling a buddy of mine, 'If the movie bombs, I'm f***ed. If the movie hits, I'm f***ed! I was just scared. I realized my whole decision-making process was fear-based, and you never want to make a decision out of fear. I can't believe I was almost too chicken to play Captain America".[5] He ultimately agreed to the role, saying, "I think Marvel is doing a lot of good things right now, and it's a fun character.... I think the story of Steve Rogers is great. He's a great guy. Even if it [were] just a script about anybody, I would probably want to do it. So it wasn't necessarily about the comic itself."[6] Regarding the extent of the character's abilities Evans remarked, "He would crush the Olympics. Any Olympic sport he's gonna dominate. He can jump higher, run faster, lift stronger weight, but he can be injured. He could roll an ankle and be out for the season. He's not perfect, he's not untouchable. So a lot of the effects, if I'm going to punch someone they're not going to put them on a cable and fly them back 50 feet, but he's going to go down, probably not getting back up, which I think humanizes it. It makes it something that, again, I think everyone can relate to a little bit more, which I really like."[7]

Kevin Feige, Joe Johnston, Chris Evans and Hugo Weaving at the 2010 San Diego Comic-Con International.

- Hayley Atwell as Peggy Carter:

  An officer with the Strategic Scientific Reserve and the love interest of Captain America. Regarding her preparation for the role, she said, "I'm training at the moment six days a week to make her a bit more military and make it convincing that I could kick butt."[8] About the character Atwell stated, "I likened her character to that famous Ginger Rogers quote. She can do everything Captain America can do, but backwards and in high heels. She's an English soldier through and through, although she always looks fabulous. She might stand there with a machine-gun shooting Nazis, but she's obviously gone to the loo beforehand and applied a bit of lipstick. She doesn't need to be rescued. That's exciting to me – her strength".[9] "I think she's quite stubborn, a slightly frustrated woman who struggles with being a woman in that time. But more importantly she's a modern woman and she sees something in Captain America that she relates to, and becomes kindred spirits. He treats her very differently to how she's been treated by lots of men, in this kind of dominated world she lives in. So she's very much a fighter."[10]

- Hugo Weaving as Johann Schmidt / Red Skull:

  Captain America's nemesis and Adolf Hitler's head of advanced weaponry, whose own plan for world domination involves a magical object known as the Tesseract.[5] [11] [12] In the film, Red Skull is the commander of the terrorist organization HYDRA.[13] Weaving stated that he patterned Red Skull's accent on those of Werner Herzog and Klaus Maria Brandauer.[14] About the character, Weaving remarked, "I think the major difference between Skull and Cap, they've both had the serum, and the serum seems to augment certain qualities that each of them have. Cap is much more in tune with other people I think. Schmidt is in tune with himself, and his own needs, and his own ego, so I suppose it augments that. From that point of view, they're quite opposite."[15]

- Sebastian Stan as Sgt. James "Bucky" Barnes:

  Steve Rogers' best friend. Stan has signed on for "five or six pictures".[16] Stan revealed that he didn't know anything about the comic books but watched a lot of documentaries and films about World War II in preparation for the role, calling *Band of Brothers* "very helpful". About the role, Stan stated, "Steve Rogers and Bucky are both orphans and kind of like brothers. They kind of grow up together and look after each other. It's a very human, relatable thing.... I also wanted to look out for how their relationship changes once Steve Rogers becomes Captain America. There's always a competition and they're always one-upping each other. I paid attention to how Bucky is affected by Steve's change and suddenly Steve is this leader".[17]

- Tommy Lee Jones as Col. Chester Phillips:

  In the early comics, Phillips recruited Steve Rogers to join Project Rebirth, the secret experiment that created the Super Soldier known as Captain America. The character was updated for the film.[18] Jones described his character as "the one you've seen in a thousand movies: the gruff, skeptical officer overseeing a team of talented, slightly sarcastic, specially talented soldiers".[19]

- Dominic Cooper as Howard Stark:

  The father of Tony Stark, who worked on various government projects dating back to the World War II era.[20] [21] Rogers, unsatisfied with his USO-issued Captain America costume, turns to Stark to design a sensible ensemble made of sophisticated fabrics.[22] About the role Cooper stated, "It's an opportunity where you can see his future because I know the guy who becomes my son and I see myself as an older version in *Iron Man 2* which is great for an actor to have those tools. All I know of him is that he's a fantastic engineer and inventor and a very slick Howard Hughes type that's into aviation and women!"[23]

- Neal McDonough as Timothy "Dum Dum" Dugan:

  A member of Steve Rogers' squad of commandos. McDonough said he grew Dugan's trademark mustache and wore the character's signature bowler hat. About his role in film he remarked, "Oh, I'm going to see a lot of action. [I'm] the go-to guy, so I'm very happy with that".[24]

- Derek Luke as Gabe Jones:

  An African-American member of Rogers' squad of commandos. Luke said he was cast without a script or much of a description of the character. As to why he took the part, "I just believed that Marvel was doing some really great work, great messages in films. The good versus evil and I was just like, 'How can I be down?'"[25]

- Stanley Tucci as Dr. Abraham Erskine:

The scientist who created the Super Soldier Serum.[26] Tucci said that what drew him to the role was the opportunity to do a German accent, which was something he always wanted to try.[27]

- Kenneth Choi as Jim Morita:

  A Japanese-American member of Rogers' squad of commandos. Choi said he was the last actor to audition for the part and that he read sides from *Saving Private Ryan*. About his preparation for the role, Choi said, "[I] did a lot of WWII research especially in regards to the 'Nisei' soldiers, or Japanese-American soldiers. I wanted to get as much true, real-life information for a guy like Jim Morita fighting in WWII. I felt that if I had built a factual basis for him, I could then let go and permit the character to exist in the Marvel Universe, which allows for a lot of imaginative circumstances."[28]

- Bruno Ricci as Jacques Dernier:

  A French member of Rogers' squad of commandos. Ricci auditioned for and got the part while filming the French series *The Hawk*.[29]

- J. J. Feild as James Montgomery Falsworth:

  A British member of Rogers' squad of commandos. Feild called his part in the film "a very physical job. I play one of the Captain's sidekicks so I've been running around shooting things and blowing things up and trying to look cool for about a year."[30]

Additionally, Toby Jones was cast as Arnim Zola, a biochemist for the Nazi party.[31] Richard Armitage portrays Heinz Kruger, the Red Skull's top assassin.[32] Samuel L. Jackson reprises his role as Nick Fury, the director of the super-spy agency, S.H.I.E.L.D.[33] Stan Lee has a cameo appearance as a general.[34]

Production

Development

"He [Captain America] wants to serve his country, but he's not this sort of jingoistic American flag-waver. He's just a good person. We make a point of that in the script: Don't change who you are once you go from Steve Rogers to this super-soldier; you have to stay who you are inside, that's really what's important more than your strength and everything... It's also the idea that this is not about America so much as it is about the spirit of doing the right thing. It's an international cast and an international story. It's about what makes America great and what make the rest of the world great too."

Joe Johnston, director of *Captain America: The First Avenger*, about the film.[35]

In April 1997, Marvel was in negotiations with Mark Gordon and Gary Levinsohn to produce *Captain America*. In addition, Larry Wilson and Leslie Bohem were set to write a script.[36] In May 2000, Marvel teamed with Artisan Entertainment to help finance the film.[37] However, a lawsuit arose between Marvel Comics and Joe Simon over the ownership of Captain America copyrights, disrupting the development process of the film. The lawsuit was eventually settled in September 2003.[38] In 2005, Marvel received a $525 million investment from Merrill Lynch, allowing them to independently produce ten films, including *Captain America*. Paramount Pictures agreed to distribute the film.[37] [39] [40] Originally, the film would stand alone; producer Kevin Feige said "about half" the movie would be set during World War II before moving into the modern day.[41] Producer Avi Arad said, "The biggest opportunity with Captain America is as a man 'out of time', coming back today, looking at our world through the eyes of someone who thought the perfect world was small-town United States. Sixty years go by, and who are we today? Are we better?" He cited the *Back to the Future* trilogy as an influence, and claimed he had "someone in mind to be the star, and definitely someone in mind to be the director".[42] In February 2006, Arad hoped to have a summer 2008 theatrical release date.[43] Jon Favreau approached Arad to direct the film as a comedy, but he chose to make *Iron Man* instead.[44] In July 2006, David Self was hired to write the script.[45] He explained Captain America was his favorite superhero as a child because "my dad told me I could one day be Captain America".[46] Joe Johnston met with Marvel to discuss directing the film.[47]

Captain America was put on hold during the 2007–2008 Writers Guild of America strike. However, in January 2008, Marvel Entertainment reached an interim comprehensive agreement with the Writers Guild of America that would put writers immediately back to work on various projects that were under the company's development.[48] On May 5, 2008, (after the success of *Iron Man*), Marvel announced the film *The First Avenger: Captain America* for a May 6, 2011 release (before being slightly pushed back to July 22).[49] *The Incredible Hulk* director Louis Leterrier viewed some of the concept art being created for the film, and was impressed enough to offer his services, but Marvel turned him down.[50] Johnston finally signed on in November 2008,[47] and he hired Christopher Markus and Stephen McFeely to rewrite.[51] Feige cited Johnston's directorial work on *October Sky* and *The Rocketeer* and his special effects work on the original *Star Wars* trilogy as to why he was an appropriate choice. *Raiders of the Lost Ark* will be an influence on the film, because they hope the film will not feel like a period piece.[52]

When asked whether anti-U.S. sentiments would affect the film's box office, Feige said, "Marvel is perceived pretty well around the world right now, and I think putting another uber-Marvel hero into the worldwide box office would be a good thing. [...] We have to deal with much the same way that Captain America, when thawed from the Arctic ice, entered a world that he didn't recognize," similar to the way Stan Lee and Jack Kirby reintroduced the character in the 1960s.[41] Likewise, Arad noted, "Captain America stands for freedom for all democracies, for hope all around the world. He was created to stop tyranny and the idea of stopping tyranny is important today as it was then and unfortunately it's not going to change because that's how the world works. So I think that we will have some interesting challenges but at the end of the day if the movie is terrific and the movie talks to the world, it's not about one place, it's about the world and I think [on] that basis it will be very successful."[53] Later, after the election of US President Barack Obama, Feige commented, "'The idea of change and hope has permeated the country, regardless of politics, and that includes Hollywood. Discussions in all our development meetings include the Zeitgeist and how it's changed in the last two weeks. Things are being adjusted".[54]

Pre-production

In December 2009, director Joe Johnston indicated he planned to start filming in April 2010.[55] In a separate interview that month, he described the film's pre-production: "Rick Heinrichs is production-designing and we're set up down in Manhattan Beach[, California].... We have eight or ten really talented artists, and we all just sit around all day and draw pictures and say, 'Hey, wouldn't it be cool if we could do this?' It's that phase of the production where money doesn't matter: 'Let's put all the greatest stuff up on the wall and [then later] see what we can afford.'" The film, he said, will begin "in 1942, 1943" during World War II. "The stuff in the '60s and '70s [comic books] we're sort of avoiding. We're going back to the '40s, and then forward to what they're doing with Captain America now."[56] In February 2010, Johnston stated that the World War II-era super team the Invaders will appear in "the entire second half" of the film,[57] though in November he shot down speculation that the Sub-Mariner, an Invaders team-member in the comics, would be included.[58] He later explained that "the Invaders" had been discussed simply as a possible name for the squad of commandos Captain America leads in the film.[59]

Variety reported in March 2010, that Chris Evans was cast as Captain America, and Hugo Weaving as the Red Skull.[11]

In April 2010, Sebastian Stan, who had been mentioned in media accounts as a possibility to play the title role of Captain America, was cast as Bucky Barnes. Stan is contracted for multiple films.[16] Also in April it was announced that Hayley Atwell had been cast as Peggy Carter as well as the changing of the film's name from *The First Avenger: Captain America* to *Captain America: The First Avenger*.[60] The next day it was reported that Joss Whedon would be re-writing the script for Joe Johnston's *Captain America: The First Avenger* as part of his negotiation to write and direct *The Avengers*. However the extent of Whedon's polish on Christopher Markus and Stephen McFeely's script remained unknown.[61] Whedon later clarified in an August interview that "I just got to make some character connections. The structure of the thing was really tight and I loved it, but there were a couple of opportunities to find his voice a little bit – and some of the other characters – and make the connections so that you understood exactly why he wanted to be who he wanted to be. And progressing through the script to flesh it out a little bit".[62] Samuel L. Jackson revealed in an interview that he will reprise his role as Nick Fury in the film.[33] Kevin Fiege later confirmed that Fury's elite special unit of US Army Rangers, the Howling Commandos would appear.[63] Screenwriter Markus later explained that the unnamed group of commandos Rogers leads was "called the Howling Commandos in the script, but no one says that out loud."[59] Director Johnston said the group at one point was to have been called the Invaders, which led to fan speculation that the Marvel superhero team of that name would appear in the film.[59]

In May 2010, Marvel Studios confirmed Hugo Weaving would play the Red Skull.[64] Toby Jones entered final negotiations to play Arnim Zola.[31] *Iron Man* director Jon Favreau said a younger Howard Stark would appear in the film, played by Dominic Cooper.[20] [21] Hayley Atwell revealed that Tommy Lee Jones will have a role in the film.[65] By June, Neal McDonough was in talks to play Dum Dum Dugan.[66] Four days later, McDonough confirmed he was taking the part.[67] On the same day, Stanley Tucci joined the cast as Dr. Abraham Erskine, the scientist who created the Super Soldier Serum.[26]

Filming

Photo taken in Manchester on the set of *Captain America: The First Avenger*.

Production began on June 28, 2010.[68] The same day, Marvel confirmed that actor Tommy Lee Jones had been cast to play US Army Colonel Chester Phillips.[18] The next day Marvel confirmed Dominic Cooper will portray the younger version of Howard Stark, the character played by John Slattery in *Iron Man 2*.[69] The film was announced to shoot in London, England, in late July, and was expected to include scenes featuring key London landmarks.[70] War scenes were filmed in September at the former Royal Navy Propellant Factory in the Welsh village of Caerwent.[71] [72] Filming was scheduled to take place that month in the Northern Quarter of Manchester, England, where parts of the 2004 film *Alfie* and the 2009 *Sherlock Holmes* had been shot,[73] followed by Liverpool's Stanley Dock area, both doubling for the period's Lower East Side of Manhattan, New York.[74] Scenes were scheduled to be shot in Liverpool's Albert Dock.[75]

In July 2010, Marvel Studios head Kevin Feige said that both this film and *Thor* would be released in 3-D.[76] Johnston did a one-day test shooting with a 3-D rig, as opposed to shooting in 2-D and converting, and found it "a nightmare" due to bulky gear, calibration issues and restricted filmmaking options. Regardless, he said he believes 3-D is "a new challenge and it's exciting". Producer Kevin Feige insisted that the conversion would not compromise the film's image quality, as the decision to release the film in 3-D was made early in development, and that "an unprecedented amount of time" would be devoted to the conversion process, with all the film's visual effects being rendered in true 3-D.[76]

Post-production

In November 2010, actor Stanley Tucci stated he completed filming his scenes and that the rest of the production would wrap in about three weeks.[77] In February 2011, Alan Silvestri was announced to compose the film score.[78] In March 2011, CraveOnline reported that *Captain America: The First Avenger* would be undergoing reshoots in the United Kingdom and in Los Angeles in April 2011.[79] [80] A scene was also filmed in New York City's Times Square on April 23, 2011.[81]

Chris Evans as pre-serum Steve Rogers before (top) and after (bottom) he was visually reduced.

The film features nearly 1,600 visual effect shots that were split between thirteen different companies.[82] To achieve the effects of the skinny, pre-super-serum Steve Rogers, director Joe Johnston stated that he used two major techniques:

> Most of the shots were done by an L.A. company called LOLA that specializes in digital "plastic surgery." The technique involved shrinking Chris in all dimensions. We shot each skinny Steve scene at least four times; once like a normal scene with Chris and his fellow actors in the scene, once with Chris alone in front of a green screen so his element could be reduced digitally, again with everyone in the scene but with Chris absent so that the shrunken Steve could be re-inserted into the scene, and finally with a body double mimicking Chris's actions in case the second technique were required. When Chris had to interact with other characters in the scene, we had to either lower Chris or raise the other actors on apple boxes or elevated walkways to make skinny Steve shorter in comparison. For close-ups, Chris' fellow actors had to look at marks on his chin that represented where his eyes would be after the shrinking process, and Chris had to look at marks on the tops of the actor's head to represent their eyes. ... The second technique involved grafting Chris's head onto the body double. This technique was used mostly when Chris was sitting or lying down, or when a minimum of physical acting was required....[83]

Captain America's shield, which serves as both a defensive tool and a weapon, consisted of four types: metal, fiberglass, rubber, and CG.[82] Prop master Barry Gibbs specified that, "We had the 'hero shield,' which was made of aluminum, for our beauty shots [and] close-up work. We then created a lighter shield that was aluminum-faced with a fiberglass back, for use on a daily basis.... And then we had a stunt shield made of polyurethane, which is sort of a synthetic rubber ... and we made an ultrasoft one we put on [Evans'] back, so that if there were an accident, it wouldn't hurt him."[84] Visual effects supervisor Christopher Townsend said Evans "would practice swinging the practical shield so he knew the arc and the speed at which he should move. We would take the shield from him and shoot the scene with him miming it. Then we would add in a CG shield".[82]

Hugo Weaving, who portrayed the Red Skull, wore a latex mask conceived by prosthetic makeup designer David White. However, the visual effects team had to manipulate his face considerably due to the bulkiness of the mask and make it look like tight skin wrapped around a very boney structure. The team thinned out Weaving's cheeks and lower lip, hollowed out his eyes, and removed his eyelashes and nose to make him appear more like the Red Skull character.[82]

Closing credits were created by the visual effects firm Rok!t via a 3D/Stereoscopic processing that utilized such iconic American propaganda images from World War Two as James Montgomery Flagg's Uncle Sam recuitment poster and Rosie the Riveter.[85]

Soundtrack

In June 2011, Buena Vista Records announced the details for the soundtrack release of *Captain America: The First Avenger*. The album includes the original score by Alan Silvestri, as well as the original song "Star Spangled Man" with music by Alan Menken and lyrics by David Zippel. The soundtrack was recorded at Air Studios in London and was released on July 19, 2011.[86]

Release

The world premiere of *Captain America: The First Avenger* was held on July 19, 2011, at the El Capitan Theatre in Hollywood, California.[87] The film was screened at the San Diego Comic-Con International on July 21, 2011.[88] *Captain America: The First Avenger* was commercially released in the United States and Canada on July 22, 2011.[89] [90]

El Capitan Theatre in Hollywood, California before the movie's world premiere.

Paramount opted against altering the American-centric title when distributing to foreign territories, instead offering international markets a choice between the official title and the alternative *The First Avenger*. Many international distributors chose to retain the original title, believing the franchise name is more identifiable than the alternative and they would otherwise risk losing ticket sales. Three countries chose the alternative title: Russia, South Korea, and Ukraine. An "insider" speaking to *The New York Times* described the reasoning behind the name change in these countries as stemming from cultural and political concerns, though Marvel and Paramount both declined to state an official reason.[91] In July 2011 there was consideration that the film would not see release in China due to a policy limiting the number of foreign films to be screened in the country per year,[91] but it eventually opened there the second weekend in September.[92]

Marketing

Early footage of the film was shown at the 2010 San Diego Comic-Con International with director Joe Johnston noting filming had begun four days prior to this presentation at the San Diego Convention Center.[14] The first television advertisement aired during Super Bowl XLV on the Fox network in the United States. Paramount paid $3 million dollars to run the 30-second ad.[93] The first full trailer was released in March 2011.[94] In May 2011, the USO girls from the film performed aboard the USS Intrepid as a part of the 2011 Fleet Week celebration in New York City.[95] In June 2011, Dunkin' Donuts and Baskin-Robbins teamed with Marvel to search for real-life Super-Soldiers. The contest sought nominations for veterans or active U.S. servicepersons making a difference where they live or serve.[96] In July 2011, Paramount Pictures promoted the film during an Independence Day celebration hosted by the Chicago White Sox.[97] Promotional partners include Harley-Davidson, Dunkin' Donuts and Baskin-Robbins.[98]

In February 2011, Marvel Comics launched the eight-issue digital comic *Captain America: First Vengeance*, the same day the first trailer aired. Written by Fred Van Lente and featuring a rotation of artists, the story is set in the

Marvel Cinematic Universe. Each of the eight issues focuses on a specific character from the movie, heroes and villains alike, and what brought them to the point where the movie begins.[99]

Sega announced a video game tie-in titled, *Captain America: Super Soldier*, that was released in 2011, for the Xbox 360, PlayStation 3, Wii and Nintendo DS.[100] Marvel released the mobile game, *Captain America: Sentinel of Liberty* in July 2011.[101] A toy line was released as well.[102]

Home media

Captain America: The First Avenger was released on Blu-ray, Blu-ray 3D and DVD on October 25, 2011. The three-disc set includes the film on Blu-ray in high-definition 3D and in high definition 2D, as well as on standard definition DVD with a digital copy. The two-disc Blu-ray/DVD combo pack includes a high definition presentation of the film, plus a standard definition presentation with a digital copy. Both sets include over an hour of bonus material including the short film, *A Funny Thing Happened on the Way to Thor's Hammer*, a sneak peek of *The Avengers*, six behind-the-scenes featurettes, and deleted scenes with commentary by director Joe Johnston, director of photography Shelly Johnson and editor Jeff Ford.[103]

Reception

Box office

Captain America: The First Avenger opened on July 22, 2011, in the United States and earned $4 million in midnight showings, outgrossing other 2011 original superhero movies like *Thor* and *Green Lantern* as well as the prequel *X-Men: First Class*, which all did between $3.25 million and $3.5 million in Friday midnights.[104] On Friday, the film opened at the number one spot at the American and Canadian box office with $25.7 million.[105] It then went on to make $65.1 million, which was the second highest-grossing opening weekend for a superhero film in 2011 behind *Thor* ($65.7 million).[106] As of November 6, 2011, *Captain America: The First Avenger* has grossed an estimated $176,640,000 in the U.S.A and Canada as well as $190,817,019 internationally, for a total of $367,457,019 worldwide.[3]

Critical reaction

Captain America: The First Avenger has received generally positive reviews from film critics. The film has a 79% approval rating on the review aggregator website Rotten Tomatoes, based on 210 reviews with an average rating of 6.9/10, and the consensus: "With plenty of pulpy action, a pleasantly retro vibe, and a handful of fine performances, Captain America is solidly old-fashioned blockbuster entertainment."[107] Metacritic, which assigns a weighted average score, gave the film a 66 out of 100 based on 36 reviews from critics.[108]

Roger Moore of the *Orlando Sentinel* gave *Captain America: The First Avenger* a positive review stating, "Johnston has delivered a light, clever and deftly balanced adventure picture with real lump in the throat nostalgia, with Nazis – who make the best villains, and with loving references to *Star Wars* and *Raiders of the Lost Ark*.'"[109] Roger Ebert of the *Chicago Sun-Times* remarked, "I enjoyed the movie. I appreciated the 1940s period settings and costumes, which were a break with the usual generic cityscapes. I admired the way that director Joe Johnston propelled the narrative. I got a sense of a broad story, rather than the impression of a series of sensational set pieces. If Marvel is wise, it will take this and *Iron Man* as its templates".[110] A. O. Scott of *The New York Times* declared it "pretty good fun".[111]

Conversely, Karina Longworth of *The Village Voice* gave the film a negative review, calling it "[A] hokey, hacky, two-hour-plus exercise in franchise transition/price gouging, complete with utterly unnecessary post-converted 3-D".[112] Peter Debruge of *Variety* said, "Captain America: The First Avenger" plays like a by-the-numbers prequel for Marvel Studios' forthcoming "The Avengers" movie".[113] Kirk Honeycutt of *The Hollywood Reporter* had mixed feelings about the film, writing, "As the last Marvel prequel that includes two Iron Man and Incredible Hulk movies before next summer's *The Avengers*, this one feels perhaps a little too simplistic and routine".[114]

Accolades

Award	Category	Winner/Nominee	Result
2011 Teen Choice Awards[115]	Choice Summer: Movie		Nominated
	Choice Summer Movie Star: Male	Chris Evans	Nominated
2011 Scream Awards[116]	The Ultimate Scream		Nominated
	Best Science Fiction Movie		Nominated
	Best Science Fiction Actress	Hayley Atwell	Nominated
	Best Science Fiction Actor	Chris Evans	Nominated
	Best Villain	Hugo Weaving as Red Skull	Nominated
	Best Superhero	Chris Evans as Captain America	Won
	Best Supporting Actor	Tommy Lee Jones	Nominated
	Breakout Performance - Female	Hayley Atwell	Nominated
	Fight Scene of the Year	Final Battle: Captain America vs. Red Skull	Nominated
	Best 3-D Movie		Nominated
	Best Comic Book Movie		Nominated
2012 People's Choice Awards[]	Favorite Movie Superhero	Chris Evans	Pending

Sequel

Screenwriters Stephen McFeely and Christopher Markus said in April 2011, that they have been writing a sequel for Marvel Studios.[117] In a June 2011 interview, the duo stated, "The story will likely be in the present day. We're experimenting with flashback elements for more period World War II stuff. I can't say much more than that but we made it baggy enough to refer to more stories in the past".[118] In September 2011, star Chris Evans said a sequel may not be released until 2014.[119]

References

[1] "Captain America – The First Avenger" (http://www.bbfc.co.uk/CFF277297/). British Board of Film Classification. July 13, 2011. .

[2] Ryan, Mike (2010-05-19). "Should We Now Call Him 'Captain England'?" (http://movies.yahoo.com/feature/movie-talk-should-we-now-call-him-captain-england.html). Yahoo!. Archived (http://www.webcitation.org/5zskkU7iS) from the original on 2011-07-22. . Retrieved 2010-06-28.

[3] *Captain America: The First Avenger* (http://www.boxofficemojo.com/movies/?id=captainamerica.htm) at Box Office Mojo

[4] Graser, Marc (2010-03-22). "Chris Evans to play 'Captain America'" (http://www.variety.com/article/VR1118016757.html). *Variety*. Archived (http://www.webcitation.org/5yDf8FIJ2) from the original on 2011-04-25. . Retrieved 2010-03-23.

[5] Jensen, Jeff (2010-10-28). "This week's cover: An exclusive first look at *Captain America: The First Avenger*" (http://popwatch.ew.com/2010/10/28/captain-america-chris-evans-2). *Entertainment Weekly*. Archived (http://www.webcitation.org/5zva0i0mC) from the original on 2011-07-04. . Retrieved 2010-10-28.

[6] Keyes, Rob (2010-04-05). "Chris Evans Talks Captain America" (http://screenrant.com/chris-evans-talks-captain-america-rob-52360). ScreenRant.com. Archived (http://www.webcitation.org/5zva0yTWB) from the original on 2011-07-04. . Retrieved 2010-07-09.

[7] Mortimer, Ben (2011-06-24). "*Captain America: The First Avenger* Set Visit!" (http://www.superherohype.com/features/articles/167663-captain-america-the-first-avenger-set-visit). Superhero Hype!. Archived (http://www.webcitation.org/5zva12RxE) from the original on 2011-07-04. . Retrieved 2011-06-27.

[8] Bently, David (2010-05-27). "Hayley Atwell talks Captain America, confirms Tommy Lee Jones in cast" (http://blogs.coventrytelegraph.net/thegeekfiles/2010/05/hayley-atwell-talks-captain-am.html). *Coventry Telegraph*. Archived (http://www.webcitation.org/5zvaAHVgG) from the original on 2011-07-04. . Retrieved 2010-07-09.

[9] Green, Graeme (2010-11-15). "Hayley Atwell on Any Human Heart and flirting with Captain America" (http://www.heraldscotland.com/arts-ents/more-arts-entertainment-news/hayley-atwell-on-any-human-heart-and-flirting-with-captain-america-1.1068462). *Scotland Herald*. Archived (http://www.webcitation.org/5zvaAYA4a) from the original on 2011-07-04. . Retrieved 2010-11-15.

[10] "Hayley Atwell's machine gun fun" (http://www.belfasttelegraph.co.uk/entertainment/film-tv/news/hayley-atwells-machine-gun-fun-16001688.html). *The Belfast Telegraph*. 2011-05-18. Archived (http://www.webcitation.org/5zx6gDYOn) from the original on 2011-07-05. . Retrieved 2011-05-2o.

[11] Graser, Marc (2010-03-22). "Chris Evans to play 'Captain America'" (http://www.variety.com/article/VR1118016757.html). *Variety*. Archived (http://www.webcitation.org/5zspettOB) from the original on 2011-07-22. . Retrieved 2010-03-23.

[12] "Hugo Weaving confirmed as Red Skull in *Captain America*" (http://www.comingsoon.net/news/movienews.php?id=65732) (Press release). Marvel Studios. May 4, 2010. Archived (http://www.webcitation.org/5zva45L7T) from the original on 2011-07-04. . Retrieved May 4, 2010.

[13] "Comic-Con 2010: 'Captain America'" (http://www.ew.com/ew/video/0,,20399642_20399689,00.html?bcpid=109297042001&bclid=207616944001&bctid=260706587001). *Entertainment Weekly*. Archived (http://www.webcitation.org/5zva4nYi4) from the original on 2011-07-04. . Retrieved 2010-03-23.

[14] "MARVEL-OUS STAR WATTAGE: Actors Assemble For Comic-Con Panel Including 'The Avengers', 'Captain America', & 'Thor'" (http://www.deadline.com/2010/07/star-wattage-marvel-assembles-the-avengers-for-comic-con-panel). Deadline.com. July 24, 2010. Archived (http://www.webcitation.org/5zx6k1EnB) from the original on 2011-07-05. . Retrieved July 25, 2010.

[15] Mortimer, Ben (2011-06-24). "Captain America: The First Avenger Set Visit!" (http://www.superherohype.com/features/articles/167663-captain-america-the-first-avenger-set-visit?start=1). Superhero Hype!. Archived (http://www.webcitation.org/5zva5QjFR) from the original on 2011-07-04. . Retrieved 2011-06-24.

[16] Bruno, Mike (2010-04-02). "'Captain America': Sebastian Stan cast as Bucky Barnes" (http://popwatch.ew.com/2010/04/02/captain-america-bucky-barnes). *Entertainment Weekly*. Archived (http://www.webcitation.org/5zx6hxNms) from the original on 2011-07-05. . Retrieved 2010-10-27.

[17] Ditzian, Eric (2011-01-12). "Sebastian Stan Talks 'Captain America' Casting And His Year Ahead" (http://www.mtv.com/news/articles/1655751/sebastian-stan-talks-captain-america-casting-his-year-ahead.jhtml). MTV News. Archived (http://www.webcitation.org/5zx6i5YVj) from the original on 2011-07-05. . Retrieved 2011-01-12.

[18] "Captain America Movie: Col. Phillips Cast" (http://marvel.com/news/moviestories.12985.captain_america_movie~colon~_col~dot~_phillips_cast). Marvel Comics. 2010-06-28. Archived (http://www.webcitation.org/5zxBt0ALJ) from the original on 2011-07-05. . Retrieved 2010-06-28.

[19] Flaherty, Mike (2011-02-11). "Tommy Lee Jones Tolerates Us for a Talk on HBO's Sunset Limited, Men in Black 3, and Captain America" (http://nymag.com/daily/entertainment/2011/02/interview.html). *New York*. Archived (http://www.webcitation.org/5zspzQ5rc) from the original on 2011-07-02. . Retrieved 2011-02-11.

[20] Marshall, Rick (2010-05-04). "Tony Stark's Father Will Have A Role In 'Captain America,' Says Jon Favreau" (http://splashpage.mtv.com/2010/05/04/iron-man-2-tony-stark-howard-stark-captain-america-movie-jon-favreau). MTV Splash Page. Archived (http://www.webcitation.org/5zva5fwTW) from the original on 2011-07-04. . Retrieved 2010-06-30.

[21] Fischer, Russ (2010-05-24). "Dominic Cooper Says He's Howard Stark in Captain America" (http://www.slashfilm.com/2010/05/24/dominic-cooper-says-hes-howard-stark-in-captain-america). /Film. Archived (http://www.webcitation.org/5zva6HGQv) from the original on 2011-07-04. . Retrieved 2010-06-30.

[22] Ames, Jeff (2010-10-28). "More Images From Captain America: The First Avenger; First Look at Hugo Weaving and Stanley Tucci" (http://www.collider.com/2010/10/28/captain-america-the-first-avengers-movie-images-weaving-tucci). Collider. Archived (http://www.webcitation.org/5zva70Uxi) from the original on 2011-07-04. . Retrieved 2010-11-13.

[23] "Captain America: The First Avenger – Dominic Cooper on Playning Howard Stark" (http://uk.ign.com/videos/2010/10/06/dominic-cooper-on-playing-howard-stark-in-captain-america). IGN. 2010-10-06. Archived (http://www.webcitation.org/5zva77tTg) from the original on 2011-07-04. . Retrieved 2010-10-07.

[24] Wigler, Josh (2010-06-07). "Neal McDonough Confirms 'Captain America' Role (And Bowler Hat), Talks Howling Commandos" (http://splashpage.mtv.com/2010/06/07/neal-mcdonough-confirms-captain-america-role-bowler-hat-howling-commandos). MTV News. Archived (http://www.webcitation.org/5zva87wWW) from the original on 2011-07-04. . Retrieved 2010-07-09.

[25] Morales, Wilson (2011-06-09). "Derek Luke Talks HawthoRNe, Captain America" (http://www.blackfilm.com/read/2011/06/derek-luke-talks-hawthorne-captain-america/). Blackfilm.com. Archived (http://www.webcitation.org/5zva9A8w9) from the original on 2011-07-04. . Retrieved 2011-06-23.

[26] McNary, Dave (2010-06-07). "Stanley Tucci joins *Captain America*" (http://www.variety.com/article/VR1118020306?refCatId=13). *Variety*. Archived (http://www.webcitation.org/5zxBrkSq5) from the original on 2011-07-05. . Retrieved 2011-03-23.

[27] Clark, Kyrstal (2010-08-29). "Stanley Tucci Says Captain America Has a Very Good Script" (http://screencrave.com/2010-08-29/stanley-tucci-says-captain-america-has-a-very-good-script). ScreenCrave.com. Archived (http://www.webcitation.org/5zva9rq3R) from the original on 2011-07-04. . Retrieved 2010-08-29.

[28] Coratelli, Carlo (2011-05-07). "Intervista a Kenneth Choi – Jim Morita in "Captain America: The First Avenger"" (http://www.comicus.it/blog/movie-comics/item/48872-intervista-a-kenneth-choi-jim-morita-in-captain-america-the-first-avenger). ComicUS.it. Archived (http://www.webcitation.org/5zx6irO7j) from the original on 2011-07-05. . Retrieved 2011-05-09.. Scroll down to English translation.

[29] "Bruno Ricci à l'affiche de *Captain América*, dans les salles le 17 août" (http://www.infosculture.com/actualite-cinema/bruno-ricci-a-laffiche-de-captain-america-dans-les-salles-le-17-aout/). InfosCulture.com. Archived (http://www.webcitation.org/5zx6jSksR) from the original on 2011-07-05. . Retrieved 2011-07-02.

Quote: "En plein tournage de la série française «L'Epervier», Bruno participe au casting de Captain America ... et est sélectionné! ...en interprétant Jacques Dernier ... qui combat aux côtés de Captain America et de ses quatre autres coéquipiers...."

Translation: "While filming the French series *The Hawk*, Bruno participated in the casting of Captain America ... and was selected! ... [He portrays] Jacques Dernier ... fighting alongside Captain America and his four other teammates...."

[30] "JJ Feild's heavy burden for film" (http://www.belfasttelegraph.co.uk/entertainment/news/jj-feilds-heavy-burden-for-film-15153814.html). *The Belfast Telegraph*. 2011-05-10. Archived (http://www.webcitation.org/5zx6jqsaS) from the original on 2011-07-05. . Retrieved 2011-06-23.

[31] "Toby Jones to Play Arnim Zola in Captain America" (http://www.comingsoon.net/news/movienews.php?id=65809). ComingSoon. 2010-05-07. Archived (http://www.webcitation.org/5zxBqgHiU) from the original on 2011-07-05. . Retrieved 2011-03-23.

[32] Jensen, Jeff. "An Exclusive First Look at 'Captain America: The First Avenger'", *Entertainment Weekly*, November 5, 2010. Time Warner.

[33] Wayland, Sara (2010-04-19). "Samuel L. Jackson Talks *Iron Man 2*, *Nick Fury*, *Captain America*, *Thor* and *The Avengers*" (http://www.collider.com/2010/04/19/samuel-l-jackson-talks-iron-man-2-nick-fury-captain-america-thor-and-the-avengers). Collider. Archived (http://www.webcitation.org/5zxBpVh6i) from the original on 2011-07-05. . Retrieved 2010-04-23.

[34] Lee, Stan (2011-03-15). "Cameo time approacheth! First, my classic cameo in the new Spider-Man cinematic triumph! Then cometh Captain America and others" (http://twitter.com/TheRealStanLee/status/47718376818229248). Twitter. Archived (http://www.webcitation.org/5zx6lLrpx) from the original on 2011-07-05. . Retrieved 2011-03-16.

[35] Boucher, Geoff (2010-07-21). "COMIC-CON 2010: 'Captain America' director has different spin on hero: 'He's not a flag-waver'" (http://latimesblogs.latimes.com/herocomplex/2010/07/captain-america-comiccon-2010-captain-america-chris-evans-joe-johnston.html). *Los Angeles Times*. Archived (http://www.webcitation.org/5zx6mC2nT) from the original on 2011-07-05. . Retrieved 2010-07-23.

[36] Fleming, Michael (1997-04-14). "A Mania For Marvel" (http://www.variety.com/article/VR1117434784.html). *Variety*. Archived (http://www.webcitation.org/5zspMVa45) from the original on 2011-07-22. . Retrieved 2008-03-02.

[37] Fleming, Michael (2000-05-16). "Artisan deal a real Marvel" (http://www.variety.com/article/VR1117781709.html). *Variety*. Archived (http://www.webcitation.org/5zspAYPBV) from the original on 2011-07-22. . Retrieved 2008-03-02.

[38] Amdur, Meredith (2003-10-09). "Marvel sees big stock gains" (http://www.variety.com/article/VR1117893720.html). *Variety*. Archived (http://www.webcitation.org/5zsowQg3T) from the original on 2011-07-22. . Retrieved 2008-03-02.

[39] Archive of Fritz, Ben, and Dana Harris (2005-04-27). "Paramount pacts for Marvel pix" (http://www.variety.com/article/VR1117921812.html). *Variety*. Archived (http://www.webcitation.org/5zsogrOMh) from the original on 2011-07-22. . Retrieved 2008-03-02.

[40] McClintock, Pamela (2005-06-21). "$500 mil pic fund feeds Warner Bros." (http://www.variety.com/article/VR1117924871.html). *Variety*. Archived (http://www.webcitation.org/5zsoYdDhG) from the original on 2011-07-22. . Retrieved 2008-03-02.

[41] "Captain America is Coming" (http://uk.movies.ign.com/articles/796/796582p1.html). IGN. 2007-06-14. Archived (http://www.webcitation.org/5zx6mO5Xb) from the original on 2011-07-05. . Retrieved 2008-10-07.

[42] Carroll, Larry (2005). "Future Shocks: What's ahead for Avi Arad and his Marvel empire" (http://www.mtv.com/shared/movies/interviews/a/arad_avi_062005). MTV. Archived (http://www.webcitation.org/5zx6nDrCP) from the original on 2011-07-05. . Retrieved 2008-03-02.

[43] Zeitchick, Steven (2006-02-23). "Marvel stock soars on rev outlook" (http://www.variety.com/article/VR1117938775.html). *Variety*. Archived (http://www.webcitation.org/5zx6nxeuD) from the original on 2011-07-05. . Retrieved 2008-03-02.

[44] Douglas, Edward (2006-07-26). "Exclusive: Jon Favreau on *Iron Man*" (http://web.archive.org/web/20080215002628/http://www.superherohype.com/news.php?id=4568). Superhero Hype!. Archived from the original (http://www.superherohype.com/news.php?id=4568) on 2008-02-15. . Retrieved 2008-03-02.

[45] Gardner, Chris (2006-07-18). "Where things stand on 5 stalled superheroes" (http://www.variety.com/article/VR1117947046.html). *Variety*. Archived (http://www.webcitation.org/5zx6oTPy1) from the original on 2011-07-05. . Retrieved 2008-03-02.

[46] Kit, Borys (2006-04-28). "Marvel Studios outlines slew of superhero titles" (http://web.archive.org/web/20080429223947/http://www.hollywoodreporter.com/hr/search/article_display.jsp?vnu_content_id=1002424612). *The Hollywood Reporter*. Archived from the original (http://www.hollywoodreporter.com/hr/search/article_display.jsp?vnu_content_id=1002424612) on 2008-04-29. . Retrieved 2008-10-07.

[47] Kit, Borys (2008-11-09). "'Captain America' recruits director" (http://www.hollywoodreporter.com/news/captain-america-recruits-director-122606). *The Hollywood Reporter*. Archived (http://www.webcitation.org/5zsl3VRxw) from the original on 2011-07-22. . Retrieved 2008-11-10.

[48] McNary, Dave (2008-01-24). "Lionsgate signs as WGA talks go on" (http://www.variety.com/article/VR1117979610.html). *Variety*. Archived (http://www.webcitation.org/5zx6pTssm) from the original on 2011-07-05. . Retrieved 2008-03-02.

[49] Edward Douglas (2008-05-05). "Marvel Studios Sets Four More Release Dates!" (http://www.superherohype.com/news/topnews.php?id=7165). Superhero Hype!. Archived (http://www.webcitation.org/5zx6pomFX) from the original on 2011-07-05. . Retrieved 2008-05-05.

[50] Franklin, Garth (2008-07-21). "Leterrier On More "Hulk", "United States"" (http://www.darkhorizons.com/news08/080721k.php). Dark Horizons. Archived (http://www.webcitation.org/5zx6q2zeo) from the original on 2011-07-05. . Retrieved 2008-10-07.

[51] Kit, Borys, and Jay A. Fernandez (2008-11-18). "'Captain America' enlists two scribes" (http://www.hollywoodreporter.com/news/captain-america-enlists-two-scribes-123195). *The Hollywood Reporter*. Archived (http://www.webcitation.org/5zxs4qFXf) from the original on 2011-07-05. . Retrieved 2008-11-19.. (First paragraph; subscription required for full story.)

[52] Billington, Alex (2009-06-07). "Profile on Marvel Studios with Big Updates from Kevin Feige" (http://www.firstshowing.net/2009/06/07/profile-on-marvel-studios-with-big-updates-from-kevin-feige). FirstShowing.net. Archived (http://www.webcitation.org/5zva6hNsx) from the original on 2011-07-04. . Retrieved 2009-06-12.

[53] Sanchez, Robert (2007-04-21). "Exclusive Interview: Avi Arad and the IESB Go 1:1!" (http://iesb.net/index.php?option=com_content&task=view&id=2344&Itemid=99). IESB. Archived (http://www.webcitation.org/5zx6qE3r3) from the original on 2011-07-05. . Retrieved 2008-10-07.

[54] Svetkey, Benjamin (2008-11-21). "Barack Obama: Celebrity In Chief" (http://www.ew.com/ew/article/0,,20241874,00.html). *Entertainment Weekly*. Archived (http://www.webcitation.org/5zx6qSSww) from the original on 2011-07-05. . Retrieved 2011-05-06.

[55] Salisbury, Mark (2009-12-23). "Terror Tidbits (Fango #290): THE WOLFMAN: Hair Today, Gore Tomorrow" (http://fangoria.com/component/content/article/119-terror-tidbits/4817-terror-tidbits-fango-290-the-wolfman-hair-today-gore-tomorrow.html). Fangoria. Archived (http://www.webcitation.org/5zx6rG4OQ) from the original on 2011-07-05. . Retrieved 2009-12-29.

[56] Lovece, Frank. "Wolfman in London: Joe Johnston resurrects a Universal horror legend" (http://www.filmjournal.com/filmjournal/content_display/esearch/e3i84347827022cc793ce558ba986c2e3b9?pn=2). *Film Journal International*. January 25, 2010. Archived (http://www.webcitation.org/5zx6rSOwO) 5 July 2011 at WebCite

[57] Drees, Rich (2010-02-07). "The Invaders Are Joining *Captain America*" (http://www.filmbuffonline.com/FBOLNewsreel/wordpress/2010/02/07/the-invaders-are-joining-captain-america). FilmBuff Newsreel. Archived (http://www.webcitation.org/5zx6s2u6J) from the original on 2011-07-05. . Retrieved 2010-06-30.

[58] Bentley, David. "Captain America director says Namor the Sub-Mariner is not in the movie" (http://blogs.coventrytelegraph.net/thegeekfiles/2010/11/captain-america-director-says.html). *Coventry Telegraph*. November 9, 2010. WebCitation Archive (http://www.webcitation.org/5uCLUbOZn).

[59] Lovece, Frank (July 14, 2011; print version July 17, 2011). "Red, White and True Blue 'Captain America'" (http://www.webcitation.org/60KXM5Vuo). *Newsday*. Archived from the original (http://www.newsday.com/entertainment/movies/red-white-and-true-blue-captain-america-1.3025849) on 2011-07-20. . Retrieved 2010-07-20.

[60] "Captain America Movie: Peggy Carter Cast" (http://marvel.com/news/all.12060.captain_america_movie~colon~_peggy_carter_cast). Marvel Comics. 2010-04-14. Archived (http://www.webcitation.org/5zvaACDGQ) from the original on 2011-07-04. . Retrieved 2010-04-14.

[61] Goldberg, Matt (2010-04-15). "Joss Whedon Re-Writing *Captain American: The First Avenger*?" (http://www.collider.com/2010/04/15/joss-whedon-re-writing-captain-america-the-first-avenger). Collider. Archived (http://www.webcitation.org/5zx6slszr) from the original on 2011-07-05. . Retrieved 2010-08-18.

[62] Gross, Ed (2010-08-17). "Joss Whedon Discusses His Contributions to The First Avenger: Captain America" (http://www.earthsmightiest.com/fansites/captainamerica/news/?a=7535). Earth's Mightiest. Archived (http://www.webcitation.org/5zxBnxPjy) from the original on 2011-07-05. . Retrieved 2010-08-18.

[63] Faraci, Devin (2010-04-23). "Exclusive: Captain America Will Meet the Howling Commandos" (http://chud.com/articles/articles/23496/1/EXCLUSIVE-CAPTAIN-AMERICA-WILL-MEET-THE-HOWLING-COMMANDOS/Page1.html). Chud. Archived (http://www.webcitation.org/5zxBq6r6w) from the original on 2011-07-05. . Retrieved 2010-04-23.

[64] "Hugo Weaving confirmed as Red Skull in Captain America" (http://www.comingsoon.net/news/movienews.php?id=65732). Archived (http://www.webcitation.org/5zva45L7T) from the original on 2011-07-04. . Retrieved May 4, 2010.

[65] "Tommy Lee Jones Confirmed for *Captain America*" (http://www.comingsoon.net/news/movienews.php?id=66418). ComingSoon.com. 2010-05-27. Archived (http://www.webcitation.org/5zxBr1Z95) from the original on 2011-07-05. . Retrieved 2010-06-30.

[66] Fleming, Michael. "Neal McDonough in *Captain America* Chatter" (http://www.deadline.com/2010/06/neal-mcdonough-in-captain-america-chatter). Deadline.com. June 3, 2010. Archived (http://www.webcitation.org/5zva83TLT) 4 July 2011 at WebCite

[67] Lesnick, Silas (2010-06-08). "Neal McDonough Confirmed for *Captain America*" (http://www.superherohype.com/news/articles/102213-neal-mcdonough-confirmed-for-captain-america). SuperheroHype.com. Archived (http://www.webcitation.org/5zxBrMQqR) from the original on 2011-07-05. . Retrieved 2010-06-30.

[68] "Marvel's "Captain America," have opened a production office at Shepperton Studios, principle photography is scheduled to begin June 28th" (http://twitter.com/prodweek/status/13018769705). Production Weekly via Twitter. 2010-04-28. . Retrieved 2010-09-27.

[69] "Captain America Movie: Howard Stark Cast" (http://marvel.com/news/moviestories.13004.captain_america_movie~colon~_howard_stark_cast). Marvel Comics. 2010-06-29. Archived (http://www.webcitation.org/5zxBth3g1) from the original on 2011-07-05. . Retrieved 2010-06-30.

[70] "Summer in the City" (http://filmlondon.org.uk/news/2010/july/summer_in_the_city). Film London. 2010-07-07. Archived (http://www.webcitation.org/5zxBuP0VR) from the original on 2011-07-05. . Retrieved 2010-07-09.

[71] "Caerwent is scene for Captain America movie" (http://www.southwalesargus.co.uk/news/9165974.Caerwent_is_scene_for_Captain_America_movie/). *South Wales Argus*. 2011-07-28. Archived (http://www.webcitation.org/60XUyTLr0) from the original on 2011-07-29. . Retrieved 2011-07-28.

[72] Bently, David (2010-07-07). "Captain America to film war scenes in Wales" (http://blogs.coventrytelegraph.net/thegeekfiles/2010/07/captain-america-to-film-war-sc.html). *Coventry Telegraph*. Archived (http://www.webcitation.org/5v62f5icZ) from the original on 2011-07-22. . Retrieved 2010-10-21.

[73] Thompson, Dan (2010-08-03). "Northern Quarter to Be Set for Captain America Film Blockbuster" (http://menmedia.co.uk/manchestereveningnews/news/s/1312830_northern_quarter_to_be_set_for_captain_america_film_blockbuster). *Manchester Evening News*. . Retrieved 2010-08-03.

[74] Collinson, Dawn (2010-09-16). "Captain America Filming to Get Underway on Liverpool Docklands" (http://www.liverpooldailypost.co.uk/liverpool-news/regional-news/2010/09/16/captain-america-filming-to-get-underway-on-liverpool-docklands-92534-27278123/2). *Liverpool Daily Post*. Archived (http://www.webcitation.org/5v617I6oR) from the original on 2011-07-22. . Retrieved 2010-09-27.

[75] Siddle, John (2010-07-39). "Captain America: The First Avenger to be filmed in Liverpool" (http://www.liverpoolecho.co.uk/liverpool-news/local-news/2010/07/30/captain-america-the-first-avenger-to-be-filmed-in-liverpool-100252-26960985). *Liverpool Echo*. Archived (http://www.webcitation.org/5v62qdbTm) from the original on 2011-07-22. . Retrieved 2010-08-03.

[76] Boucher, Geoff (2010-07-14). "It's official: 'Thor' and 'Captain America' will be 3-D films" (http://latimesblogs.latimes.com/herocomplex/2010/07/thor-3d-captain-america-3d-comiccon-marvel-studios.html). *Los Angeles Times*. Archived (http://www.webcitation.org/5zspo35dM) from the original on 2011-07-22. . Retrieved 2010-07-14.

[77] JimmyO (2010-11-14). "IAR Exclusive: Stanley Tucci Talks 'Captain America" (http://www.iamrogue.com/news/movie-news/item/1672-iar-exclusive-stanley-tucci-talks-captain-america.html). IAmRogue.com. Archived (http://www.webcitation.org/5zxBvZufb) from the original on 2011-07-05. . Retrieved 2011-01-23.

[78] "BREAKING NEWS: Alan Silvestri to score 'Captain America'" (http://filmmusicreporter.wordpress.com/2011/02/28/breaking-news-alan-silvestri-to-score-captain-america). *Film Music Reporter*. 2011-02-28. Archived (http://www.webcitation.org/5zxBw5wJ8) from the original on 2011-07-05. . Retrieved 2011-03-01.

[79] Childress, Ahmad (2011-03-21). "Captain America Reshoots?" (http://www.craveonline.com/entertainment/film/article/captain-america-reshoots-126481). CraveOnline. Archived (http://www.webcitation.org/5zxBwNkEx) from the original on 2011-07-05. . Retrieved 2011-03-21.

[80] Silas Lesnick. "Captain America Shooting in Los Angeles" (http://www.superherohype.com/news/articles/164467-captain-america-shooting-in-los-angeles). Superhero Hype!. Archived (http://www.webcitation.org/5zxBwTUXX) from the original on 2011-07-05. .

[81] "Captain America Scene Filmed in New York on Saturday" (http://www.superherohype.com/news/articles/166519-captain-america-scene-filmed-in-new-york-on-saturday). *Superhero Hype!* (April 24, 2011). Retrieved May 2, 2011. Archived (http://www.webcitation.org/5zxBwpaQ2) 5 July 2011 at WebCite

[82] Hogg, Trevor (2011-07-27). "Raising the Shield: The Making of Captain America: The First Avenger" (http://www.cgsociety.org/index.php/CGSFeatures/CGSFeatureSpecial/captain_america). CGSociety.org (Society of Digital Artists). Archived (http://www.webcitation.org/60XVGqH7s) from the original on 2011-07-29. . Retrieved 2011-07-28.

[83] Alter, Ethan (2011-06-27). "'Avenger' auteur: Joe Johnston shapes a muscular 'Captain America" (http://www.filmjournal.com/filmjournal/content_display/news-and-features/features/movies/e3if59b6538fcf8c6c637df82f5a7cf3d79). *Film Journal International*. Archived (http://www.webcitation.org/5zxBxGv1F) from the original on 2011-07-05. . Retrieved 2011-06-30.

[84] Lovece, *Newsday*, " The Man Behind the Shield of 'Captain America' (http://www.newsday.com/entertainment/movies/red-white-and-true-blue-captain-america-1.3025849)" (article sidebar). WebCitation archive (http://www.webcitation.org/60KXM5Vuo).

[85] "Interview: A Q&A with creative director Steve Viola of Rok!t" (http://www.artofthetitle.com/2011/08/30/captain-america/?WLXID=d0fa98c0-1d28-458e-9ffa-e99c24eca99d&RID=1bd4104bd3c&TID=1316709786605&lid=). *Captain America: The First Avenger*. Art of the Title. . Retrieved 2011-09-22.

[86] "'Captain America: The First Avenger' Soundtrack Details" (http://filmmusicreporter.com/2011/06/12/captain-america-the-first-avenger-soundtrack-details). *FilmMusicReporter.com*. 2011-06-12. Archived (http://www.webcitation.org/5zxBxqXFA) from the original on 2011-07-05. . Retrieved 2011-06-13.

[87] "Watch the Captain America Red Carpet Premiere LIVE on Marvel.com" (http://marvel.com/news/story/16296/watch_the_captain_america_red_carpet_premiere_live_on_marvelcom). Marvel Comics. 2011-07-15. . Retrieved 2011-07-18.

[88] "See Captain America: The First Avenger Early at Comic-Con" (http://marvel.com/news/story/16330/see_captain_america_the_first_avenger_early_at_comic-con). Marvel Comics. 2011-07-18. . Retrieved 2011-07-19.

[89] "Marvel Movie Update: New Release Schedule!" (http://marvel.com/news/.7214.Marvel_Movie_Update~colon~_New_Release_Schedule). Marvel Comics. 2009-03-12. Archived (http://www.webcitation.org/5zsqEyYKW) from the original on 2011-07-22. . Retrieved 2010-03-28.

[90] "Global sites & Release Dates" (http://captainamerica.marvel.com/intl/releasedates/release-dates.html). Paramount Pictures. Archived (http://www.webcitation.org/5zva04fKI) from the original on 2011-07-04. . Retrieved 2011-05-06.

[91] Barnes, Brooks (July 3, 2011). "Soft-Pedal Captain America Overseas? Hollywood Says No" (http://mediadecoder.blogs.nytimes.com/2011/07/03/soft-pedal-captain-america-overseas-hollywood-says-no/). *The New York Times*. Archived (http://www.webcitation.org/5zxObt19Z) from the original on 2011-07-22. . Retrieved 2011-07-07.

[92] Segers, Frank (September 11, 2011). "Foreign Box Office: 'The Smurfs' Squeak Out Another Victory Overseas" (http://www.hollywoodreporter.com/news/foreign-box-office-smurfs-squeak-233896). *The Hollywood Reporter*. Archived (http://www.webcitation.org/61g880VeH) from the original on September 13, 2011. . Retrieved September 13, 2011.

[93] McClintock, Pamela (2011-01-19). "Studios Set Super Bowl Ads; 'Pirates,' 'Transformers,' 'Captain America'" (http://www.hollywoodreporter.com/news/studios-set-super-bowl-ads-73548). *The Hollywood Reporter*. Archived (http://www.webcitation.org/5zsnfT318) from the original on 2011-07-22. . Retrieved 2011-01-20.

[94] "Watch the Debut Trailer for Captain America: The First Avenger" (http://marvel.com/news/story/15471/watch_the_debut_trailer_for_captain_america_the_first_avenger). Marvel Comics. 2011-03-23. Archived (http://www.webcitation.org/5zxBxziFm) from the original on 2011-07-05. . Retrieved 2011-03-24.

[95] "Cap's USO Girls Salute the USS Intrepid" (http://marvel.com/news/story/16002/caps_uso_girls_salute_the_uss_intrepid). Marvel Comics. 2011-05-31. Archived (http://www.webcitation.org/5zxByIlrc) from the original on 2011-07-05. . Retrieved 2011-06-01.

[96] "Dunkin' Donuts and Baskin-Robbins Launch National Search for "America's Super-Soldiers"" (http://www.reuters.com/article/2011/06/27/idUS131964+27-Jun-2011+PRN20110627). Dunkin' Donuts / Baskin-Robbins / Marvel Entertainment press release via Reuters. 2011-06-27. Archived (http://www.webcitation.org/5zsoGEy05) from the original on 2011-07-22. . Retrieved 2011-06-28.

[97] "White Sox Host Independence Day Celebration" (http://mlb.mlb.com/news/press_releases/press_release.jsp?ymd=20110701&content_id=21243198&vkey=pr_cws&fext=.jsp&c_id=cws). Major League Baseball. 2011-07-01. Archived (http://www.webcitation.org/5zxByytRD) from the original on 2011-07-05. . Retrieved 2011-07-01.

[98] "Premiere Of "Captain America: The First Avenger"" (http://www.reuters.com/article/2011/07/18/idUS162389+18-Jul-2011+PRN20110718). Reuters. 2011-07-18. Archived (http://www.webcitation.org/60K07Mkmd) from the original on 2011-07-20. . Retrieved 2011-07-20.

[99] Truitt, Brian (2011-02-01). "Captain America commands attention in digital comic, film" (http://www.usatoday.com/life/movies/news/2011-02-01-captainamerica01_ST_N.htm). *USA Today*. Archived (http://www.webcitation.org/5zxs93nFf) from the original on 2011-07-05. . Retrieved 2011-02-01.

[100] Rosenberg, Adam (2010 10 06). "'Captain America' Movie Gets Video Game Tie-In: 'Captain America: Super Soldier'" (http://splashpage.mtv.com/2010/10/05/captain-america-movie-video-game-captain-america-super-soldier). MTV News. Archived (http://www.webcitation.org/5zxsA5yMr) from the original on 2011-07-05. . Retrieved 2010-10-06.

[101] "Download Captain America: Sentinel of Liberty Now!" (http://marvel.com/news/story/16292/download_captain_america_sentinel_of_liberty_now). Marvel.com. 2011-07-14. Archived (http://www.webcitation.org/612LtogiQ) from the original on 2011-08-18. . Retrieved 2011-07-14.

[102] "Tons of New THOR & CAPTAIN AMERICA Movie-Based Toy Line Images" (http://www.dailyblam.com/news/2011/02/03/tons-of-new-images-of-captain-america-thor-movie-based-toy-lines). . Retrieved February 3, 2011.

[103] "Bring Captain America Home on Blu-ray & DVD 10/25" (http://www.webcitation.org/61rdm7nep). *Marvel Comics*. 2011-09-20. Archived from the original (http://marvel.com/news/story/16689/bring_captain_america_home_on_blu-ray_dvd_1025) on 2011-09-21. . Retrieved 2011-09-21.

[104] Finke, Nikki (2011-07-22). "'Captain America' Opens To $4M Midnights" (http://www.deadline.com/2011/07/captain-america-opens-to-4m-midnights/). Deadline.com. Archived (http://www.webcitation.org/60NI2VeFh) from the original on 2011-07-22. . Retrieved 2011-07-22.

[105] Box office update: 'Captain America' soars into first place with $25.7 million on Friday (http://insidemovies.ew.com/2011/07/23/friday-box-office-captain-america-harry-potter-friends-with-benefits/)

[106] Weekend Report: 'Captain America' Rockets to the Top, 'Potter's Bubble Bursts (http://boxofficemojo.com/news/?id=3221&p=.htm)

[107] "Captain America: The First Avenger (2011)" (http://www.rottentomatoes.com/m/captain-america/). *Rotten Tomatoes*. Flixster accessdate=2011-08-04. .

[108] "Captain America: The First Avenger" (http://www.metacritic.com/movie/captain-america-the-first-avenger). *Metacritic*. CBS Interactive. . Retrieved 2011-07-28.

[109] Moore, Roger (2011-07-20). "Movie Review: Captain America, the First Avenger" (http://blogs.orlandosentinel.com/entertainment_movies_blog/2011/07/movie-review-captain-america-the-first-avenger.html). *Orlando Sentinel*. Archived (http://www.webcitation.org/60K8HEZCZ) from the original on 2011-07-20. . Retrieved 2011-07-20.

[110] Ebert, Roger (2011-07-20). "Captain America" (http://rogerebert.suntimes.com/apps/pbcs.dll/article?AID=/20110720/REVIEWS/110729997/1001/reviews). *Chicago Sun-Times*. Archived (http://www.webcitation.org/60LHUVKkA) from the original on 2011-07-21. . Retrieved 2011-07-21.

[111] Scott, A. O. (2011-07-21). "Hey, Brooklyn, Where Did You Get Those Muscles?" (http://movies.nytimes.com/2011/07/22/movies/captain-america-with-chris-evans-review.html). *The New York Times*. Archived (http://www.webcitation.org/60LIgPgZ9) from the original on 2011-07-21. . Retrieved 2011-07-21.

[112] Longworth, Karina (2011-07-20). "Captain America: The First Avenger: Film Review" (http://www.villagevoice.com/2011-07-20/film/captain-america-movie-ignores-its-roots-for-easy-money/). *The Village Voice*. Archived (http://www.webcitation.org/60K1yC2J6) from the original on 2011-07-20. . Retrieved 2011-07-20.

[113] Debruge, Peter (2011-07-20). "Captain America: The First Avenger" (http://www.variety.com/review/VE1117945677). *Variety*. Archived (http://www.webcitation.org/60K7sf6G5) from the original on 2011-07-20. . Retrieved 2011-07-20.

[114] Honeycutt, Kirk (2011-07-20). "Captain America: The First Avenger: Film Review" (http://www.hollywoodreporter.com/review/captain-america-first-avenger-film-213287). *The Hollywood Reporter*. Archived (http://www.webcitation.org/60K1FEuC2) from the original on 2011-07-20. . Retrieved 2011-07-20.

[115] Ng, Philiana (2011-07-19). "Teen Choice Awards 2011: 'Pretty Little Liars,' Rebecca Black Added to List of Nominees" (http://www.webcitation.org/60UVrjVi4). *The Hollywood Reporter*. Archived from the original (http://www.hollywoodreporter.com/news/teen-choice-awards-2011-pretty-212996) on 2011-07-27. . Retrieved 2011-07-27.

[116] "SCREAM 2011" (http://www.spike.com/events/scream-awards-2011/). *Spike TV*. . Retrieved 2011-09-07.

[117] Marshall, Rick (April 14, 2011). "'Captain America' Writers Talk Sequel, Post-'Avengers' Plans, And The Marvel Movie-Verse" (http://splashpage.mtv.com/2011/04/14/captain-america-movie-sequel-avengers). MTV Splash Page. Archived (http://www.webcitation.org/5zxsAqHPq) from the original on 2011-07-05. . Retrieved 2011-04-14.

[118] Topel, Fred (2011-06-20). "'Captain America' Sequel Already In The Works" (http://www.webcitation.org/60NJMvmhS). ScreenJunkies.com. Archived from the original (http://www.screenjunkies.com/movies/movie-news/captain-america-sequel-already-in-the-works/) on 2011-07-22. . Retrieved 2011-07-22.

[119] Toro, Gabe (2011-09-22). "Chris Evans Says 'Captain America' Sequel Might Not Arrive Until 2014" (http://blogs.indiewire.com/theplaylist/archives/exclusive_chirs_evans_says_captain_america_wont_pop_up_in_non-cap_marvel_mo/#). indieWire. . Retrieved 2011-09-22.

External links

- Official website (http://www.captainamerica.com/)
- *Captain America: The First Avenger* (http://www.allrovi.com/movies/movie/v451108) at AllRovi
- *Captain America: The First Avenger* (http://www.imdb.com/title/tt0458339/) at the Internet Movie Database
- *Captain America* Movie Hub (http://marvel.com/movies/captain_america.the_first_avenger~colon~_captain_america) at Marvel Comics

What's Your Number?

What's Your Number?	
Theatrical release poster	
Directed by	Mark Mylod
Produced by	Beau Flynn Tripp Vinson
Screenplay by	Gabrielle Allen Jennifer Crittenden
Based on	*20 Times a Lady* by Karyn Bosnak
Starring	Anna Faris Chris Evans
Music by	Aaron Zigman
Cinematography	J. Michael Muro
Editing by	Julie Monroe
Studio	Regency Enterprises New Regency
Distributed by	20th Century Fox
Release date(s)	September 30, 2011
Running time	106 minutes
Country	United States
Language	English
Budget	$20 million[1]
Box office	$26,091,205 (worldwide estimate as of October 2011)[2]

What's Your Number? is a 2011 romantic comedy film starring Anna Faris and Chris Evans. It is based on Karyn Bosnak's book *20 Times a Lady*. The film was released on September 30, 2011.

Plot

Ally Darling, read an article in a magazine about the average amount of sex partners a women has. She is far above average, so she goes looking for the one out of her exes when she realizes that they could have changed for the better. She enlists the help of her neighbour, Colin (Evans) making a deal that if he helps her find her exes, she'll provide an escape from his one night stands.

Cast

- Anna Faris as Ally Darling
- Chris Evans as Colin Shea
- Joel McHale as Roger
- Blythe Danner as Ava Darling
- Ed Begley, Jr. as Mr. Darling
- Andy Samberg as Gerry Perry
- Zachary Quinto as Rick
- Oliver Jackson-Cohen as Eddie Vogel
- Thomas Lennon as Dr. Barrett Ingold
- Mike Vogel as Dave Hansen
- Chris Pratt as Disgusting Donald
- Dave Annable as Jake Adams
- Martin Freeman as Simon
- Anthony Mackie as Tom Piper
- Ari Graynor as Daisy Darling
- Eliza Coupe as Shelia
- Heather Burns as Eileen
- Kate Simses as Katie
- Tika Sumpter as Jamie
- Denise Vasi as Cara

Reception

The film has received mostly negative reviews from critics. It has a 25% rating at Rotten Tomatoes based on 101 reviews.[3] The film's rating on metacritic is "generally unfavourable", receiving a score of 35% from 31 professional critics.[4]

References

[1] Kaufman, Amy (September 29, 2011). "Movie Projector: Holdovers likely to beat '50/50,' 'Dream House'" (http://latimesblogs.latimes.com/entertainmentnewsbuzz/2011/09/box-offfice-dream-house-5050-whats-your-number.html). *Los Angeles Times*. . Retrieved September 30, 2011.

[2] "What's Your Number" (http://www.boxofficemojo.com/movies/?id=whatsyournumber.htm). *Box Office Mojo*. October 2, 2011. . Retrieved October 2, 2011.

[3] "What's Your Number? (2011)" (http://www.rottentomatoes.com/m/whats_your_number/). *Rotten Tomatoes*. . Retrieved October 1, 2011.

[4] http://www.metacritic.com/movie/whats-your-number/critic-reviews

External links

- Official site (http://www.whatsyournumbermovie.com/)
- *What's Your Number?* (http://www.imdb.com/title/tt0770703/) at the Internet Movie Database

The Avengers (2012 film)

The Avengers	
Teaser poster	
Directed by	Joss Whedon
Produced by	Kevin Feige
Screenplay by	Joss Whedon
Based on	*The Avengers* by Stan Lee Jack Kirby
Starring	• Robert Downey, Jr. • Chris Evans • Mark Ruffalo • Chris Hemsworth • Scarlett Johansson • Jeremy Renner • Samuel L. Jackson
Music by	Alan Silvestri
Cinematography	Seamus McGarvey[1]
Editing by	• Paul Rubell[1] • Jeffrey Ford[1]
Studio	Marvel Studios
Distributed by	Walt Disney Pictures[1]
Release date(s)	May 4, 2012
Country	United States
Language	English
Budget	$220 million[2]

The Avengers is an upcoming American superhero film produced by Marvel Studios and distributed by Walt Disney Pictures[1], based upon the Marvel Comics superhero team of the same name. It is part of the Marvel Cinematic Universe, which crosses over several Marvel superhero films including *Iron Man* (2008), *The Incredible Hulk*

(2008), *Iron Man 2* (2010), *Thor* (2011) and *Captain America: The First Avenger* (2011). The film is written and directed by Joss Whedon and features an ensemble cast, which includes Robert Downey, Jr., Chris Evans, Mark Ruffalo, Chris Hemsworth, Scarlett Johansson, Jeremy Renner and Samuel L. Jackson. In *The Avengers*, Nick Fury, director of the peacekeeping organization S.H.I.E.L.D., recruits Iron Man, Hulk, Thor, and Captain America to save the world from destruction.

Development of *The Avengers* began when Marvel Studios received a grant from Merrill Lynch in April 2005. After the success of the film *Iron Man*, Marvel announced that *The Avengers* would be released in July 2011. With the signing of Scarlett Johansson in March 2009, the film was pushed back for a 2012 release. Whedon was brought on board in April 2010 and rewrote the screenplay that was originally written by Zak Penn. Production began in April 2011 in Albuquerque, New Mexico, before moving to Cleveland, Ohio, in August and New York City in September.

The Avengers is scheduled for release on May 4, 2012 in the United States.

Premise

When an unexpected enemy emerges who threatens global safety and security, Nick Fury, the director of the international peacekeeping agency known as S.H.I.E.L.D., finds himself in need of a team of superheroes to pull the world back from the brink of disaster.[1]

Cast

- Robert Downey, Jr. as Tony Stark / Iron Man:

  A billionaire industrialist who seeks to pacify the world with a mechanical suit of armor of his own invention. Downey was cast as part of his four-picture deal with Marvel Studios, which includes *Iron Man 2* and *The Avengers*.[3] Downey stated that he initially pushed Whedon to make Stark the lead revealing, "Well, I said, 'I need to be in the opening sequence. I don't know what you're thinking, but Tony needs to drive this thing.' He was like, 'Okay, let's try that.' We tried it and it didn't work, because this is a different sort of thing, the story and the idea and the theme is the theme, and everybody is just an arm of the octopus."[4]

- Chris Evans as Steve Rogers / Captain America:

  A World War II veteran who was enhanced to the peak of human physicality by an experimental serum. Evans was cast as part of a deal to star in three Marvel films, in addition to *The Avengers*.[5] Evans stated that Steve Rogers is much darker in *The Avengers* explaining, "It's just about him trying to come to terms with the modern world. You've got to imagine, it's enough of a shock to accept the fact that you're in a completely different time, but everybody you know is dead. Everybody you cared about... He was a soldier, obviously, everybody he went to battle with, all of his brothers in arms, they're all dead. He's just lonely. I think in the beginning it's a fish out of water scene, and it's tough. It's a tough pill for him to swallow. Then comes trying to find a balance with the modern world."[4] Regarding the dynamic between Captain America and Tony Stark, Evans remarked, "I think there's certainly a dichotomy—this kind of friction between myself and Tony Stark, they're polar opposites. One guy is flash and spotlight and smooth, and the other guy is selfless and in the shadows and kind of quiet and they have to get along. They explore that, and it's pretty fun".[6]

- Mark Ruffalo as Dr. Bruce Banner / Hulk:

  A genius scientist who, because of exposure to gamma radiation, transforms into a monster when enraged or excited. Ruffalo was cast after negotiations between Marvel and Edward Norton broke down.[7] About replacing Edward Norton, Ruffalo said, "I'm a friend of Ed's, and yeah, that wasn't a great way for all that to go down. But the way I see it is that Ed has bequeathed this part to me. I look at it as my generation's *Hamlet*." About the character he stated, "He's a guy struggling with two sides of himself—the dark and the light—and everything he does in his life is filtered through issues of control. I grew up on the Bill Bixby TV series, which I thought was a really nuanced and real human way to look at the Hulk. I like that the part has those qualities".[8] Regarding the Hulk's place on the team Ruffalo said, "He's like the teammate none of them are sure they want on their team. He's a loose cannon. It's like, 'Just throw a grenade in the middle of the group and let's hope it turns out well"![9] Ruffalo also told *New York* magazine that unlike previous incarnations, he will actually play the Hulk, "I'm really excited. No one's ever played the Hulk exactly, they've always done CGI. They're going to do the *Avatar* stop-action, stop-motion capture. So I'll actually play the Hulk. That'll be fun".[10] About his preparation for the role Ruffalo joked, "I've lost 15 pounds and I've put another five on of just strapping, pure USDA beef... They want me mean and lean, but they don't want me big and buff".[11]

- Lou Ferrigno will voice the Hulk.[12] [13]

- Chris Hemsworth as Thor:

  The Norse god of thunder. Hemsworth was cast as part of a multiple movie deal.[14] He had previously worked with Joss Whedon on *The Cabin in the Woods*.[15] Hemsworth stated that he was able to maintain the strength he built up for *Thor* by increasing his food intake, consisting of a number of chicken breasts, fish, steak and eggs a day. When asked exactly how much, Hemsworth joked, "My body weight in protein pretty much!"[16] About Thor's motivations Hemsworth remarked, "I think [Thor's] motivation is much more of a personal one, in the sense that it's his brother that is stirring things up. Whereas everyone else, it's some bad guy who they've gotta take down. It's a different approach for me, or for Thor. He's constantly having to battle the greater good and what he should do vs. it's his little brother there... I've been frustrated with my brothers at times, or family, but I'm the only one who is allowed to be angry at them. There's a bit of that."[4]

Cast of *The Avengers* at the 2010 San Diego Comic-Con International, with Joss Whedon and Kevin Feige.

- Scarlett Johansson as Natasha Romanoff:

  A highly trained spy working for the international peacekeeping organization, S.H.I.E.L.D.[17] Whedon confirmed that Johansson's Romanoff would be the only female member of the Avengers, but not the only female character in the film.[18] Regarding the character's abilities to measure up to her teammates Johansson recounted, "The other day we were doing this big reveal shot of all the Avengers. Thor has got his hammer, Cap's got his shield, Hawkeye has his bow and arrow, and Hulk is huge. Then it pans over to me and I've got guns. Iron Man's like, hovering above all of us, ready to go... I was like, 'Joss… um… do I look okay holding these guns?' and he responded 'She's a total badass. She's a killing machine.'"[4]

- Jeremy Renner as Clint Barton:

  A S.H.I.E.L.D. agent and master archer known in the comics as "Hawkeye".[19] Renner said it was a very physical role and that he trained physically and practiced archery as much as possible in preparation.[20] About Hawkeye's dynamic with the Black Widow and place in the film, Renner stated, "The only sort of thing I cling to is the relationship of past experiences with Scarlett's character, with them both being human. I can cling to that." However Renner said there's no insecurity explaining, "He's the only one who can really take down The Hulk with his tranq tip arrows. He knows his limitations. But when it comes down to it, there has to be a sense of confidence in any superhero."[4]

- Samuel L. Jackson as Nick Fury:

  The director of S.H.I.E.L.D., who was revealed in previous films to be coordinating the "Avenger Initiative". Jackson was brought to the project with a deal containing an option to play the character in up to nine Marvel films.[21]

- Tom Hiddleston as Loki:

The Norse god of mischief.[14] In regard to his character's evolution from the film *Thor*, Hiddleston stated, "I think the Loki we see in *The Avengers* is further advanced. You have to ask yourself the question: how pleasant an experience is it disappearing into a wormhole that has been created by some kind of super nuclear explosion of his own making? So I think by the time Loki shows up in *The Avengers* he's seen a few things."[22] About Loki's motivations, Hiddleston remarked, "At the beginning of *The Avengers*, he comes to Earth to subjugate it and his idea is to rule the human race as their king. And like all the delusional autocrats of human history, he thinks this is a great idea because if everyone is busy worshipping him, there will be no wars so he will create some kind of world peace by ruling them as a tyrant. But he is also kind of deluded in the fact that he thinks unlimited power will give him self respect so I haven't let go of the fact that he is still motivated by this terrible jealousy and kind of spiritual desolation".[23]

- Cobie Smulders as Maria Hill:

  A S.H.I.E.L.D. agent who works closely with Jackson's Nick Fury.[24] Smulders, whom Joss Whedon once considered for his unproduced live-action Wonder Woman film, was selected from a short list of potential actresses including Morena Baccarin. Smulder's deal would integrate her into nine films.[25] [26] Regarding her preparation, Smulders stated, "I hired this amazing black-ops trainer to teach me how to hold a gun, take me to a shooting range, how to hit, how to hold myself, how to walk and basically how to look. I don't do a ton of fighting in the movie, which is why I wasn't offered a trainer, but I wanted to look like I had the ability to. And I really just got down and dirty with the character, but then I finally went on set; when you're about to roll, all the "blubbity blue" you've been working on kind of messes with you. And you become a little bit detached." [*sic*][27] On relating to the character, Smulders commented, "I can relate to her being a mom and being a business woman and trying to work full time and raising a family and having a career. We're asked to do a lot of things these days. I feel she is just all about her job and keeping things going."[28]

Clark Gregg and Stellan Skarsgård reprise their roles from previous films as Phil Coulson and Erik Selvig respectively.[29] [30] Paul Bettany returns to voice JARVIS.[31] Avengers co-creator Stan Lee will have a cameo appearance.[32]

Production

Development

"It goes back to the very first incarnation of The Avengers, it goes to The Ultimates, it goes to everything about it. It makes no sense, it's ridiculous. There's a thunder god, there's a green "ID" giant rage monster, there's Captain America from the 40s, there's Tony Stark who definitely doesn't get along with anybody. Ultimately these people don't belong together and the whole movie is about finding yourself from community. And finding that you not only belong together but you need each other, very much. Obviously this will be expressed through punching but it will be the heart of the film."

Joss Whedon, director of *The Avengers*, about the film.[33]

Marvel Studios chair-CEO Avi Arad first announced plans to develop an *Avengers* film in April 2005 after Marvel Enterprises declared independence by pacting with Merrill Lynch to produce a slate of films that would be distributed by Paramount Pictures.[34] In September 2006 Marvel confirmed their crossover plans in a brief presentation to Wall Street analysts. The studio's plan was to release individual films for the main characters, to establish their identities and familiarize audiences with them, before merging the characters together in an Avengers movie.[35] Marvel Studios announced in July 2007 that screen writer Zak Penn, who wrote *The Incredible Hulk*, had been hired to write the film and will be titled, *The Avengers*.[36] Penn confirmed his involvement but said he did not believe work would begin soon.[37]

In January 2008, Marvel struck a deal with the striking Writers Guild of America so that the company could go back to work on films based on its comic book characters, including Captain America, Ant-Man and The Avengers.[38] After the successful release of *Iron Man* in May, Marvel announced that *The Avengers* is scheduled for release in

July 2011.[39] In September Paramount signed an agreement with Marvel Studios that locks Paramount in as the worldwide distributor of Marvel's next five self-produced feature films. The partnership extended a 2005 agreement that saw Paramount agreeing to distribute as many as ten Marvel films.[40] In October it was announced that Robert Downey, Jr. and Don Cheadle would reprise their *Iron Man 2* roles as Iron Man and War Machine respectively in *The Avengers*. However Don Cheadle later revealed in a January 2011 interview that he will not be appearing in *The Avengers* despite previous reports.[41] It was also announced that Jon Favreau will executive produce the film.[3] Also in October, Marvel Studios signed a long-term lease with Raleigh Studios to film four big-budget movies at Raleigh's Manhattan Beach, California complex. The films are *Iron Man 2*, *Thor*, *Captain America: The First Avenger* and *The Avengers*.[42] Lou Ferrigno, who voiced Hulk in 2008's *The Incredible Hulk*, stated that he would be involved in the film.[12]

In February 2009, Samuel L. Jackson signed a nine-picture deal with Marvel Entertainment to play the role of Nick Fury in *Iron Man 2* and other films including vehicles for Captain America, Thor, the Avengers, and S.H.I.E.L.D.[21] In March it was reported that Scarlett Johansson had replaced Emily Blunt in *Iron Man 2*, a deal that also tied her to *The Avengers*.[17] The following day Marvel announced that the release date for *The Avengers* had been pushed back to May 4, 2012, almost a full year later.[43] In June, Marvel's president of production Kevin Feige confirmed that Chris Hemsworth and Tom Hiddleston would reprise their roles as Thor and Loki, respectively, in *The Avengers*.[14]

In July screenwriter Zak Penn talked about the crossover process, stating, "My job is to kind of shuttle between the different movies and make sure that finally we're mimicking that comic book structure where all of these movies are connected... There's just a board that tracks 'Here's where everything that happens in this movie overlaps with that movie'... I'm pushing them to do as many animatics as possible to animate the movie, to draw boards so that we're all working off the same visual ideas. But the exigencies of production take first priority".[44] The following month, Marvel Studios chief Kevin Fiege stated he would introduce more characters into *The Avengers* and that the Hulk would factor in the film.[45] In September, Edward Norton stated that he was open to returning as The Hulk for *The Avengers*.[46] The next month, executive producer Jon Favreau stated that he would not direct the film but will "...definitely have input and a say". Favreau also expressed concerns stating, "It's going to be hard, because I was so involved in creating the world of Iron Man and Iron Man is very much a tech-based hero, and then with 'Avengers' you're going to be introducing some supernatural aspects because of Thor. ... [Mixing] the two of those works very well in the comic books, but it's going to take a lot of thoughtfulness to make that all work and not blow the reality that we've created".[47]

In January 2010, Kevin Feige was asked if it will be difficult to meld the fantasy of *Thor* with the high-tech science fiction in *Iron Man* and *The Avengers*. "No," he said, "because we're doing the Jack Kirby/Stan Lee/Walt Simonson/J. Michael Straczynski *Thor*. We're not doing the blow-the-dust-off-of-the-old-Norse-book-in-your-library *Thor*. And in the *Thor* of the Marvel Universe, there's a race called the Asgardians. And we're linked through this Tree of Life that we're unaware of. It's real science, but we don't know about it yet. The 'Thor' movie is about teaching people that".[48] In March it was reported that Zak Penn had completed the first draft of the script, and that Marvel editor-in-chief Joe Quesada and *Avengers* comic-book writer Brian Michael Bendis had received copies.[49] Also in March it was reported that Chris Evans would reprise the role of Captain America in *The Avengers*.[5] In April 2010, *Variety* reported that Joss Whedon was close to completing a deal to direct the film, and to rework Penn's script.[50]

Pre-production

Whedon at the 2010 San Diego Comic-Con International.

At the 2010 Wizard World convention *Avengers* creator Stan Lee and Marvel Studios CEO Avi Arad confirmed Joss Whedon's involvement.[51] Arad praised the decision by stating, "My personal opinion is that Joss will do a fantastic job. He loves these characters and is a fantastic writer... It's part of his life so you know he is going to protect it... I expect someone like him is going to make the script even better".[52]

In June 2010, it was reported that Jeremy Renner was in final negotiations to play Hawkeye in the film.[19]

The following month, Marvel Comics said it declined to have Edward Norton reprise his role as Bruce Banner.[53] The next day Kevin Feige, the president of Marvel Studios, confirmed the report stating, "We have made the decision to not bring Ed Norton back to portray the title role of Bruce Banner in *The Avengers*. Our decision is definitely not one based on monetary factors, but instead rooted in the need for an actor who embodies the creativity and collaborative spirit of our other talented cast members. The Avengers demands players who thrive working as part of an ensemble, as evidenced by Robert, Chris H, Chris E, Samuel, Scarlett, and all of our talented casts. We are looking to announce a name actor who fulfills these requirements, and is passionate about the iconic role in the coming weeks."[54] In response Norton's agent Brian Swardstrom called Feige's statement "purposefully misleading" and an "inappropriate attempt to paint our client in a negative light".[55]

Joss Whedon announced at the 2010 San Diego Comic-Con International that he is directing *The Avengers*. Whedon mentioned that he was a fan of the early *Avengers* comics while growing up.[56] He also said he is still writing an outline for the film and that what drew him to the movie is that he loves how "these people shouldn't be in the same room let alone on the same team—and that is the definition of family".[57] Whedon also confirmed that Jeremy Renner would play Hawkeye.[58] It was reported during the convention that Mark Ruffalo would replace Edward Norton as Bruce Banner in a deal reached by Ruffalo's agency with Marvel.[7] During the Marvel Studios panel, it was announced Clark Gregg would reprise his role as S.H.I.E.L.D. Agent Phil Coulson.[29]

In August 2010, it was reported that Paramount Pictures and Marvel Studios were planning to start shooting in February.[59] It was also reported that the film would be shot in 3-D.[60]

In October 2010, it was reported that Marvel Studios will shoot *The Avengers* partly at Grumman Studios in Bethpage, New York[61] and at Steiner Studios in Brooklyn, New York City.[62] Set construction was slated to begin in November.[61] Also in October, The Walt Disney Company agreed to pay Paramount at least $115 million for the worldwide distribution rights to *Iron Man 3* and *The Avengers*.[63] The deal also allowed Paramount to continue to collect the 8% box office fee it would have earned for distributing the film and placement of the company's logo on marketing materials, even though Marvel's films are fully owned, distributed and marketed by Disney. Paramount's Epix also retained pay TV rights.[64]

In December 2010, New Mexico Governor Bill Richardson and Marvel Studios Co-president Louis D'Esposito announced *The Avengers* would film primarily in Albuquerque, New Mexico, with principal photography scheduled for April through September 2011. Parts of the film were also scheduled to be shot in Michigan,[65] but a plan to film in Detroit ended after Governor Rick Snyder issued a budget proposal that would eliminate a film tax incentive.[66]

In February 2011, Marvel began conducting screen tests for the role of a key member of S.H.I.E.L.D. who Samuel L. Jackson described as Nick Fury's sidekick.[25] Four days later it was reported that Cobie Smulders was wrapping up a deal for the role later revealed to be that of Maria Hill.[26]

In March 2011, Stellan Skarsgård confirmed he would play the same role as he did in *Thor*, Doctor Selvig.[30] Also in March, Ohio Governor John Kasich announced before Mayor Frank G. Jackson's State of the City address that

The Avengers will film in Cleveland.[67]

The Science & Entertainment Exchange provided science consultation for the film.[68]

Filming

United States Army Reserve soldiers on the set of *The Avengers* in Cleveland, Ohio.

Part of *The Avengers* film set on Park Avenue in New York City.

On an estimated $220 million budget[2] , principal photography began on April 25, 2011 in Albuquerque, New Mexico with filming scheduled to continue in Cleveland, Ohio and New York City.[1] The following day Paul Bettany confirmed he would return to voice Tony Stark's computerized assistant, JARVIS.[31] In May 2011, Gwyneth Paltrow stated that she might "possibly" appear very briefly in the film as Pepper Potts.[69] Also in May, Stan Lee confirmed through his Twitter account that he will have a cameo appearance in the film unless they "shoot it on the moon".[32] In June, stuntman Jeremy Fitzgerald injured his head while attempting a stunt involving a 30-foot fall from a building after getting hit by an arrow. A Marvel spokesperson later told TMZ.com that, "[Fitzgerald] was fine. He slid briefly along the side of the building. He got right back up and did several more takes."[70] In July 2011, it was reported that secondary filming took place about an hour outside of Pittsburgh, Pennsylvania in the Butler area.[71]

In August 2011, production moved to Cleveland, Ohio for four weeks. The city's East 9th Street was chosen as a double for New York City's 42nd Street to be used in climactic battle scenes.[72] Army Reserve soldiers assigned to the Columbus, Ohio-based 391st Military Police Battalion provided background action during the battle scenes in Cleveland. Staff Sgt. Michael T. Landis stated the use of real soldiers made the scenes more realistic and helped portray the Army in a more positive light, explaining that, "It's easy for us to make on-the-spot corrections to tactics and uniforms, the director actually took our recommendation on one scene and let us all engage the enemy as opposed to only the gunners in the trucks engaging".[73] Filming also took place in the large vacuum chamber at the NASA Plum Brook Station near Sandusky, Ohio.[74] The station's Space Power Facility was used to portray a S.H.I.E.L.D. research facility.[75] A series of explosions were filmed at the Chevrolet powertrain plant in Parma, Ohio as part of the battle sequence that began in Cleveland.[76] Scenes from the film were also shot on Public Square and the Detroit–Superior Bridge.[77] The southwest quadrant of Public Square was turned into Stuttgart, Germany, for filming.[78]

In September 2011, production moved to New York City for two days to wrap up filming.[79] Filming locations in New York City included Park Avenue and Central Park.[80] [81]

Post-production

Visual effects for the film were created by Industrial Light & Magic (*Iron Man*, *Iron Man 2*), Legacy Effects (*Iron Man 2*, *Thor*) and Luma Pictures (*Thor*, *Captain America: The First Avenger*).[82] [83] [84]

Music

Alan Silvestri, who scored *Captain America: The First Avenger*, composed music for *The Avengers*.[85]

Marketing

The film was promoted at the 2010 San Diego Comic-Con International, during which a teaser trailer narrated by Samuel L. Jackson was shown followed by an introduction of the cast.[29] In June 2011, Marvel Studios announced that it would not hold a panel at the 2011 San Diego Comic-Con International after studios executives decided it wasn't prepared to compete with its own past and fan expectations with filming still in production.[86]

Chris Evans, Tom Hiddleston, Cobie Smulders and Clark Gregg promoting *The Avengers* at the 2011 New York Comic Con.

In July 2011, a teaser trailer that was meant to be the post-credits scene of *Captain America: The First Avenger* was briefly leaked online. *Entertainment Weekly* speculated it came from a preview screening and described the footage as "shaky, fuzzy, flickering and obviously filmed on a cell phone".[87]

In August 2011, Walt Disney Studios, Pixar Animation Studios and Marvel Studios presented a look at Walt Disney Studios' upcoming film slate, which included Marvel's *The Avengers*, at the D23 Expo in Anaheim, California. The presentation featured footage from the film and appearances by the cast members.[88] Also in August, Disney dismissed Marvel's executive vice president of worldwide marketing, vice president of worldwide marketing and manager of worldwide marketing to bring their functions in-house.[89]

In October 2011, Marvel Studios held a presentation at the New York Comic Con that featured new footage and a panel discussion including producer Kevin Feige and several cast members.[90] The first full-length trailer was also released in October. *Comic Book Resources* said, "The two-minute teaser handily establishes the movie's premise" and is "heavy on the assembling, but fans are also treated to plenty of action, as well glimpses [*sic*] of Iron Man's new armor and, best of all, the new take on the Incredible Hulk. Naturally, Robert Downey Jr.'s Tony Stark gets the best lines".[91] However, *The Hollywood Reporter* called it "Awesome. Or it would be if we hadn't seen all of this before and expected every single thing that we saw in the trailer".[92] The trailer which debuted exclusively on iTunes Movie Trailers, was downloaded over 10 million times in its first 24 hours, breaking the website's record for the most-viewed trailer.[93]

Video game

A video game based on the film was planned for concurrent release. The game was to be a first-person shooter brawler for the Xbox 360, PlayStation 3 and Microsoft Windows and published by THQ, with THQ Studio Australia developing of the console versions and Blue Tongue Entertainment the PC version. After THQ closed both studios, the game was cancelled.[94] Intellectual property rights for an Avengers video game reverted to Marvel, which said it was exploring potential publishing and licensing opportunities.[95]

Sequel

In October 2011, producer Kevin Feige hinted at a sequel to *The Avengers* during the New York Comic Con stating, "*Iron Man 3* will be the first of what we sort of refer to as phase two of this saga that will culminate, God willing, in *Avengers 2*".[96]

Notes

1 As part of the negotiation deal of transferring the distribution rights of future releases of Marvel Studios films to Walt Disney Pictures, Paramount Pictures's logo appears on marketing materials and not Disney's.[64]

References

[1] "Marvel's The Avengers Begins Production" (http://marvel.com/news/story/15733/marvels_the_avengers_begins_production). Marvel.com press release. 2011-04-26. . Retrieved 2011-04-26.. WebCitation Archive (http://www.webcitation.org/5yF6sRDUv)

[2] Breznican, Anthony (Oct 07, 2011). "First Look at The Avengers: Dream Team". *Entertainment Weekly* (Time Inc.) (1175): 37. "At risk is not only the movie's estimated $220 million budget, but also one of the most promising tent pole franchises in Hollywood."

[3] "Downey Jr., Favreau & Cheadle Suit Up for The Avengers" (http://www.superherohype.com/news/ironmannews.php?id=7763). Marvel Comics press release via SuperheroHype.com. 2008-10-28. Archived (http://www.webcitation.org/5yDIh7m8P) from the original on April 25, 2011. . Retrieved 2010-04-14.

[4] Breznican, Anthony (2011-09-29). "'The Avengers' Dis-Assembled! Exclusive Cast Portraits Revealed" (http://insidemovies.ew.com/2011/09/29/the-avengers-dis-assembled-exclusive-cast-portraits-revealed/). *Entertainment Weekly*. Archived (http://www.webcitation.org/624KaS4rJ) from the original on 2011-07-29. . Retrieved 2011-07-29.

[5] Graser, Marc (2010-03-22). "Chris Evans to play 'Captain America'" (http://www.variety.com/article/VR1118016757.html?categoryid=13&cs=1). *Variety*. . Retrieved 2010-04-14.. WebCitation Archive (http://www.webcitation.org/5yDf7jzfG).

[6] Marshall, Rick (2011-04-25). "EXCLUSIVE: 'Captain America' Star Talks 'Avengers,' Looks Forward To 'Friction' With Iron Man" (http://splashpage.mtv.com/2011/04/25/captain-america-avengers-chris-evans-iron-man). MTV News. Archived (http://www.webcitation.org/5zxBnzavF) from the original on 2011-07-05. . Retrieved 2011-04-27.

[7] Finke, Nikki (July 23, 2010). "Toldja! Marvel & Ruffalo Ink Hulk Deal" (http://www.deadline.com/2010/07/toldja-marvel-ruffalo-reach-hulk-deal). Deadline.com. . Retrieved July 23, 2010.. WebCitation Archive (http://www.webcitation.org/5yDfrDrMs).

[8] Jensen, Jeff (July 29, 2010). "'Avengers': New Hulk Mark Ruffalo on replacing Edward Norton, plus Oscar buzz for 'The Kids Are All Right'" (http://popwatch.ew.com/2010/07/29/avengers-new-hulk-mark-ruffalo). *Entertainment Weekly*. . Retrieved August 2, 2010.. WebCitation Archive (http://www.webcitation.org/5yF72hS8x)

[9] Jimmy Kimmel Live! (2011-04-26). "Mark Ruffalo on Jimmy Kimmel Live PART 2" (http://www.youtube.com/watch?v=1IJE4H2vRr4). *YouTube*. Archived (http://www.webcitation.org/5zxBoFszX) from the original on 2011-07-05. . Retrieved 2011-04-28.

[10] Vilensky, Mike (2010-09-24). "Mark Ruffalo on 'Actually' Playing the Hulk in The Avengers" (http://nymag.com/daily/entertainment/2010/09/mark_ruffalo_on_actually_playi.html). *New York*. . Retrieved 2010-09-25.. WebCitation Archive (http://www.webcitation.org/5yF7IcsHQ).

[11] Malkin, Brett; Malec (2011-03-03). "Mark Ruffalo "Getting Hard" for the Hulk" (http://www.eonline.com/uberblog/b228980_mark_ruffalo_getting_hard_hulk.html). *Entertainment Weekly*. Archived (http://www.webcitation.org/5zx6qnVH4) from the original on 2011-07-05. . Retrieved 2011-03-07.

[12] YouTube (2008-12-16). "Nuke The Fridge Interviews Lou Ferrigno" (http://www.youtube.com/watch?v=cmLT0tmSrWY). *YouTube*. Archived (http://www.webcitation.org/5yDgoZif9) from the original on 2011-04-25. . Retrieved 2009-05-16.

[13] Ron Messer (2010-10-10). "NY Comic Con: Lou Ferrigno Interview – Opens Up about *The Avengers*, Mark Ruffalo as the Hulk, and *Chuck*" (http://www.collider.com/2010/10/10/lou-ferrigno-interview-the-hulk-the-avengers-nycc). *Collider*. Archived (http://www.webcitation.org/5zva6AKlJ) from the original on 2011-07-04. . Retrieved 2010-10-10.

[14] Bellington, Alex (2009-06-07). "Profile on Marvel Studios with Big Updates from Kevin Feige" (http://www.firstshowing.net/2009/06/07/profile-on-marvel-studios-with-big-updates-from-kevin-feige). *First Showing*. Archived (http://www.webcitation.org/5zva6hNsx) from the original on 2011-07-04. . Retrieved 2010-04-14.

[15] Brian Warmoth (2010-07-26). "Comic-Con: Chris Hemsworth Shares Joss Whedon's Fascination With Avengers Drama" (http://splashpage.mtv.com/2010/07/26/chris-hemsworth-shares-joss-whedons-fascination-with-avengers-drama/#more-38230). MTV News. Archived (http://www.webcitation.org/5zx6kglPd) from the original on 2011-07-05. . Retrieved 2010-07-26.

[16] Malkin, Marc and Malec, Brett (2010-12-17). "Avengers Flick Update: Where's the Script?" (http://www.eonline.com/uberblog/marc_malkin/b216448_avengers_flick_update_wheres_script.html). *E!*. Archived (http://www.webcitation.org/5zx6nTej1) from the original on 2011-07-05. . Retrieved 2011-01-05.

[17] Finke, Nikki (2009-03-11). "Another 'Iron Man 2' Deal: Scarlett Johansson to Replace Emily Blunt as Black Widow for Lousy Lowball Money" (http://www.deadline.com/2009/03/another-iron-man-2-exclusive-scarlett-johansson-will-replace-emily-blunt-in-iron-man-2).

Deadline Hollywood. . Retrieved 2010-04-14.. WebCitation Archive (http://www.webcitation.org/5yDg3GmuW).

[18] "Whedon : Black Widow won't be the only female character in *Avengers*" (http://www.moviehole.net/201026096-whedon-black-widow-wont-be-the-only-female-character-in-avengers). Moviehole.net. 2010-08-22. Archived (http://www.webcitation.org/5zx6r0Mhb) from the original on 2011-07-05. . Retrieved 2011-03-25.

[19] Kit, Borys and Kit, Zorianna (2010-06-04). "Jeremy Jeremy Renner near deal to join Marvel's 'Avengers'" (http://www.webcitation.org/60UTnWqQ5). Reuters. Archived from the original (http://www.reuters.com/article/2010/06/04/us-renner-idUSTRE65310E20100604) on 2011-07-27. . Retrieved 2011-07-27.

[20] Farley, Christopher John (2010-09-17). "Jeremy Renner on 'The Town,' 'The Avengers' and the New 'Mission: Impossible'" (http://blogs.wsj.com/speakeasy/2010/09/17/jeremy-renner-on-the-town-the-avengers-and-the-new-mission-impossible). *The Wall Street Journal*. Archived (http://www.webcitation.org/5zx6liDtR) from the original on 2011-07-05. . Retrieved 2010-09-18.

[21] Fleming, Micheal (2009-02-25). "Samuel Jackson joins 'Iron' cast" (http://www.variety.com/article/VR1118000573.html?categoryid=1236&cs=1). *Variety*. . Retrieved 2010-04-14.. WebCitation Archive (http://www.webcitation.org/5yDhMjeCo).

[22] Philbrick, Jami (2011-05-01). "Exclusive: Tom Hiddleston Discusses Loki's Role in 'The Avengers'" (http://www.iamrogue.com/news/movie-news/item/3534-exclusive-tom-hiddleston-discusses-lokis-role-in-the-avengers.html). IAmRogue.com. Archived (http://www.webcitation.org/5zxBoOBUw) from the original on 2011-07-05. . Retrieved 2011-05-01.

[23] THR staff (2011-08-20). "'Avengers' Tom Hiddleston Talks the Return of Loki (Video)" (http://www.webcitation.org/618UtAbKg). *The Hollywood Reporter*. Archived from the original (http://www.hollywoodreporter.com/heat-vision/avengers-tom-hiddleston-talks-return-225649) on 2011-08-22. . Retrieved 2011-08-22. "(from video) At the beginning of The Avengers, he comes to earth to subjugate it and his idea is to rule the human race as their king. And like all the delusional autocrats of human history, he thinks this is a great idea because if everyone is busy worshipping him, there will be no wars so he will create some kind of world peace by ruling them as a tyrant. But he is also kind of deluded in the fact that he thinks unlimited power will give him self-respect so I haven't let go of the fact that he is still motivated by this terrible jealousy and kind of spiritual desolation."

[24] O'Connell, Mikey (2011-03-25). "'Avengers' star Cobie Smulders on spending her hiatus in a catsuit" (http://blog.zap2it.com/pop2it/2011/03/avengers-star-cobie-smulders-on-spending-her-hiatus-in-a-catsuit.html). Zap2It.com. Archived (http://www.webcitation.org/5zx6rWZsv) from the original on 2011-07-05. . Retrieved 2011-03-25.

[25] Kit, Borys (2011-02-03). "'V' Star Morena Baccarin Among Actresses on 'Avengers' Shortlist (Exclusive)" (http://www.webcitation.org/5wE8wQt12). *The Hollywood Reporter*. Archived from the original (http://www.hollywoodreporter.com/blogs/heat-vision/v-star-morena-baccarin-actresses-95741) on 2011-02-03. . Retrieved 2011-02-03.

[26] Graser, Marc (2011-02-07). "Cobie Smulders joins 'Avengers' cast" (http://www.variety.com/article/VR1118031688). *Variety*. . Retrieved 2011-02-07.. WebCitation Archive (http://www.webcitation.org/5yDfEndIX).

[27] " The Best Man (http://itunes.apple.com/us/podcast/how-i-met-your-mother/id464893076?ign-mpt=uo=4)". *How I Met Your Mother Podcast*. CBS. 2011-09-20. No. 1, season 7. Event occurs at 7:40. Retrieved on 2011-09-24.

[28] Ford, Rebecca (2011-08-21). "'The Avengers' at D23: Cobie Smulders Reveals the Scene that Made her Sweat (Video)" (http://www.webcitation.org/617zglAKM). *The Hollywood Reporter*. Archived from the original (http://www.hollywoodreporter.com/heat-vision/avengers-at-d23-cobie-smulders-225731) on 2011-08-22. . Retrieved 2011-08-22.

[29] "Marvel-ous Star Wattage: Actors Assemble For Comic-Con Panel Including 'The Avengers', 'Captain America', & 'Thor'" (http://www.deadline.com/2010/07/star-wattage-marvel-assembles-the-avengers-for-comic-con-panel). Deadline.com. July 24, 2010. Archived (http://www.webcitation.org/5zx6k1EnB) from the original on 2011-07-05. . Retrieved July 25, 2010.

[30] "Stellan Skarsgård klar för ny superhjältefilm" (http://www.expressen.se/noje/film/1.2351661/stellan-skarsgard-klar-for-ny-superhjaltefilm) (in Swedish). *Expressen*. 2011-03-03. Archived (http://www.webcitation.org/5zx6odEiZ) from the original on 2011-07-05. . Retrieved 2011-03-03. "The Avengers is the dream team of superheroes, a group consisting of among others Iron Man, the Hulk, Captain America and Thor. The film is planned to premier in 3D in May of next year. Stellan Skarsgård confirms to *TT Spektra* that he will play the same role as in the upcoming *Thor*: Doctor Selvig. Not much is yet known about the character apart from that Selvig is a scientist in New Mexico."

[31] Davidson, Danica (2011-04-26). "Paul Bettany Confirms 'Avengers' Role, Will Return As Voice Of J.A.R.V.I.S." (http://splashpage.mtv.com/2011/04/26/paul-bettany-confirms-avengers-role-will-return-as-voice-of-jarvis). MTV News. Archived (http://www.webcitation.org/5zx6sQRRg) from the original on 2011-07-05. . Retrieved 2011-04-27.

[32] "Stan Lee Talks Upcoming Cameo Roles" (http://www.superherohype.com/news/articles/167299-stan-lee-talks-upcoming-cameo-roles). SuperheroHype.com. 2011-05-17. Archived (http://www.webcitation.org/5zxBobWWA) from the original on 2011-07-05. . Retrieved 2011-05-17.

[33] Woerner, Meredith (2010-07-24). "Joss Whedon says Captain America and Iron Man won't be pals in his "Avengers" (http://io9.com/5595293/will-joss-whedons-avengers-movie-include-marvels-civil-war-we-asked-him). *io9*. Archived (http://www.webcitation.org/61MIFwfMs) from the original on 2011-08-31. . Retrieved 2011-08-31.

[34] McClintock, Pamela (2005-04-28). "Marvel touts Par's hero worship" (http://www.variety.com/article/VR1117921854.html?categoryid=1350&cs=1&query=marvel+touts+par's+hero+worship). *Variety*. Archived (http://www.webcitation.org/60tBDuloX) from the original on 2011-08-12. . Retrieved 2011-08-12.

[35] "Marvel Avengers Update" (http://www.cinematical.com/2006/09/14/marvel-avengers-update). *Cinematical*. 2006-09-14. Archived (http://www.webcitation.org/5zva1BydW) from the original on 2011-07-04. . Retrieved August 2, 2010.

[36] Kit, Borys (2007-06-14). ""Avengers" are heroes on horizon" (http://www.reuters.com/article/2007/06/15/film-avengers-dc-idUSN1439793620070615). *Reuters*. Archived (http://www.webcitation.org/5zva1JlS4) from the original on 2011-07-04. . Retrieved 2011-04-26.

[37] Davis, Erik (2007-05-04). "Tribeca Interview: 'The Grand' Director Zak Penn" (http://www.cinematical.com/2007/05/04/tribeca-interview-the-grand-director-zak-penn). *Cinematical*. Archived (http://www.webcitation.org/5zva4I4Mk) from the original on 2011-07-04. . Retrieved 2010-04-14.

[38] White, Michael & Andy Fixmer (2008-01-25). "Lions Gate, Marvel Reach Accords With Striking Film, TV Writers" (http://www.bloomberg.com/apps/news?pid=20601103&sid=a4QS2Pyn4T3M&refer=us). *Bloomberg*. Archived (http://www.webcitation.org/5zva4wVY5) from the original on 2011-07-04. . Retrieved 2010-04-14.

[39] "Marvel Studios Sets Four More Release Dates!" (http://www.superherohype.com/features/articles/96489-marvel-studios-sets-four-more-release-dates). SuperheroHype.com. 2008-05-05. Archived (http://www.webcitation.org/5zva53o8q) from the original on 2011-07-04. . Retrieved 2010-04-14.

[40] Fernandez, Jay A. (2008-09-28). "Paramount, Marvel ink new distrib deal" (http://web.archive.org/web/20081202183120/http://www.hollywoodreporter.com/hr/content_display/film/news/e3if965d7b680521402238dbeccba1cd031). The Hollywood Reporter. Archived from the original (http://www.hollywoodreporter.com/hr/content_display/film/news/e3if965d7b680521402238dbeccba1cd031) on December 2, 2008. . Retrieved 2010-04-14.

[41] Marshall, Rick (2011-01-21). "Don Cheadle Says 'War Machine' Movie Has A Writer, Won't Show Up In 'Avengers'" (http://splashpage.mtv.com/2011/01/21/war-machine-movie-don-cheadle-avengers). MTV News. Archived (http://www.webcitation.org/5zx6nwqVL) from the original on 2011-07-05. . Retrieved 2011-01-21.

[42] Kit, Borys (2008-10-06). "Marvel signs long-term lease with Raleigh" (http://web.archive.org/web/20090104152049/http://www.hollywoodreporter.com/hr/content_display/film/news/e3i3ccdd00902078c244d32d5b416e56215). The Hollywood Reporter. Archived from the original (http://www.hollywoodreporter.com/hr/content_display/film/news/e3i3ccdd00902078c244d32d5b416e56215) on January 4, 2009. . Retrieved 2010 04 14.

[43] Jessica Barnes (2009-03-12). "New Dates for Thor, Captain America, and The Avengers" (http://www.cinematical.com/2009/03/12/new-dates-for-thor-captain-america-and-the-avengers). *Cinematical*. Archived (http://www.webcitation.org/5zva6WVtF) from the original on 2011-07-04. . Retrieved 2010-04-14.

[44] Topel, Fred (2009 07 08). "Avengers movie update with Zak Penn" (http://www.craveonline.com/entertainment/film/article/avengers-movie-update-with-zak-penn-80387). Crave Online. Archived (http://www.webcitation.org/5zva6xZTG) from the original on 2011-07-04. . Retrieved 2010-04-14.

[45] Fred Topel (2009-08-18). "Kevin Fiege talks about Marvels movie line up" (http://www.webcitation.org/60UUNxJ6N). *Crave Online*. Archived from the original (http://www.craveonline.com/film/interviews/144328-kevin-fiege-talks-about-marvels-movie-line-up) on 2011-07-27. . Retrieved 2011-07-27.

[46] Ditzian, Eric (2009-09-24). "Edward Norton Open To Returning As The Hulk For 'Avengers' Movie" (http://www.mtv.com/movies/news/articles/1622158/story.jhtml). MTV News. Archived (http://www.webcitation.org/5zva7plzL) from the original on 2011-07-04. . Retrieved 2010-04-14.

[47] Rick Marshall (2009-10-14). "EXCLUSIVE: Jon Favreau Won't Direct 'Avengers,' Explains 'Iron Man 2' Tie-In Process" (http://splashpage.mtv.com/2009/10/14/exclusive-jon-favreau-wont-direct-avengers-explains-iron-man-2-tie-in-process). MTV News. Archived (http://www.webcitation.org/5zva7xlGi) from the original on 2011-07-04. . Retrieved 2010-04-14.

[48] "Kevin Feige on Upcoming Marvel Studios Films" (http://www.superherohype.com/news/thornews.php?id=9019). SuperheroHype.com. 2010-01-26. Archived (http://www.webcitation.org/5zva8TAbL) from the original on 2011-07-04. . Retrieved 2010-04-14.

[49] Marnell, Blair (2010-03-03). "First Draft Of 'Avengers' Script Completed" (http://splashpage.mtv.com/2010/03/03/first-draft-of-avengers-script-completed). MTV News. Archived (http://www.webcitation.org/5zva8XIPg) from the original on 2011-07-04. . Retrieved 2010-04-14.

[50] Graser, Marc (2010 04 13). "Whedon to head 'Avengers'" (http://www.variety.com/article/VR1118017689.html?categoryid=10&cs=1). *Variety*. . Retrieved 2010-04-14.. WebCitation Archive (http://www.webcitation.org/5yDehLvaA).

[51] Warner, Kara (July 30, 2010). "Joss Whedon Is The 'Right Thing' For 'Avengers,' Marvel Boss Says" (http://www.mtv.com/news/articles/1644849/20100730/story.jhtml). MTV News. Archived (http://www.webcitation.org/5zx6kwRFS) from the original on 2011-07-05. . Retrieved August 2, 2010.

[52] Lesnick, Silas (2010-04-17). "Stan Lee and Avi Arad on Marvel Movies" (http://www.superherohype.com/news/featuresnews.php?id=9294). SuperheroHype.com. Archived (http://www.webcitation.org/5zva95g1S) from the original on 2011-07-04. . Retrieved 2010-04-19.

[53] McWeeny, Drew (2010-07-09). "Exclusive: Edward Norton is not the Hulk in 'The Avengers'... but he'd like to be" (http://www.hitfix.com/blogs/2008-12-6-motion-captured/posts/exclusive-edward-norton-is-not-the-hulk-in-the-avengers-but-he-d-like-to-be). HitFix.com. Archived (http://www.webcitation.org/5zva9lcPq) from the original on 2011-07-04. . Retrieved 2010-07-09.

[54] McWeeny, Drew (2010-07-10). "Exclusive: Marvel confirms they will hire new 'Hulk' for 'The Avengers'" (http://www.hitfix.com/blogs/2008-12-6-motion-captured/posts/exclusive-marvel-confirms-they-will-hire-new-hulk-for-avengers). HitFix.com. Archived (http://www.webcitation.org/5zvaARlaL) from the original on 2011-07-04. . Retrieved 2010-07-10.

[55] Ellwod, Gary, and Drew McWeeny (2010-07-11). "Exclusive: Edward Norton's agent responds to Marvel Chief's statement" (http://www.hitfix.com/articles/2010-7-11-exclusive-edward-norton-s-agent-responds-to-marvel-ceo-s-statement?m=k). HitFix.com. . Retrieved 2010-07-12.. WebCitation Archive (http://www.webcitation.org/5yDgC3nXJ).

[56] Hardawar, Devindra (2010-07-22). "Joss Whedon Officially Directing The Avengers" (http://www.slashfilm.com/2010/07/22/joss-whedon-officially-directing-the-avengers). /Film. Archived (http://www.webcitation.org/5zvaAodKG) from the original on 2011-07-04. . Retrieved 2010-07-23.

[57] Downey, Ryan J. (2010-07-22). "Comic-Con: Joss Whedon Talks 'Avengers' At EW Visionaries Panel" (http://splashpage.mtv.com/2010/07/22/comic-con-joss-whedon-avengers-ew-visionaries-panel). MTV News. Archived (http://www.webcitation.org/5zvaAtYGx) from the original on 2011-07-04. . Retrieved 2010-07-23.

[58] Corinne Heller (July 23, 2010). "Joss Whedon talks 'The Avengers': Jeremy Renner also confirmed as 'Hawkeye' (Exclusive)" (http://www.ontheredcarpet.com/2010/07/joss-whedon-on-the-avengers-jeremy-renner-confirmed-as-hawkeye.html). *OnTheRedCarpet.com*. Archived (http://www.webcitation.org/5zx6jBXPP) from the original on 2011-07-05. . Retrieved July 24, 2010.

[59] "The Avengers to Start Filming in February" (http://www.superherohype.com/news/articles/105479-the-avengers-to-start-filming-in-february). SuperheroHype.com. 2010-08-10. Archived (http://www.webcitation.org/5zx6l14o6) from the original on 2011-07-05. . Retrieved 2010-08-10.

[60] Friedman, Roger (2010-08-10). "Joss Marvel Movie "The Avengers" Will Be in...3 D!" (http://www.showbiz411.com/2010/08/10/marvel-movie-the-avengers-will-be-in-3-d). Showbiz 411. . Retrieved 2010-08-10.. WebCitation Archive (http://www.webcitation.org/5yDfSKRy6).

[61] Solnik, Claude. Cached version of "The Avengers Landing at Grumman" (http://webcache.googleusercontent.com/search?q=cache:qPvmhb9Y7TUJ:libn.com/blog/2010/10/07/the-avengers-landing-on-long-island). *Long Island Business News* (October 7, 2010). Original story (http://libn.com/blog/2010/10/07/the-avengers-landing-on-long-island), requiring subscription. Retrieved 2010-10-08.

[62] Lovece, Frank. "Marvel's 'Avengers' being shot at Grumman Studios" (http://www.newsday.com/entertainment/movies/marvel-s-avengers-being-shot-at-grumman-studios-1.2375058). *Newsday* (October 20, 2010), p. A13 of print edition. WebCitation Archive (http://www.webcitation.org/5unn9duRi).

[63] McClintock, Pamela (2010-10-18). "Disney, Paramount restructure Marvel deal" (http://www.variety.com/article/VR1118025864.html?categoryId=13&cs=1). *Variety*. Archived (http://www.webcitation.org/5zxBn7VD8) from the original on 2011-07-05. . Retrieved 2010-10-18.

[64] Graser, Marc (2011-10-11). "Why Par, not Disney, gets 'Avengers' credit" (http://www.variety.com/article/VR1118044282). *Variety*. Archived (http://www.webcitation.org/62NajSZYC) from the original on 2011-10-12. . Retrieved 2011-10-12.

[65] "Governor Bill Richardson and Marvel Studios Announce Largest Movie Production in New Mexico History" (http://www.nmfilm.com/article.php?id=1644&title=Governor+Bill+Richardson+and+Marvel+Studios+Announce+Largest+Movie+Production+in+New+Mexico+History). *Film New Mexico*. Archived (http://www.webcitation.org/5zx6mamWG) from the original on 2011-07-05. . Retrieved 2010-12-23.

[66] Hammerstein, B.J. and Hinds, Julie (2011-02-21). "Film producers not waiting to see how governor cuts tax incentives" (http://www.freep.com/article/20110221/ENT01/102210379/Film-producers-not-waiting-see-how-governor-cuts-tax-incentives?). *Detroit Free Press*. . Retrieved 2011-02-21.

[67] Sangiacomo, Michael (2011-03-03). "Upcoming 'Avengers' movie will be filmed in Cleveland" (http://blog.cleveland.com/metro/2011/03/upcoming_avengers_movie_will_b.html). *The Plain Dealer*. Cleveland, Ohio. . Retrieved 2011-03-03.. WebCitation Archive (http://www.webcitation.org/5yDgzCs9b).

[68] "Recent Projects" (http://www.scienceandentertainmentexchange.org/projects). *The Science & Entertainment Exchange*. National Academy of Sciences. Archived (http://www.webcitation.org/5zxBotExh) from the original on 2011-07-05. . Retrieved 24 May 2011.

[69] Paltrow interviewed on *Something For the Weekend*, BBC2, May 8, 2011, via Gallagher, Simon, "Gwyneth Paltrow Will 'Probably' Appear in *Iron Man 3*, and 'Possibly' in *The Avengers*" (http://www.obsessedwithfilm.com/movie-news/gwyneth-paltrow-will-probably-appear-in-iron-man-3-and-possibly-in-the-avengers.php), ObsessedWithFilm.com, May 8, 2011. Retrieved 2011-05-08. WebCitation archive (http://www.webcitation.org/5yXk7CuQp).

[70] "'Avengers' Stuntman -- SCALPED During 30-Foot Fall" (http://www.tmz.com/2011/06/27/avengers-stuntman-scalped-fall-stunt-gone-wrong-jeremy-renner-jeremy-fitzgerald-photo-bloody-hair-head/). *TMZ*. 2011-06-27. Archived (http://www.webcitation.org/5zxBp8KvF) from the original on 2011-07-05. . Retrieved 2011-06-27.

[71] Vancheri, Barbara (2011-07-01). "'Avengers' headed this way" (http://www.webcitation.org/5zr8HWxRf). *Pittsburgh Post-Gazette*. Archived from the original (http://blogs.sites.post-gazette.com/index.php/arts-a-entertainment/mad-about-the-movies/28227-avengers-headed-this-way) on 2011-07-01. . Retrieved 2011-07-01.

[72] Sangiacomo, Micheal (2011-08-08). "Avengers workers start transforming East Ninth into scene for epic battle" (http://www.webcitation.org/60n8NOQxS). *The Plain Dealer*. Cleveland, Ohio. Archived from the original (http://www.cleveland.com/avengers/index.ssf/2011/08/avengers_workers_start_transfo.html) on 2011-08-08. . Retrieved 2011-08-08.

[73] Sgt. 1st Class Mark Bell (2011-11-07). "Captain America, Reserve Soldiers share big screen" (http://www.webcitation.org/6334zhlHD). United States Army. Archived from the original (http://www.army.mil/article/68834/Captain_America__Reserve_Soldiers_share_big_screen/) on 2011-11-07. . Retrieved 2011-11-07.

[74] Jackson, Tom (2011-08-09). "'Avengers' filming starts at Plum Brook" (http://www.webcitation.org/60oJGLxwe). *Sandusky Register*. Ohio. Archived from the original (http://www.sanduskyregister.com/sandusky/news/2011/aug/08/avengers-filming-starts-plum-brook) on 2011 08 09. . Retrieved 2011-08-09.

[75] Jackson, Tom (2011-08-11). "NASA Plum Brook cast as S.H.I.E.L.D. research facility in the 'Avengers' film" (http://www.webcitation.org/60rcZ6LnU). *Sandusky Register*. Sandusky, Ohio. Archived from the original (http://www.sanduskyregister.com/perkins-twp/news/2011/aug/11/nasa-plum-brook-cast-shield-research-facility-avengers-film) on 2011-08-11. . Retrieved 2011-08-11.

[76] Sangiacomo, Micheal (2011-08-11). ""The Avengers" movie to film booming explosions in Parma next week" (http://www.webcitation.org/60rrA3dDc). *The Plain Dealer*. Cleveland, Ohio. Archived from the original (http://www.cleveland.com/avengers/index.ssf/2011/08/the_avengers_movie_to_film_boo.html) on 2011-08-11. . Retrieved 2011-08-11.

[77] Sangiacomo, Micheal (2011-08-11). "Avengers filming wrapping up at NASA facility in Sandusky" (http://www.webcitation.org/60sjWB9ub). *The Plain Dealer*. Cleveland, Ohio. Archived from the original (http://www.cleveland.com/avengers/index.ssf/2011/08/avengers_filming_wrapping_up_a.html) on 2011-08-12. . Retrieved 2011-08-12.

[78] Sangiacomo, Micheal (2011-08-17). "Avengers turning Cleveland, Ohio into Stuttgart, Germany for next round of downtown filming" (http://www.webcitation.org/611rKBIh8). *The Plain Dealer*. Cleveland, Ohio. Archived from the original (http://www.cleveland.com/avengers/index.ssf/2011/08/avengers_turning_cleveland_ohi.html) on 2011-08-18. . Retrieved 2011-08-18.

[79] Sangiacomo, Micheal (2011-08-28). "Filming of 'Avengers' in Cleveland approaches the end" (http://www.webcitation.org/61dwEGNwI). *The Plain Dealer*. Cleveland, Ohio. Archived from the original (http://www.cleveland.com/avengers/index.ssf/2011/08/avengers_filming_nears_the_end.html) on 2011-09-12. . Retrieved 2011-09-02.

[80] Lesnick, Silas (2011-09-02). "First Look at the New York Avengers Set" (http://www.superherohype.com/news/articles/168340-first-look-at-the-new-york-avengers-set). SuperheroHype.com. Archived (http://www.webcitation.org/61dwMx3in) from the original on 2011-09-12. . Retrieved 2011-09-02.

[81] "Scarlett Johansson is all smiles as she gets back to work on her new film The Avengers" (http://www.dailymail.co.uk/tvshowbiz/article-2033243/Scarlett-Johansson-smiles-gets-work-The-Avengers.html). *Daily Mail*. London, UK. 2011 09 03. Archived (http://www.webcitation.org/61dwTmCa6) from the original on 2011-09-12. . Retrieved 2011-09-03.

[82] "In Production" (http://www.ilm.com/). Industrial Light & Magic. . Retrieved 2011-09-20.

[83] "Legacy Effects Filmography" (http://www.legacyefx.com/features/LegFilm.pdf). Legacy Effects. Archived (http://www.webcitation.org/625M292Ss) from the original on 2011 09 30. . Retrieved 2011 09 30.

[84] "Projects" (http://lumapictures.com/projects). Luma Pictures. Archived (http://www.webcitation.org/625M8OTWM) from the original on 2011-09-30. . Retrieved 2011-09-30.

[85] "Filmography" (http://www.webcitation.org/62waZO14v). alansilvestri.com. Archived from the original (http://www.alansilvestri.com/Alan_Silvestri/Filmography.html) on 2011-11-04. . Retrieved 2011-11-04.

[86] Boucher, Geoff (2011-06-22). "Marvel makes it official: No Hall H panel at Comic-Con" (http://herocomplex.latimes.com/2011/06/22/marvel-makes-it-official-no-hall-h-panel-at-comic-con/). *Los Angeles Times*. Archived (http://www.webcitation.org/60Gya6xKF) from the original on 2011-07-22. . Retrieved 2011-07-18.

[87] Breznican, Anthony (2011-07-18). "Avenge Me! Post-Captain America teaser for The Avengers copied, pasted, deleted" (http://www.webcitation.org/60UUukhwF). *Entertainment Weekly*. Archived from the original (http://insidemovies.ew.com/2011/07/18/avengers-teaser/) on 2011-07-27. . Retrieved 2011-07-24.

[88] "The Walt Disney Studios Takes Fans Behind the Scenes at the D23 Expo" (http://www.webcitation.org/60ocZGrrt). Go.com. 2011-08-09. Archived from the original (http://d23.disney.go.com/expo/articles/080911_BN_ExpoStudios.html) on 2011-08-09. . Retrieved 2011-08-09.

[89] Finke, Nikki (2011-08-23). "Disney Fires Marvel's Marketing Department" (http://www.webcitation.org/61CbIcgFx). Deadline Hollywood. Archived from the original (http://www.deadline.com/2011/08/disney-fires-marvels-marketing-department/) on 2011-08-25. . Retrieved 2010-08-25.

[90] "Marvel's The Avengers Comes to NYCC" (http://marvel.com/news/story/16772/marvels_the_avengers_comes_to_nycc). Marvel.com. 2011-10-04. Archived (http://www.webcitation.org/62CvrjUyq) from the original on 2011-10-05. . Retrieved 2011-10-05.

[91] "Marvel Studios Debuts "The Avengers" Trailer" (http://www.comicbookresources.com/?page=article&id=34844). Comic Book Resources. 2011-10-11. Archived (http://www.webcitation.org/62MJDljlw) from the original on 2011-10-11. . Retrieved 2011-10-11.

[92] Fernandez, Jay A. (2011-10-11). "'The Avengers' Trailer Verdict: More Hulk, Less Stark, Less Loki, More Dark" (http://www.webcitation.org/62Nj0BfMQ). *The Hollywood Reporter*. Archived from the original (http://www.hollywoodreporter.com/heat-vision/avengers-trailer-verdict-more-hulk-246726) on 2011-10-12. . Retrieved 2011-10-12.

[93] ""Marvel's The Avengers" Trailer Downloaded over 10 Million Times in First 24 Hours on iTunes Movie Trailers" (http://www.webcitation.org/62R5c4GRw). Burbank, California: Business Wire. 2011-10-14. Archived from the original (http://www.businesswire.com/news/home/20111014005986/en/âMarvelâs-Avengersâ-Trailer-Downloaded-10-Million-Times) on 2011-10-14. . Retrieved 2011-10-14.

[94] Lien, Tracey (2011-09-15). "What Was THQ Brisbane Working On Before the Studio Closed?" (http://www.kotaku.com.au/2011/09/what-was-thq-brisbane-working-on-before-the-studio-closed/). Kotaku. Archived (http://www.webcitation.org/61iULFxoq) from the original on 2011-09-15. . Retrieved 2011-09-15.

[95] Sinclair, Brendan (2011-09-19). "Marvel looking for Avengers game partner" (http://www.gamespot.com/news/6335430/marvel-looking-for-avengers-game-partner). GameSpot. Archived (http://www.webcitation.org/61q8uJs60) from the original on

2011-09-20. . Retrieved 2011-09-20.
[96] Szalai, Georg (2011-10-15). "'Avengers' Producer Hints at Sequel at New York Comic-Con" (http://www.webcitation.org/62VEEruHF). *The Hollywood Reporter*. Archived from the original (http://www.hollywoodreporter.com/heat-vision/avengers-sequel-comic-con-mark-ruffalo-249014) on 2011-10-17. . Retrieved 2011-10-17.

External links

- Official website (http://marvel.com/avengers_movie)
- *The Avengers* (http://www.imdb.com/title/tt0848228/) at the Internet Movie Database

Opposite Sex (TV series)

Opposite Sex	
Intertitle	
Genre	Comedy-drama
Created by	Marc Silverstein Abby Kohn
Starring	Milo Ventimiglia Margot Finley Kyle Howard Chris Evans Allison Mack Lindsey McKeon
Composer(s)	Anna Waronker
Country of origin	United States
Language(s)	English
No. of seasons	1
No. of episodes	8
Production	
Executive producer(s)	Rick Kellard Randall Zisk
Producer(s)	Lewis Abel
Editor(s)	Jeff Betancourt Joanna Cappuccilli Mark Gerstein
Cinematography	Johnny E. Jensen
Running time	43 minutes
Broadcast	
Original channel	FOX
Original run	July 17, 2000 – September 4, 2000

Opposite Sex is an American comedy-drama series that aired during FOX's summer 2000 schedule. The series was one of the first teen dramas to primarily use independent artists on its soundtrack by such acts as Elliott Smith and Ben Lee.

Synopsis

The series chronicles the life of Jed Perry (Milo Ventimiglia), a 15-year-old boy who moves to Northern California along with his father shortly after the death of his mother. After enrolling at the prestigious Evergreen Academy, Jed finds out the school was formerly for girls that recently became co-ed. Along with Jed, two other boys attended the school; Philip Steffan (Kyle Howard) and Cary Baston (Chris Evans). The boys run into problems when the girls of the school are resistant to the changes and make it clear that their presence is unwanted.

It was initially shot in 1999 for the 1999–2000 season, but for various reasons the series was delayed until Summer 2000. The series lasted eight episodes before being canceled. It is unknown if anything from episodes 9–13 were filmed or completed.

Cast

- Milo Ventimiglia – Jed Perry
- Kyle Howard – Philip Steffan
- Chris Evans – Cary Baston
- Margot Finley – Miranda Mills
- Lindsey McKeon – Stella
- Allison Mack – Kate Jacobs
- Chris McKenna – Rob Perry

Reception

Carole Horst of *Variety* wrote of the series, "Clever concept, sleek production values, a nice cast and thoughtful writing (for a teen show) add up to the enjoyable *Opposite Sex*". In concluding her review she stated, "Despite all the good things in this gentle comedy-drama, it's hard to say who the series is aimed at: It's not intellectual enough for "*Freaks*" fans and too grounded for the WB crowd. Young auds will have to seek it out. And therein lies the rub."[1] Barry Garron of *The Hollywood Reporter* described *Opposite Sex* as a "far-fetched, overly earnest teen-oriented show" that "never manages to overcome its contrived premise and establish real emotional connections." He went on to say that "*My So-Called Life* and *Freaks & Geeks* have raised the bar for teen drama by providing keen insight into the awkwardness of adolescence" and that while not on the same level this series is "not nearly as cartoonish" as *Saved By The Bell*.[2] Joel Brown, a *New York Times* syndicated columnist published in *The Spokesman-Review* found that "Ventimiglia conveys Jed's frustration well" but that "bad TV cliches overwhelm this show's mild promise."[3] *The Modesto Bee's* TV critic, Kevin McDonough, describes the series as "hardly the worst teen show of the year." He continues by stating that "it lacks the soft-core exploitation that permeates *Young Americans*."[4]

Episodes

Series #	Title	Writer(s)	Director	Original Airdate
1	**"Pilot"**	Abby Kohn, Marc Silverstein	Randall Zisk	July 17, 2000
Jed Perry becomes one of the first boys ever to attend Evergreen Academy when he moves to a new town. He quickly bonds with the only other male students, Cary (Chris Evans) and Phil (Kyle Howard), when the girls, led by Stella (Lindsey McKeon), ostracize them. But when Miranda Mills (Margot Finley), a free-spirited Sophomore, takes an interest in Jed she helps the boys gain acceptance with a stunt at the annual Evergreen talent show.				
2	**"The Virgin Episode"**	Abby Kohn, Marc Silverstein	Randall Zisk	July 24, 2000
Miranda's birthday party is approaching, a legendary event where two virgins are "sacrificed". Jed, the only one of the boys who openly admits to be a virgin, is naturally selected and his friendship with Kate (Allison Mack), another suspected virgin, develops. Meanwhile, Cary, who has been flaunting his sexual experience, becomes the target of Stella's campaign to remove the boys from school. The boys discover that the school has a history of expelling girls with an unwholesome reputation, so they decide to track them down in the hopes of gleaning some information that might save Cary's place at Evergreen.				
3	**"The Drug Episode"**	Abby Kohn, Marc Silverstein	Danny Leiner	July 31, 2000
After the boys discover the janitor's stash of marijuana, the school hires a new drug counselor, Greg Tillman (Dax Griffin), to speak with the students. Jed instantly forms a strong dislike of him, due to his good looks and the lust he provokes in the entire student body, including Miranda and Kate. When word gets out that Cary is "hooked up" and he instantly becomes popular with some of the girls, he decides to play up to his new reputation. Meanwhile, Phil runs an ill-fated campaign for city council with a strong position against drugs.				
4	**"The Homosexual Episode"**	Nick Harding	Randall Zisk	August 7, 2000
It's Bow Down week at Evergreen Academy, an annual tradition in which Seniors select a Junior to be their personal slave for a week. Jed is picked by Joely (Nicki Aycox), an out lesbian, who begins to show a strong attraction to him. Completely confused, he tries to work out whether he's just imagining it. Meanwhile, Cary incures the wrath of popular girl Cassie Schreiber (Joanna García) after he leads a revolt against the seniors, and is threatened with the mythical "360".				
5	**"The Dance Episode"**	Rick Kellard	Kenneth Fink	August 14, 2000
The boys wonder if they're losing their masculinity. As a school dance approaches, a rift is formed in the boys' friendship when Phil starts to pursue Kate, much to Jed's chagrin. Meanwhile, Cary is humiliated by a student from the nearby military school Fort Union and vows to get revenge.				
6	**"The Field Trip Episode"**	Carole Real	Ian Toynton	August 21, 2000
The juniors of Evergreen Academy travel to New York for a Model U.N. summit, where Jed is reunited with his ex-girlfriend, Lisa (Christine Lakin). When Lisa and Kate, Jed's current love interest, become awfully friendly with each other, Cary persuades Jed that a "ménage à trois" is on the cards. Meanwhile, Phil befriends some boys from Fort Union, and sparks fly between Cary and Stella.				
7	**"The Fantasy Episode"**	Abby Kohn, Marc Silverstein	Randall Zisk	August 28, 2000
When Stella gets severely drunk on Miranda's hidden supply of everclear just as the student body is leaving for a field trip, the boys, along with Miranda and Kate, smuggle her back into the now empty school. With only the supervision of Greg Tillman, the drug counselor who they called to help with Stella, the gang spend the night on the Evergreen campus, where Miranda asks Jed to sleep with her, Phil and Kate bond in the school kitchens, and Cary comes to Stella's rescue.				
8	**"The Car Episode"**	Abby Kohn, Marc Silverstein	Adam Nimoy	September 4, 2000
When he finds himself dating both Miranda and Kate at the same time, Jed is forced to decide who he really wants to be with. He chooses Kate, but shortly afterwards she learns about his two-timing and breaks up with him. Phil, with his eye on the newly single Kate, decides that he needs a driver's license to win her heart. Meanwhile, Cary and Stella are forced to cater to a band geek's every whim in order to keep their relationship secret. Having finally decided on Kate, Jed goes to extreme lengths to try to get her back.				

References

[1] Horst, Carole (28 June 2000). "Opposite Sex" (http://www.variety.com/review/VE1117787472.html?categoryid=32&cs=1). Variety. . Retrieved 14 November 2005.

[2] Garron, Barry (28 June 2000). "Tv Review: 'opposite Sex'" (http://www.allbusiness.com/services/motion-pictures/4862707-1.html). The Hollywood Reporter. . Retrieved 19 February 2010.

[3] Brown, Joel (17 July 2000). "'Opposite Sex' much too predictable" (http://news.google.ca/newspapers?id=X7szAAAAIBAJ&sjid=Q_IDAAAAIBAJ&pg=2676,5385330&dq=opposite-sex+tv+review+2000&hl=en). The Spokesman-Review. pp. B4. . Retrieved 19 February 2010.

[4] McDonough, Kevin (17 July 2000). "'Opposite' distracts" (http://news.google.ca/newspapers?id=VS8uAAAAIBAJ&sjid=L9YFAAAAIBAJ&pg=1390,3144390&hl=en). The Modesto Bee. pp. D-4. . Retrieved 19 February 2010.

External links

- *Opposite Sex* (http://www.imdb.com/title/tt0202513/) at the Internet Movie Database
- *Opposite Sex* (http://www.tv.com/show/2379/summary.html) at TV.com
- *Opposite Sex* (http://epguides.com/OppositeSex_2000) at epguides.com

Article Sources and Contributors

Chris Evans (actor) *Source*: http://en.wikipedia.org/w/index.php?oldid=459668344 *Contributors*: 1988, 6afraidof7, A. B., AP1787, Abraingame, Acalamari, Acjelen, Akral, Alessandriana, All Hallow's Wraith, Allstarecho, Alphathon, Andrewlp1991, Angelic Wraith, Angr, Antonio Lopez, Antonrojo, Aremith, Arendedwinter, Arniep, Art1991, Artemisboy, Auntof6, Azucar, Baird, Balsa10, Bart Versieck, Bencey, Bender235, BiH, Bill william compton, Billde, Blacqston, BlastOButter42, Blotski, Bmclaughlin9, Bobo192, Bongwarrior, Bookman1124, BostonRed, Boutrie, Bovineboy2008, Boycool42, Bratz angel14, Brian1979, BrokenSphere, BrownHairedGirl, Buddy Thulasi101, Bunchofgrapes, Byped, Caitlin0799, Caknuck, Calvin 1998, CaptainMorgan, Cbl62, Cerrot, Ceyockey, ChesterG, Chrisrevans, Cinemaniac86, Closedmouth, Commander Keane, CommonsDelinker, CovenantD, Cresix, Crystallina, DStoykov, DaChoppa, Dancter, Dante.antonio, Danteorange123, Dark Shikari, David Gerard, Davodd, DeadEyeArrow, Deb, DepressedPer, DerHexer, Deutsch fil, DiePerfekteWelle, Dismas, Disney22, Djbj16, Doniago, Dprabhu, Dr. McGrew, EJBanks, Ebyabe, Effer, Ejfetters, ElBoricua, Empty Buffer, Encyclopedia77, Epbr123, Erebus Morgaine, Erik9, Esc2003, Evanreyes, Evanswikigirl, Fallout boy, Fandraltastic, FastLizard4, Fastilysock, Fierce134, FireInMySoul, Frankgorshin, FrickFrack, Fylgiar, GORIZARD, Garda40, Gary King, GcSwRhIc, Geeness, Gene Nygaard, Gifford924, Gilliam, Gimmetoo, Glclancy, Glennlowney, Gocubs17, GoingBatty, Gonzonoir, Granpuff, Gregfitzy, Griffithstrife, Gryffindor, Guat6, Gunslinger, HOT L Baltimore, HX, HaeB, Hall Monitor, Hammersfan, Handtalker, Hashmi, Usman, Hcblue, Headstrong neiva, Hede2000, Hologram900, Hotwiki, Hux, Hyliad, Hyukan, ILovePlankton, Ich, Iridescent, Italiangel95, J-stan, J.delanoy, JDspeeder1, JNW, JXtra, JYi, Jack Merridew, Jack O'Lantern, JackO'Lantern, Jagfan71, JamesB3, Jaranda, Jasonfred1980, Jeffrey O. Gustafson, JennieC2005, JerzeyHellboy, Jg325, Jmorgan, John254, Joliboy, JonathanKao1, Jvcdude, KGasso, Karone, Kath090, Kauczuk, Kbdank71, Kcufy, Khosein84, King Lopez, Kollision, Krishan 25, L Kensington, Lacon432, Lano'reillygid, Lauragia, Laurascudder, Laydee Lyca, Leclaird, Lmenthe, Loyal Jen, Lukep913, MacTire, Manishearth, Marcd30319, Marcus Brute, Marokwitz, Martarius, MarvelCinematicUniverseFan, Materialscientist, Mccajor, Mccott, Mdebets, Mephistophelian, Metagraph, Metao, Metfan722, Mh raul, Missmonroe09, Mjpieters, Monegasque, Movieguru2006, Mrs. kiwi, Mtjaws, Mustang dvs, NP Chilla, Namzie11, Nanouk, Naomi19, Ndenison, NedBigby3, Nehrams2020, Nick C, Nicki797, Nsaa, Nv8200p, Nymf, ONEder Boy, Oatmeal batman, Obi-WanKenobi-2005, Ohnoitsjamie, One Night In Hackney, Onecanadasquarebishopsgate, Onlymystory, P.B. Pilhet, PeaceNT, Peptuck, PeterSymonds, Philip Trueman, Pinkadelica, Plasticup, Pogokidd2, Postdlf, Princessruby, Provelt, Rafael.minogue, Rakaha, Ravanacker, RealGer, Realdiamonds, Revenged heart23, Rhstowell, Risehalloween, River4ever, Rje, Rjwilmsi, Ro9ue, Sagitario, Salamurai, Sam, Sam Blacketer, Sauj, SelfDestructButton, Shadowjams, Shakirfan, Shojego, SidP, SkweekyDawn, SkyWalker, Slideways, Slysplace, Snorkyorky70, SoCalSuperEagle, Someone111111, Souhardyo, SpLoT, Spanglej, Spartakingleo, Sry85, Staka, Stemonitis, Superhero111, Sweetlew13, TMC1982, TOMKURTZ, Taroaldo, Tbhotch, Tell-Tale Ghost, Tenebrae, Terminator50, The 80s chick, The Editor 155, The Hacker 1, The wub, TheAznSensation, TheFeds, TheRealFennShysa, Thecheesykid, Thomasav, Thuresson, Tisdale90210, Tomkurts, Toughpigs, TransUtopian, Tregoweth, TriiipleThreat, Tweetyma15, Twinsday, UNFORGIVEN, VCA, Venicemenace, Vixen 47, Vizcarra, Vovan7349, Vulturell, WIKI-GUY-16, WLU, WOSlinker, Waghhhh, Wakamoley, Ward3001, Willscrlt, Wowsters, Wrestlinglover, Yamla, ZX81, Zalgo, Zeta26, Zythe, 780 anonymous edits

Not Another Teen Movie *Source*: http://en.wikipedia.org/w/index.php?oldid=458385418 *Contributors*: *drew, 07chill07, 5150pacer, 803290, ACE Spark, AEMoreira042281, Aaaxlp, Aaporter 87, AaronWK, Abomasnow, AbsoluteGleek92, Achin4aiken15, Actsofism, Adamwankenobi, Addict 2006, Afed, Alan smithee, Alasdairmacdonald, Alexandru Stanoi, All Hallow's Wraith, Allixpeeke, Americus55, Andrzejbanas, Angel caboodle, AngelOfMusic, Anthony Hogg, AshTFrankFurter2, Aspects, Aubreyclark, Beardo, Before My Ken, Bencey, Bezapt, Billydeeuk, Bitbitz.xx, Blackrvn, BladesCrusade, BluePhoenix12, Boadrummer, Bovineboy2008, Brianchi, Britannicus, BurningZeppelin, Burntorange493, Bushi, CJ, Callmarcus, Can't sleep, clown will eat me, Canadaolympic989, Cartmankenny, Cbrown1023, Celebith, ChanelDisney, Chantessy, CharlesMartel, ChesterG, Cjd4life, Cjewell, Ckatz, Computerjoe, CrazyLegsKC, Crumbsucker, Cubs Fan, DH85868993, DLand, DarkMissy, Darren Lee, Darrenhusted, Darth Mike, Darwinek, Dasani, David Costello, David Gerard, Dcd139, DearPrudence, Defrosted, Dekkanar, Deltabeignet, DepressedPer, Dflav1138, Diaz, Diberri, Discospinster, Doctat3, Doczilla, Doidimais Brasil, Dpower, Drblubox, Drdr1989, DreDaKid16, Drmagic, DropDeadGorgias, Dudesleeper, Dynamite XI, EHonkoop, EagleOne, Eaglestorm, Elcapitane, Elephantissimo, Elvoret, Emperor001, Enter Movie, Ericaquinton, Esprit15d, Evanreyes, EveryDayJoe45, Evil Monkey, FMAFan1990, Fallout boy, Farcical, FatalError, Flibirigit, Flowerkiller1692, Flyer22, Format, Fourthords, Frankie0607, Freakofnurture, Freezing the mainstream, Freikorp, Frogan, Furrykef, Gabbe, GeeFour, Gracz54, Graveyarder, Guinea pig warrior, Gw2005, Hairy Dude, Harlot, Hearfourmewesique, Hearttocats, Hede2000, HelloAnnyong, Hypermagic, Ianjones50, Iapetus, Ich, Iceaturtles, Ig88b, ItsAlwaysLupus, ItsTheClimb17, J-Kama-Ka-C, J.delanoy, JYi, Jadexoxo, Jaeger5432, Jaldridge86, JamesBurns, Jbm867, Jeepday, Jeff Muscato, Jetsin07, Jimathane, JimmyMcJim, Jmeden2000, Jogers, John, John5008, JohnABerring27A, Johnred32, Juggernautthunderclap, Jwein, Kakashi-sensei, Kane5187, Kirby119, Ktpedia, Kyle C Haight, Lach Graham, LadyNorbert, Layzie the kid, Levelistchampion, Levineps, LinkToddMcLovinMontana, LittleMenace2K3, Liverpoolpaddy, Logical Fuzz, Lord Seth, Lore aura, Lots42, LouScheffer, Lukasz Lukomski, MSchnitzler2000, MWB1138, Markoff Chaney, Marpicco, MartinRe, Master of Puppets, Matt.smart, Matthew238, Mbertsch, McSly, Mcope123456789, Mercury, Mes tex, Messy Thinking, Metroid690, MicahDCochran, Michaelritchie200, Michig, Mike Payne, Mikecraig, MisterBadIdea, Moose Boy, Mrjeff, Musicpvm, Mütze, NTMfan10, Navysealxray, Nehrams2020, Nerdmaster, NickBush24, NickMartin, Nightscream, Noclevername, Norb6672, Nufy8, Num1dgen, ONEder Boy, OOODDD, OS2Warp, Oberto22, Ocatecir, Oliver202, PFHLai, Pacholeknbnj, Paranoid117, Paul730, PaulHammond2, Perfecto, PhilHibbs, Phoenix 964, Pi, Polylerus, Polystrength1, Poofdd, Proofreader77, QuasyBoy, R00m c, RaseaC, Rbb l181, Redvers, RexNL, Reywas92, Riana, Rje, Rjwilmsi, Roaring Siren, RobJ1981, Rockerbaberonnie, Rowbull, Rudjek, Rwiggum, SQGibbon, SW4ever, Sabrewing, Sadisticality, Sasquatch, Satori Son, ScottJ, SeanDuggan, Secret Saturdays, Seqsea, Seraphurin, Shadowolf, Shamrock27, Shatterband, Sheepnacidadegrande, ShelfSkewed, Sjö, SkyWalker, Slgrandson, Sohmc, Sohollywood, Someoneinmyheadbutit'snotme, Sorcha, Sottolacqua, Spadoodle, Specs112, SpikeToronto, StarScream1007, StephenBuxton, Steven Zhang, Suckstobeabum, TBSfan1223, TKD, TMC1982, Tassedethe, Tattau, Tavilis, Ted87, The Cool Kat, The IPS, The Transhumanist, Thevaliant, Thryduulf, Timclare, Tlogmer, Tokyogirl79, TracyLinkEdnaVelmaPenny, Tregoweth, TreuBoy680, Treplacements90, TreyMarsh20, Treybien, Trubye, Tubbino, TyDwiki, Typhoon966, UNCLAX72, Ubardak, UltimatePyro, Unregistered.coward, Usien6, Utelprob, Valermos, Vaughnstull, Vladar86, Volker89, Wakuran, Ward3001, Weedle McHairybug, Weirdling, Wiikipedian, Wikipediarocks17, Wohz, Woohookitty, Wt is this, Wumbo, Xx kidschoice xx, Yahel Guhan, Zchris87v, ~shuri, 874 anonymous edits

The Perfect Score *Source*: http://en.wikipedia.org/w/index.php?oldid=450234148 *Contributors*: 28421u2232nfenfcenc, AN(Ger), Angelfirenze, Appraiser, Bender235, Beyond My Ken, Biblbroks, Booyabazooka, Brainscar, Cbrown1023, Chandler, Ckatz, Closedmouth, David Gerard, Duja, EamonnPKeane, Eleos, FMAFan1990, Felicity Tepper, Freshh, Helplessstar88207, Hierophantasmagoria, Hoptsur42, Jagged 85, JamesBWatson, Jonnyboy88, Jonyyeh, Kerowyn, Lord of Illusions, Mallanox, Moez, Mvergall, Nightscream, Nqnpipnr, PM800, Paul Erik, PaulHammond2, Rajrajmarley, Rje, Rjwilmsi, Roaring Siren, Rwxrwxrwx, RyanGerbil10, SabreMau, Salamurai, Sango123, Shining.Star, TMC1982, TakuyaMurata, TheMovieBuff, Tingrin87, ToadX, Treybien, Uglyricky, Vcelloho, Vickser, VolatileChemical, Wikipedian314, Woodshed, Xezbeth, Zr2d2, Мурад 97, 99 anonymous edits

Cellular (film) *Source*: http://en.wikipedia.org/w/index.php?oldid=459052677 *Contributors*: AbsolutDan, Accounting4Taste, Ahoerstemeier, AjaxSmack, Aldo samulo, Alex G, All Hallow's Wraith, Allhailtoyin, Amikake3, Andrzejbanas, Andycjp, Aranea Mortem, BR9000, Billdorr, Black Falcon, Bluerules, Boomer929, Bovineboy2008, Breno, Brich2929, Bswee, Can't sleep, clown will eat me, Carc5959, Cbrown1023, CelticJobber, Chrisminter, Cigammagicwizard, Ciroslive, ColdFusion650, Coolcaesar, Counsell, Crumbsucker, D.brodale, Darklilac, Dav-FL-IN-AZ-id, Del91, DepressedPer, Desdenova, Dodgerblue777, Dogah, EALacey, Edward, Elkman, Emperor, Fist of Glory, FoxieSlavik, FrankRizzo2006, Func, Geeness, Gilliam, H-b-g, Harikvr, HennessyC, Horkana, Iridescent, J04n, Jayunderscorezero, Jeffrey Mall, Jonjames1986, Kaarvok, Kollision, Lots42, MSchnitzler2000, Marcel flaubert, Martarius, Mckinley99, Mdumas43073, Melyssa57, Mensurs, Misza13, Moshe Constantine Hassan Al-Silverburg, Nalkoff, Nehrams2020, Nicolas1981, Noctibus, Norm mit, Okki, Perfecter, Pjoef, Quentin X, RLipstock, RadioKirk, Rje, Rm999, SamIAm22, Sheady 16, SidP, Skybunny, SpNeo, Sraan, Sugar Bear, Sumsum2010, Supapuerco, TCL, Tam1hibs, Tanner65, The Rhymesmith, TheMovieBuff, Thedoctor98, Thief12, Ukexpat, Useight, Wikirocks, Wrightbus, Wwoods, Xezbeth, АлександрВв, 220 anonymous edits

Fierce People (film) *Source*: http://en.wikipedia.org/w/index.php?oldid=453454152 *Contributors*: AbsoluteGleek92, AndrewHowse, Bluefooeyes, Bronayur, Buldożer, Cornellrockey, Crisco 1492, Djflem, Easchiff, Ekabhishek, FrankRizzo2006, Grandpafootsoldier, ItsTheClimb17, LcawteHuggle, Lugnuts, Moondeep, NcSchu, Ospinad, Parkwells, Pascal666, Plasticspork, Promking, Shining.Star, TJ Spyke, Tiptoety, Treybien, Woohookitty, Վազգեն, 33 anonymous edits

Fantastic Four (film) *Source*: http://en.wikipedia.org/w/index.php?oldid=455888567 *Contributors*: 23skidoo, 2Pac, A man alone, Acjelen, Adambro, After Midnight, Ahpook, Akcarver, Alientraveller, Alison9, AndrewHowse, Andrzejbanas, Andycjp, Apartmento, Apedia, Apostrophe, Ardenn, ArglebargleIV, Art1991, Asenine, B.d.mills, BOne, Bacteria, Badcoverversion, Batman2005, Bendragonbrown47, Betty Logan, BigCow, Bignole, Billium 91, Blue Spider, Bolman Deal, Boris Crépeau, Bovineboy2008, BoydRE, Bradtcordeiro, Briaboru, Buchanan-Hermit, Bufflo, Burks821, C777, CIreland, Canek, CapDac, Cheesemeister, Chris McFeely, ChristTrekker, Cobaltcigs, Coder Dan, ContiAWB, CovenantD, Creepy Crawler, Crotchety Old Man, Curps, DaffyDuck619, Dark Eagle (usurped), Darrenhusted, David Gerard, DavidA, DeadEyeArrow, DeansFA, Deposuit, Discospinster, Dismas, DoctorWho42, Doczilla, Downfall Guy, Dr who1975, Dr. McGrew, DragoLink08, Drat, Drpickem, Dubbya9, Dudesleeper, Dynesclan, Empty2005, Erik, Erik9, Evil Monkey, Evilgidgit, Explicit, Fabiogramos, Falcon373, Ferdinand Pienaar, FigmentJedi, Fluffybun, Fordmadoxfraud, Freemarket, Fusek71, GHcool, Gabriel Duvall, Gaius Cornelius, Gambitx18, Garion96, Gin and Tonic, GoingBatty, Good Olfactory, Granpuff, Gregalodon, Guat6, Gurch, Harish, Hotwiki, I am a jedi, Imaudihere, Imladros, Incredi-Player, Indiedude, Indignantpenguin, Indrek, InfamousPrince, Inwind, Iron Ghost, J Greb, J.delanoy, JJoseph145, JamminBen, Jeffrey O. Gustafson, Jevansen, Johnalexgolden, Joizashmo, Jonkerz, Joriel1995, Joseph Q Publique, Josh Parris, Joylock, Jtalledo, Juandope, Jump Guru, K1Bond007, Kal-El, Kanjilearner55, Kbdank71, Kchishol1970, Keeves, Keith D, Kidlittle, Kirujoy, Kollision, LEX LETHAL, Lacrimosus, Laughlikecrazy42, Lgl6spears, Liftarn, Lovellama, Lowellian, Luigi-ish, Luna Santin, Lwc, M2K 2, MER-C, MITalum, MWCRR7, Maciste, Magnocrusher2007, Mallanox, Marcd30319, MarnetteD, Martinsizon, Marwan soft, Master Yugin, MattSutton1, Mclay19, Meatwod, Mermaid from the Baltic Sea, Methosruby, Michael Devore, Mike 41000000000, Mike Selinker, Mild Bill Hiccup, Millahnna, MisterHand, Mokwella, Mrblondnyc, Musicpvm, NawlinWiki, Nehrams2020, Newyorkballadeer, Nlu, Noirish, Notmicro, Nshady16, Oleg Alexandrov, Onomatopoeia, OutRider2003, PTSE, Paradoxdreamer, Passive, Patchallel, Paul A, Paulrach, Pax:Vobiscum, Pc13, Pengo, Peterqm, Piano non troppo, Postdlf, Prem555, Pukachu, Quadratus, RVDDP2501, RadicalBender, Ralphy512, RandomP, Rapscallion, Raz.you.up, Redranger241, Riana, Richfife, Rje, Rjwilmsi, RobJ1981, Ronark, Ronhjones, Rtkat3, Russ is the sex, SGCommand, SMegatron, Salamurai, Scottree, Sdkfdslkf, Septegram, Sesshomaru, Sestet, Shermantankboy, Shnierland, Silent Tom, SirNuke, Skymt, Slysplace, Smart-edd, SoM, Son of Kong, SpNeo, Speeddemon2992, Spidey104, Steam5, StuffOfInterest, TMC1982, Tenebrae, The 4th Snake, The Clawed One, The Filmaker, The Missing Piece, The wub, TheFatJamoc, TheGreenFaerae, TheMovieBuff, TheRealFennShysa, Thecheesykid, Thedarkside, Thunderbrand, ThuranX, TijhofGraphics, Tim0907, Tmdscore, Tommyt, ToxicAllure, Travisbell, Trevgreg, TurabianNights, Typhoon966, UnicornTapestry, Vader200591, Valfontis, Vorratt, Voxparadox, WatchAndObserve, WhiteAvenger, WikiFew, Willgee, Willie D, Xezbeth, Youngandrestless, Zajabys, Zotdragon, Zzyzx, 524 anonymous edits

London (2006 film) *Source*: http://en.wikipedia.org/w/index.php?oldid=438420004 *Contributors*: Andycjp, Arniep, Bagel7, Bart133, Bungle, Chrishmt0423, Clashfrankcastle, Kross, LewisHamiltonTR, Mattbuck, Owen, Phawn, Phil Boswell, ProveIt, Rheubie, Rockfang, SidP, Supernumerary, Treybien, Wackelpudding, Wiikipedian, Xandrus, 51 anonymous edits

TMNT (film) *Source*: http://en.wikipedia.org/w/index.php?oldid=456530075 *Contributors*: Acebloo, AdamDeanHall, Afluent Rider, After Midnight, Agustinaldo, Alakazam, Alaric Deschain, Alexfb, Alice Mudgarden, Alksub, Amalga, An Useok, Andrewrost3241981, Andrzejbanas, Anetode, Arrowned, Arxiloxos, Ashmoors, Aspects, Atlan, Atomic Duck!, Austin316ejd, Avenged Eightfold, Bando26, BarryTheUnicorn, Beetstra, Benjwong, Berserkerz Crit, Betamax the Flyer, Betty Logan, BhushanHDamle, Bigger Boss, Bignole, Blaarg, Blood sliver, Bnl79, BoersSkinsPunx, Bovineboy2008, Brant Jones, Braydwilde, Brian Kendig, BuickCenturyDriver, Bushcarrot, Buslady, C777, CNGLITCHINFO, CartmanUK26, Cartoonist Will, Ceauntay13, Ceauntay31, Chavando, Chris McFeely, Chris1219, Christine5797, Cnota, Crazy4metallica, Crumbsucker, Cujo27, CyberSkull, Cybninja, Da Vynci, Dale Arnett, DanDud88, Danchan22, Danger, Dangerous-Boy, Danteorange123, Darknessthecurse, Darkwind, Darth Mike, DarthScorcho, Davey4, David Gerard, David Shankbone, Davidhorman, Dee15gon, Diemi, Digata200, Disinclination, Doberman Pharaoh, Doc502, Dominicbillings, Doobsmcgee, Dposse, Dr. R.K.Z, Duhman0009, Dynesclan, ESkog, Eldarsevenstar, Elijya, Elipongo, Emurphy42, Enguerrand, Erik, Esn, Evil saltine, Exo Kopaka, FMAFan1990, Faded, FaithLehaneTheVampireSlayer, Fiery bobcat, Film freak, Flammablemonkey, Flowerparty, FlyingPenguins, Forteblast, FrankRizzo2006, Fundistraction, FuriousFreddy, Furrykef, Fusek71, FutureNJGov, GDallimore, GPanesarJatt, Gadfium, Galactic war, Garrett Albright, GarryKosmos, Geocator, German barrero, Ghostchild23, Gilliam, Girlsboy217, Gman124, Gnielson, Good Olfactory, Gundato, Halfshell, Harley Quinn hyenaholic, Heegoop, HiDrNick, Horkana, Howardho, Howdoggie, Iicatsii, Inflataman, J 1982, JAF1970, JCO312, JForget, JQF, JYi, Jake Lancaster, Janadore, Jay Cee, Jay Verdi, JenniferHeartsU, Jhsounds, Jj137, Jlpspinto, Jminternelia, JoeSmack, John, Johnny Arrombador 01, Jtalledo, Kaijucole, Karateka Farrant, KdogDS, KevinKeene85, Kingplatypus, Kitch, Koopa turtle, Krellion, Kris Classic, Kuralyov, LaNicoya, Lahiru k, Lambiam, Larrythefunkyferret, Lbdrox123, Lewisskinner, Lexicon, Lg16spears, LilHelpa, Lumaga, MMSX, Magical Duel Guy, Mallanox, Mandarax, Manfroze, Markcambrone, Martarius, Master of Pies, Materialscientist, MathUser2929, Mediadimension, MegX, MemeGeneScene, Merotoker1, Merqurial, Mike Selinker, Millahnna, Moss56, Mostly Rainy, Moviesnoop, Mr.Grave, Mtjaws, Mullet, Navex, Nehrams2020, Nejee16, New World Man, Nicknitro86, NielsenGW, NisseSthlm, NotoriousNick500, Nr1moviefan, ONEder Boy, Okajaya, OkamiDotanuki, Oknazevad, Osubuckeye, Otemple700, OutRider2003, PJ Pete, Pacer898, PantheraLeo, Patar knight, Phoenixrod, Pikawil, Pixelface, Platypus222, Porsche997SBS, Ppntori, Psychonaut, Quackslikeaduck, QuasiAbstract, RSStockdale, Rachel Cakes, Randomdoorknob, Ranhalt, Rantinghuman, RattleMan, Rayshon, Reedy, Rehevkor, Renosecond, Richfife, Rico2099, Ritchy, Rjwilmsi, Rm w a vu, RoadDogXVIII, Roaring Siren, RobJ1981, RobertHeadley, Rockysmile11, Ronark, RoyBoy, Rtkat3, Ryan the Game Master, Ryulong, SAGE01, Saberwyn, Sagaciousuk, Sambangs, Sarujo, Scarface123456789, Sdphost, Seto19, ShadowHntr, Shimgray, Shirt58, SideshowBob99, Silver Edge, Sithlordpetey, Sjones23, SkyWalker, Smash, Smgold92, Smijes08, Sn0wflake, Speed Air Man, SpikeJones, Squishy Vic, Stardust8212, Sugar Bear, Supermorff, Svetovid, TAnthony, TITROTU, TJ Spyke, TMC1982, TMNTfan, TOkKa, Tarrun, Tcclives23, Tedder, Teenwriter, TenPoundHammer, Th1rt3en, Thanos6, The Rogue Penguin, The S, The Thing That Should Not Be, The beuks, TheCoffee, Thefro552, Thinker222, ThuranX, Tiger Trek, Tigermave, Timothy989, Tommy Gun, Tony Myers, Tregoweth, Trmptboy2007, Trogga, TwilightLink, Typhoon966, UltimatePyro, UnfriendlyFire, Unkelspike, Unknown Dragon, Urness.sam, VG Cats Tipe 2, Vanwhistler, Vrray Sockpuppet1, WARendfeld, WHeimbigner, WesleyDodds, Whorchatasoto, WikHead, Wildervageta, Will Decay, Xargon666x6, XenoSphere, Xeon25, Yanksox, Ynhockey, Youal, Zarsus, Zeropunk16, Zidane4028, 1141 anonymous edits

Sunshine (2007 film) *Source*: http://en.wikipedia.org/w/index.php?oldid=458125897 *Contributors*: AC+79 3888, Ahpook, Alansohn, Alaric Deschain, Alientraveller, Alton, Amdyrowlands, An Useok, Analoguedragon, Anchoress, Andrzejbanas, Andy120290, Andycjp, Angel caboodle, AniRaptor2001, Anonymous Dissident, ApusChin, Aramir, Auz, Bailey, Barvinok, Beardo, Benk115, BigAl2k6, Bignole, Bilsonius, BlackTerror, Blacktoxic, Bobfr08, Bobo192, Bofum, Boing! said Zebedee, Booksworm, Bovineboy2008, Brandmeister (old), Brandt Luke Zorn, Brencar, Brinlong, Bronks, Bryan Derksen, Burtbarnacle, Butseriouslyfolks, C.Fred, CO, CSOCSOCSO, CambridgeBayWeather, Causa sui, CaveatLector, Ceejayoz, Chaweb, Closedmouth, CokeBear, Colvija9472, Commo1, Creature, Cyclades, DJRaveN4x, DOSGuy, Da Joe, Danleary25, Darkwind, Darrenhusted, DaveGorman, David Gerard, Davidhorman, Deuteriumcomet, Dieter Weber, Divinedegenerate, Dogah, DoktorDec, DragonflySixtyseven, Drat, Duncan, Emurphy42, Enpitsu, Entrybreak, Enviroboy, Erik, Erolos, Esss, Evanreyes, Eventhorizon55, Ewa5050, Facepaint1, Farle275, Fatzebra, Fayenatic london, Fish and karate, Fourthords, Fredrick day, FredrikLähnn, GameLegend, Gargile, Garion96, Geoff B, Gfoley4, Gilliam, Giraffedata, Gnfnrf, Greenrd, Groggy Dice, Gunslinger, Gwynand, HJensen, Halo2, Hamiltondaniel, Haon 2.0, Hede2000, Heirpixel, Hellbus, Hellcat fighter, Hibana, Hobartimus, HorrorMonkey, Hurball, IMLX, Icerve, Imaginary heroes, InspectorSands, Irazmus, IrisKawling, Irishguy, Iscaria, Jaiminthakrar, Jal11497, James Emtage, Jamhin4, Jeepday, Jimd, Jmackaerospace, John Millikin, Jon.bux, Jonathanosim, Jonny-mt, Jordanceltiscfan, Joshfriel, Jpgwriter, Js2081, Kbthompson, Kintetsubuffalo, Kitchybop, Koavf, Kontar, Kronnang Dunn, Kstraka, Kuralyov, Kurrupt3d, Lambyte, Lightmouse, Little Jimmy, Liyster, Lynea, MRSC, Madman, Mallanox, MarcoTolo, MarphyBlack, Martarius, Master Deusoma, Matthew, Maury Markowitz, Melty girl, Mentalpez, Mgiganteus1, Mike Peel, Millahnna, Million Little Gods, Molix, Monchberter, MoraSique, Moviees, Myscrnnm, Nehrams2020, Notjim, Nymf, Olyus, Omeganumber, OnBeyondZebrax, OneVeryBadMan, Ordosingularis, Oxymoron83, ParalysedBeaver, Patriarch, Patrick, PatrickOfLondon, Peter Dorey, Phil Sandifer, Pixelface, Platypus222, Populus, Portalthinking, Powerofmayhem, President David Palmer, Prodego, Quuxplusone, RODERICKMOLASAR, Ranieldule, Ratter, RedKage, Ricky81682, Riki, Riyuky, Rje, Rjwilmsi, Rlove, RobNS, Roger Roger, RyanGFilm, SGGH, SQGibbon, Salamurai, SanGatiche, Sbrockway, SchueyFan, Scorpinok123, Scottmacpherson, Sean gorter, SeanLegassick, Seb Patrick, Sebastian Goll, Shaneo632, Shnoodles, Silpion, Sin-man, Sjones23, Smoran69, Smurrayinchester, Sockatume, Sonicdeathmonkey, Spidergareth, Steve, Stevouk, Subdolous, Sunshinefan07, Swpb, TKD, Tabanger, Tassedethe, Teknolyze, Th1rt3en, Thanos777, The Anome, The penfool, TheCosmicFrog, Thief12, Tiktokman, Tim!, Time Slayer, TomEatsCake, Tommyt, Tony Sidaway, Tr8917, Tregoweth, Treybien, Turkeyphant, Typhoonchaser, TøM, VaGuy1973, Vancera, Vanished user 03, Vckeating, Vinnivince, Vjamesv, Voyagerfan5761, Wahlin, Ward3001, Wiher, WildlifeAnalysis, Winston365, Woohookitty, Wrightbus, XJamRastafire, Yettie0711, Yobmod, Yovinedelcielo, Zandperl, Zarcadia, Zelphar, ZephyrWind, ZeroJanvier, Zu Ninja, 용박인생, 724 anonymous edits

Fantastic Four: Rise of the Silver Surfer *Source*: http://en.wikipedia.org/w/index.php?oldid=459533362 *Contributors*: 1chin45, 28421u2232nfenfcenc, 29Palms.Marine, A man alone, AAA!, AJR, Acebloo, AcerJayde20, Aericanwizard, Ahoerstemeier, Akcarver, Albino2, AlexDotta, Alientraveller, AlistairMcMillan, Amarkov, Andrwsc, Andrzejbanas, Antandrus, Apostrophe, Arcayne, Arienh4, Arthur Rubin, Asaspades, Aswells, Atb129, Auronlupin, Autocracy, Bacteria, Barraki, BazookaJoe, Beto, Betty Logan, Bignole, Bingo45, Bishop2, Bkeshad, Blackmetalbaz, BlueShrek, Boltaco, Bongwarrior, Bossk-Office, Bovineboy2008, Bradtcordeiro, Briaboru, Brian Kendig, Brianstr4, Brockfreak007, Brwest06, Buchanan-Hermit, Burks821, Bvbear92, CBM, CJMylentz, Can't sleep, clown will eat me, CanadianLinuxUser, Captain Infinity, Captain america2020, Catgut, Centrx, Chad19r, Chancemichaels, Charmed fanatic, Chavando, Cheesemeister, Cherry, Chris McFeely, Chriselliswest, Chrishmt0423, ChristTrekker, Cigammagicwizard, Cobaltcigs, CommonsDelinker, ConradPino, ContiAWB, Cooldude3240, CovenantD, Creepy Crawler, Crisco 1492, Crownjewel82, Curefreak, Dahamsta7, Darkness2005, DarthBinky, David Gerard, Dbarlett, Dburnes1, Dee4leeds, Defaultdotxbe, Dekkanar, Deposuit, Diabound, Discospinster, Dismas, Disneyrocks13, Dl2000, Doc Comic, DoctorWho42, Doczilla, Donmike10, Donteatyellowsnow, Dorgana, DoubleCross, Dr. McGrew, Dragon1027, DragonChi, Drc79, Dubbya9, Duke33, EVula, Ebyabe, Eddie's Teddy, Edgar181, EgyptianSushi, Elenseel, ElmoRox, Enpitsu, EntChickie, Eran of Arcadia, Eric Wester, Erik, ErinKM, Esrever, Evice, FJPB, Fabianmty, Fastlane101, Faviang, FigmentJedi, Firetrap9254, FrankCostanza, Freemarket, Freshh, Fritz Saalfeld, Fukatsu 28, FullyClothedMike, Furuba9, FutureNJGov, GPanesarJatt, Gabriel Duvall, Gamerstats, Garion96, Geeness, Geniac, German barrero, GhostStalker, Gigasonic, GoingBatty, Gonevart, Good Olfactory, Granpuff, GroovySandwich, Guat6, Guerby, Gurko, Guthrie, Guybrush, Gwr2004, HD123, Harish, HarleyHyde2386, Havok, Hellboy42, Hellmistress, Hello32020, Henrithecute, Hero62, Hippi ippi, Horkana, Hotwiki, Hu12, IKato, Ian-turner77, Iann Lee, IllaZilla, Ilovefoxes, InShaneee, InfamousPrince, Invincible Ninja, J Greb, JLaTondre, JNW, JQF, Jaardon, Jac16888, Jak-Esz, JamesAM, JamesBWatson, JarlaxleArtemis, Jaw710, JayKeaton, Jayhawk of Justice, Jdremix, Jess Cully, Jevansen, Jheath2011, Jhenderson777, Jkid4, John K, Johnny542, Jojhutton, JokerNick, Joowwww, Joren, Journeyman, Joylock, Jrockley, Jump Guru, KNHaw, Kbdank71, Kchishol1970, Kcordina, Kellymar, Kilo-Lima, KingMorpheus, Kitch, KnowledgeOfSelf, Koavf, Kollision, Kolon3442, Konczewski, Korny O'Near, Kouichikun, Kreternal, Krylonblue83, Kungfuadam, LEX LETHAL, Laydee Lyca, LedgerJoker, Lee M, Legedevin, LeonMcNichol, Leoni2, Level, Lg16spears, Liesse00, LifeStroke420, Lord Bodak, Lord Hammu, Lord Sinestro, Lost king chro, MASTER178, Magnocrusher2007, Makeamovie, Maple Leaf, Marcd30319, Marcus Brute, MarkSutton, MarnetteD, Martarius, Marwan soft, Master Deusoma, Mat wang, Maximum power, Mclay19, Mcothier, Meatwod, Mechagio, Mhking, Midnightdreary, Mike Selinker, Mild Bill Hiccup, MinHarris32, Misza13, Mixtapeguru, Mjrmtg, Morwen, Moss56, Ms. Sarita, Mtelewicz, MuZemike, N00basbenhur, Naruto134, Naruto627886, NawlinWiki, Nehrams2020, Neopets team, Nick Cooper, Nighend, Nonagonal Spider, NorthernThunder, Nousernamesleft, ONEder Boy, Obi-WanKenobi-2005, Ohnoitsjamie, Olivier, Onorem, Oosh, Ophois, Oshaberi, Otto4711, OwenX, Panelmyth107, Paulmac2k, Pcg13, Pejorative.majeure, Peter M Dodge, Phydend, Pimpjoe esb, Pixelface, Pogokidd2, Poison the Well, Postdlf, Powerbomb1411, Powerofjuju, Prashanthns, Prem555, Pseudomonas, Psyklax, Qbking, QuasiAbstract, Quentin X, R'n'B, RabidJackal, Ranhalt, RasputinAXP, RattleMan, Ravish123, RealityTelevisionFan, Relly Komaruzaman, Rhino131, Richfife, Rilbiz, Rje, Rjwilmsi, Robbie098, Robertvan1, Romans1423, Rtkat3, Rubber cat, Rugratfan1025, Runewiki777, Ruyn, Ryankat25, Ryneweir, Ryulong, SJP, Sajman12, Salamurai, SamX13, Sarregouset, Scarlet buckeye, Sesshomaru, Shabook, Shadow Android, ShadowMan1od, Sharkface217, Shooter16101, SigmaEpsilon, Silenceofthelamb, Silent Tom, Silver Surfer, SixFourThree, SkyWalker, Smokizzy, Smyd286, Snowman Guy, So what, Somemoron, Somno, SonicNirvana, Sp8d8, SpikeJones, SportsEditor, Staffwaterboy, Starstriker7, Steam5, Stoffelofferson, Sukecchi, Sundevilesq, Supertwins, TAE15,000,000, THobern, TK421, TKD, TMC1982, Tahu90, Tank2046, Teacheorgy, Techplore, Tectar, TehPhil, Tekkenzone, Tell-Tale Ghost, Tenebrae, Terry harris, Thaimissions2006, Thanos6, That Asian Guy, The 80s chick, The Giant Puffin, The Hungarian, The Last Mystery, The MARVEL, The MeXecutioner, The Rogue Penguin, TheBalance, TheManWhoLaughs, TheMovieBuff, Theleftorium, Themeparkfanatic, Think outside the box, ThinkBlue, ThuranX, TigerK 69, TijhofGraphics, Tmdscore, Tohd8BohaithuGh1, Tomkurts, Tony Sidaway, Toorayay, Torridon1, Toughpigs, Toxicroak, Tregoweth, Tuberculosisness, Tukkaatje, Tvfan000, Twisterdk, TylerXKJ, Typhoon966, Tyw7, Ukepedia, VG Cats Tipe 2, Vader200591, Veracious Rey, Vmaldia, Voidvector, Voldemort, Vranak, WTRiker, Wagino 20100516, Ward3001, Wheelboss, Whispering, Willgee, Witwicky555, Woohookitty, WzMG5LJ, X958, Xiahou, Yinyanglightningthrash, Yjwong, Youngandrestless, Zandperl, Zidonuke, Zooba, Zu Ninja, Zythe, 1192 anonymous edits

The Nanny Diaries (film) *Source*: http://en.wikipedia.org/w/index.php?oldid=448647926 *Contributors*: Alexandru Stanoi, Alienlifeformz, All Hallow's Wraith, AndrewHowse, Andycjp, Are You The Cow Of Pain?, Beardo, Beeswax07, Bencey, Bobo192, Brian1979, Bsadowski1, Ckatz, Clamster5, Colonies Chris, Crotchety Old Man, Crzycheetah, DJ Clayworth, Daniel Case, Dannywein, Darrenhusted, David Gerard, Deanb, Destron Commander, Djflem, Edwtie, Erik, FMAFan1990, Ferrischan, Gatur, GoldFlower, Guat6, HJH Lady Renegade, HMFS, Hu12, Intractable, Iridescent, ItsTheClimb17, Jack O'Lantern, Jeremy Butler, JessPink, Jiggz84, Jnelson09, Johncatsoulis, Jonathan.s.kt, Koavf, La Lovely, LinkToddMcLovinMontana, Magioladitis, Mattbrundage, Moogle10000, MusiCitizen, Myscrnnm, Nehrams2020, Nnxion, Nricardo, Nytimes19992000, Pastoryam12, Photo me2004, Pink rose108, Pixelface, Propaniac, Radoslaw10, Rje, Robertvan1, Rockysmile11, Ryan man101, Santryl, Sarahjane10784, Schildwaechter, Tabletop, The Wrong Man, TheMovieBuff, Thomas-gough, Tinton5, TracyLinkEdnaVelmaPenny, Treybien, USN1977, Underaround, Wildhartlivie, 155 anonymous edits

Battle for Terra *Source*: http://en.wikipedia.org/w/index.php?oldid=454312738 *Contributors*: Ahkilinc, All Hallow's Wraith, Andrzejbanas, BD2412, Ben-Bopper, Bencey, BigBang616, Bovineboy2008, Chaosdruid, Chowbok, Christianster94, Chuunen Baka, ContinuityMaster, Djbj16, Erik, Esn, Fandraltastic, Fierce Beaver, Fiftytwo thirty, Forrestdfuller, Glamking, Goa103,

GrandDrake, Grandpafootsoldier, Griz44, Heighliner10191, HidariMigi, Hoborage, Holothurion, Homesun, JQF, Jagoperson, Jeturcotte, KnowBuddy, Krams, LaCp15, MikeAllen, Monkiejump, OnBeyondZebrax, Ost316, Plastikspork, Quentin X, Rockerfan37, Ronhjones, Scoutjd, Secret Saturdays, Seeleschneider, Shining.Star, Smooth Nick, TRBP, Tabletop, TechLight, Thantos963, The 80s chick, Thomas Blomberg, Tree387, Trivialist, Valkyrie Red, Varlaam, Websurfer246, WhatGuy, Wikibarista, Williamsburgland, 139 anonymous edits

Street Kings *Source*: http://en.wikipedia.org/w/index.php?oldid=456798090 *Contributors*: 21655, 6afraidof7, A Nobody, AN(Ger), Acroterion, Aesopos, Al.locke, Aleenf1, Andreas S., Andrzejbanas, AntiDAD, Ashish j29, AskFranz, Atomiser2003, Beast from da East, Beren, Bertcocaine, Big Bird, Big Money420, Bobo192, Bpauley, BrownHairedGirl, Canterbury Tail, Captain Cheeks, Catamorphism, Chris the speller, CollisionCourse, Cteist, Cubs Fan, CyberSkull, DStoykov, DamageW, DarKnight80, Darrenhusted, Dekisugi, DepressedPer, Dibol, Djbj16, Djln, DropShadow, Ecozonz, Ej926, Ejfetters, Erik, Escape Orbit, Ettrig, Ewshannon, Excirial, Explicit, Fabish Boaitey, Falcon9x5, Feudonym, Finchsnows, FlieGerFaUstMe262, FrankRizzo2006, Freaky n Ruff, Fæ, Gamer472, Gamma Spelazi, Garion96, Ghost215, Girolamo Savonarola, Guat6, Hu12, Huaiwei, Icesea, InfamousPrince, J.delanoy, JHunterJ, JNW, Jake Wartenberg, JukoFF, Keilana, Killnorth, Klknoles, Lazylaces, LedgendGamer, Lilac Soul, Live and Die 4 Hip Hop, MJBurrage, Martarius, Matthiashess, Max.sicherman, Mcanmoocanu, Mccajor, Mdy2k5, Mealy, Mgolaghaee, Midnight man, Miquonranger03, MisterHand, Mortal118, Movieguru2006, Mrblondnyc, Myscrnnm, Nehrams2020, NellieBly, Nocargo, Nunh-huh, OOODDD, Obi-WanKenobi-2005, Obriensg1, Patrick, PinkPsycho, Pixelface, Propaganda328, Pseudomonas, Qconroe, Qwerty Binary, R.M.Hale, Random Hero 791, Random User 937494, Razorflame, Rcspirit, Repmax, Rodwa4, STATicVerseatide, Safydadon, Sakletare, Scjessey, Seahorseruler, Shannon Tucker, Shawis, ShelfSkewed, Skier Dude, Slysplace, Spartan, Staffwaterboy, Standfest, TaerkastUA, The Garden Gnome, The Hungarian, The JPS, TheOnlyOne12, Theman81, Therocsfinished, Tlynne2002, Tohd8BohaithuGh1, Tomgibbons, Transity, Varlaam, Wiikipedian, Wildroot, Woohookitty, Yasiranzar, 516 anonymous edits

The Loss of a Teardrop Diamond *Source*: http://en.wikipedia.org/w/index.php?oldid=458084197 *Contributors*: AN(Ger), AlbertSM, AndrewHowse, Anthony Appleyard, Benatfleshofthestars, Bluejay Young, Cartoon Boy, Djbj16, DoubleCross, Dravecky, EdHavens, Ekabhishek, Erik, Frank Bongers, Fylgiar, G.-M. Cupertino, GTBacchus, HenkvD, InfamousPrince, J.delanoy, Jaydec, Movieguru2006, Rjwilmsi, RottenPotato, Shining.Star, SkyWalker, Staka, Stardust8212, Steve, Tjmayerinsf, Treybien, Tryptofeng, TubularWorld, Varlaam, Viking59, 40 anonymous edits

Push (2009 film) *Source*: http://en.wikipedia.org/w/index.php?oldid=459670012 *Contributors*: Adamtheaffman@hotmail.com, AlexDBNB, All Hallow's Wraith, Andrzejbanas, Angelica K, Arcayne, Arch angel gabriele, Ashlaly98, Astanhope, Axxonnfire, Basit147, Beardo, Bgs022, Bignole, Blotski, Bovineboy2008, Braffmaster, Bsadowski1, Can't sleep, clown will eat me, Ccacsmss, Ced lewis, Cedy 30, Chris the speller, Christianster94, Ckatz, Closedmouth, Coinmanj, Collegebookworm, CommonAnomaly, Crazysunshine, Cubs Fan, Cubs197, CunningWizard, DMCer, Daedae, DarkNITE, Darkyninja, Darrenhusted, DavidK93, Debresser, DepressedPer, Dh993, Discospinster, Djbj16, DoctorJest, Doniago, Donmike10, Download, Dysepsion, Egmontaz, Emperor, Epbr123, Erik, Evans1982, Fastily, Fierce Beaver, FlieGerFaUstMe262, Fourthords, FrankRizzo2006, Franklin Jebaraj, Giggletowns, Girolamo Savonarola, GlassCobra, GoingBatty, Gracelessally, Grandpafootsoldier, Greenrd, GroovyandPears, H.ehsaan, HealerSpirit, Hoof Hearted, Huntthetroll, Hyju, Hyzera, Ih.j.321, InfamousPrince, ItsTheClimb17, J.delanoy, Jal11497, Jamesbanesmith, Jbrickwood, Jevansen, Jhsounds, Jimagnus, Jimmieman, Jkm51, JoeLoeb, John of Reading, Johnnysugar, Joowwww, JoshuaGolbez, JoshuaZ, Jwas65, Kalaong, Kamots, Knight123, Kubigula, Lampak, Larrybob, Larts83, Legionsynch, Leikfaz, Lg16spears, Liav321, Liberaler Konservativer, Livethir, Lone twin, LonerXL, Ltljltlj, Macy, Maestro25, Malenien, Marasmusine, Martarius, Mdraus93, Mifter, Millahnna, Moemoe21, Mongol, Monkeytheboy, MovieManiac93, Mr. Chicago, Mr.Grave, Mrnatural, Noble12345, Ophois, Otolemur crassicaudatus, Palmer5000, Paperella21, Parsecboy, Piano non troppo, Pictureuploader, Pnpanchamia, RJHall, Radosław10, Raiku Samiyaza, Random User 937494, Reflections of Memory, Riavar, Richardcavell, Richrakh0876, Rmallins, Rob, Ryulong, Sabi76, Salamurai, Sdrawkcab, SchuminWeb, Scorpion99110, Shadowjams, Shoodinho52, Skillthknuth411, Skier Dude, SkyWalker, SnakeChess5, Space Dementina, Staka, Stargat, Steve3849, SuperFlash101, Swikid, SwisterTwister, Sylar07, TRTX, Tassedethe, Teiladnam, TenTonParasol, Th1rt3en, TheMovieBuff, Tophy, Treybien, Trogga, TubularWorld, Typhoon966, Tyrasibion, UKER, UNIT A4B1, Userblame324, VzirZ, Wondyfan, Woohookitty, XMattingly, Zombie433, 543 anonymous edits

The Losers (film) *Source*: http://en.wikipedia.org/w/index.php?oldid=459608999 *Contributors*: 3TimesALoser, 88Flowers, Agent neo 007, AgentSkrocks, Akcarver, Allecwilliams, Andrzejbanas, Anechoic Man, Anime4international, Aranea Mortem, Arsvita734, Artoasis, BLGM5, BMax15, Beemer69, BenjyC95, Blotski, Bobby122, Bovineboy2008, BrokenSphere, CameronTGD, Ceauntay59, Comayagua99, Cubs Fan, Da gr8 1, Dravecky, ERJ1024, Edlitz36, Emperor, Erik, Eumolpo, Faded, FiGhT 12, Finland911, FrankRizzo2006, GoingBatty, Gstein, Gunmetal Angel, Hehehahaheha, Horkana, InfamousPrince, J Greb, J appleseed2, Jaybling, Jdemp42, Jordanceltiesfan, KathrynLybarger, Kidlittle, Killnorth, Kintetsubuffalo, Koavf, Kolpie123, Krashlandon, LOL, Martarius, MikeAllen, Mojo15, New World Man, Nycteris86, O.neill.kid, PM800, PaPaLuigi, Portillo, ProtoBuster, ProveIt, Ranjithsutari, Realitystarr24, Reservoireddog, Rtdixon86, Salamurai, Santryl, Sara11028, Sings-With-Spirits, SirJibby, Skomorokh, Snevetsm, Sp33dyphil, Sparkdex, Steam5, Stewggrifin, Superman98962, TAE15,000,000, Tbhotch, The Mink Ermine Fox, The russians, TheMovieBuff, Tom Danson, Tommy2010, Tony1, Toxin1000, Travisharlem, Twinsday, Typeriuskirk, Typhoon966, Varlaam, Vegaswikian, Wayne Slam, Xeworlebi, ZPM, 234 anonymous edits

Scott Pilgrim vs. the World *Source*: http://en.wikipedia.org/w/index.php?oldid=459567205 *Contributors*: 10metreh, 11cookeaw1, 1234r00t, 1Matt20, Aawood, AbsoluteGleek92, Access Denied, Acidtechblood101, Adwiii, AffectionApe, Afkatk, Agrumer, AlainV, All Hallow's Wraith, Amibiased, Anaxial, Andrzejbanas, Angel caboodle, Arbero, Archaeo, Areaseven, Asarauli005, Astproxy, Asian.piano.dude, Atum World, Aylesburyape, BKMastah, Badblokebob, Baringully, Barry margolin, Ben-Bopper, Benatfleshofthestars, Bencey, Betty Logan, Billyboy01, Binkyuk, Birkenburg, Blackaqualad'snappybodyhair, Bob Castle, Bobliveson, Booboobear123, Bovineboy2008, CJMylentz, Cameron Scott, Canterbury Tail, Carbo45, Carlson288, Cashie, Cherryblossom1982, Chowbok, CommonsDelinker, CosmicJester, Counny, Cpt ricard, Crash52, DARTH SIDIOUS 2, Dallan007, Dancter, Danlev, Darkness2005, Darknessthecurse, Dashiel, Dem1995, Designerofdoom, Diannaa, Doc Strange, Dochengal, DocumentN, Doniago, Dornbiker, Dp76764, Dr heartless, DrJimothyCatface, Drpickem, Dylancraigboyes, E-Quizative, E2eamon, Eddiejake, Erik, Ewa5050, Fall Of Darkness, FrankRizzo2006, Fritz Saalfeld, Fryn, Funandtrvl, G009q, GDallimore, GageSkidmore, Gen77c, Geoff B, Gimmetoo, GoingBatty, Goldenboy, Goodbye Galaxy, Goth67, GrantyO, Gu1dry, Guinea pig warrior, Hairolfitri, HathawayThere, Havermayer, Hectorz111, Hellboy42, Hongyunsub, Horkana, Hrcolyer, Hullaballoo Wolfowitz, Hyju, Hyliad, I need a name, Immblueversion, Iota, Iridius, Irrypride, ItsTheClimb17, JForget, JaffaCakeLover, Jagged 85, JasonAQuest, Jayunderscorezero, JeffJonez, JeffreySwate, John Pannozzi, Johnc69, Johnlongbond, Jonathan.ian.ellis, Jseipel, Kajervi, Kanebell Assistant, Kchishol1970, Khazar, KieferSkunk, KimiSan, KingRaven44, Kitsunegami, Koavf, Kolma, Kronnang Dunn, Kubrickrules, Kuriboh600, Kuru, Kville2010, L Kensington, Lbr123, Leader Vladimir, Lebreadbox, LilHelpa, LtPowers, Luminum, Madchester, Magnius, Manofiorn, Marchingknight11, Marco Guzman, Jr, Marcus Brute, Martarius, Matt FJ, May Cause Dizziness, Mdedrick, Merqurial, Metao, Mice never shop, Michaelpamon828, Michig, MikeAllen, Mild Bill Hiccup, Millahnna, Minimac, Minna Sora no Shita, Misterkillboy, Mr. Chicago, MrBrightisde, Muldoon X9, MultipleTom, My76Strat, NBbeauty, NathanLands, Nbdelboy, One-Man Army Corps, OnePt618, Ordago, Orphan Wiki, Owatonnaredhayden, PM800, Paiint, ParadiseHunter, Patrick, Perthmonsit, Peter Karlsen, Phlegat, Pol098, Pol430, Prezbo, Prolog, ProtoBuster, Pumpkinking0192, Q Ramona, Qszet, Randileigh, RealAmericanHero, Reaper Eternal, Redranger241, Rehevkor, RicNrikk, Rich Farmbrough, Richiekim, Rillian, Rje, Robojorge, Ronhjones, Ru-G Corp., Russelleh, Rusted AutoParts, SCARECROW, Salamurai, SavageEdit, ScottMHoward, Shalmaneser88, SkyWalker, Slon02, Some guy, Spitfire, SudoGhost, T, Teafico, Tednikelli, Tekkaman, Teknolyze, Th1rt3en, Thanos777, The Thing That Should Not Be, TheIguana, TheMadcapLaugh, TheSilleGuy, Thirty-seven, Tiller54, Tim!, Timeoin, Tiswaser, Tommy2010, Travisharlem, Treybien, TriiipleThreat, Trogga, Truffles64, UDScott, Uncle Milty, Varanwal, Varlaam, VerasGunn, Viewdrix, Wade1210, Wayne Slam, Wbender14, WhisperToMe, Whosaysicantdance, Whywhenwhohow, WikiKong, Willy james, Wolfpax50, Wonchop, Youvebeenthundersturck, Yuefairchild, ZPM, Zap Rowsdower, Zephyr surfer, Τασουλα, Лишь человек, 831 anonymous edits

Puncture (film) *Source*: http://en.wikipedia.org/w/index.php?oldid=454282087 *Contributors*: Bovineboy2008, InfamousPrince, Lacon432, Mcclane2010, Peppage, Providern, Rhstowell, Shining.Star, The Editor 155, Treesrule, Vipinhari, 22 anonymous edits

Captain America: The First Avenger *Source*: http://en.wikipedia.org/w/index.php?oldid=459710236 *Contributors*: '63 Chesapeake, -5-, 19jduryea, 4twenty42o, 5 albert square, 95hlopez, A&ofan75, Acebloo, Acefarrukh, AdamDeanHall, Agustinaldo, AlexDotta, All Hallow's Wraith, Americanhero, And1987, Antovolk, Anythingspossibleforapossible, Arimis, Ashliveslove, Beadmatrix, Bencey, Bignole, Bobanmertiopsis, BornonJune8, Bovineboy2008, Boycool42, Bradley0110, Byakuya Truelight, Cameron Scott, CaptainCanada, Captaincool9496, Carlkevad, Chickenmonkey, ClintMalpaso, Clintp, Crazy runner, Cs-wolves, DMC30, Danratedrko, Darkwarriorblake, DavidJNock, Diabound, Dnwwn, Dodgerblue777, Dreadstar, Eagc7, Emperor, EoGuy, Erik, Facetoface333, Fandraltastic, Farpointer, Fdwar, Festermunk, Floydgeo, FormerIP, Fortdj33, Fyyer, Garrisonsurg, Gary Panser, Ged UK, Ghmyrtle, GhostFace1234, GoingBatty, Guy546, Hackidoo, HalfElfDragon, HarDNox, Hattiedog, Hawaiian717, Hellboy42, Hyju, InfamousPrince, J Greb, Jadrago, Jagfan71, Jal11497, Jamesc6969, Jar789, Jaybling, Jboncha, Jclemens, Jdcollins13, Jedi94, Jeff G., Jhenderson777, Jimknut, Jinglesthetiger, JoeLoeb, Joeboyle1987, John Smith (test), Jp8636, JustPhil, Kaxil, Kchishol1970, Killy mcgee, Kitsunegami, Konczewski, Krevans, Kuralyov, L Kensington, Lacon432, Leader Vladimir, Legend, Lg16spears, LilHelpa, Little Jimmy, LockLockBoy, Looney Guy, Luis1791, Lukep913, Lyght, Maggot 10, Mahewa, Majinsnake, Marcd30319, MarnetteD, Martarius, MattParker 119, Mattman71481, Mdriver1981, Mike Searson, MikeAllen, Millahnna, Milojthatch, Mistery Spectre, MrEmoDuck, MrRuidavets, Muhandes, Mythical Curse, NBbeauty, Namanbapna, NightmareDali, Nightscream, Noelba, Noformation, Nutiketaiel, Obi-WanKenobi-2005, Oknazevad, Orange Suede Sofa, Parousie, PeeJay2K3, Peppage, Peregrine Fisher, Philip Trueman, Planewalker Dave, Pleonic, Polisher of Cobwebs, Pottyaboutpotter1, Prem555, President Rhapsody, PsychoticLoner, Psychotron71, R'n'B, Reaper Eternal, Redranger241, Richiekim, Rigelsanchez, Rockysmile11, Rreagan007, Rtkat3, Rusted AutoParts, Salamurai, Sarahjanegrun, Sb1990, Sesshomaru, Shabby, Sij747, Sjones23, Skeleton 777, Skyrocket, Slogical, Snugalfritz, Spanglej, Spidey104, SquattyPottyJockey, Sullross, Sumampouw, Superman98962, TRON 27, Tbhotch, Tenebrae, The Filmaker, The Iceman2288, The Stick Man, Thegreat100, Thuanho, TomorrowWeDie, TravisBernard, Trevor Burnham, TriiipleThreat, Trivialist, Truthanado, Twispace3000, TylerDurdenUMD, UDScott, UbZaR, Ucucha, UnicornTapestry, Vader47000, Vapour, Varanwal, Vranak, Wayne Slam, Weedle McHairybug, WesleyDodds, Whywhenwhohow, WikiFew, WikiInformante, Wikieditor14, Wikifan12345, Wildroot, Willy105, Winter04, Xeworlebi, Xizer, XululuX, ZEVANATION, Zandperl, Zythe, Δ, 553 anonymous edits

What's Your Number? *Source*: http://en.wikipedia.org/w/index.php?oldid=459723013 *Contributors*: 19jduryea, All Hallow's Wraith, AmericanMovieBuff, Bbb23, Bovineboy2008, BreakingDexter, CalebEnglish, Charbroil, Court1286, Cubs Fan, Davejones33, Erik, Erpert, FollowGuard, FrankRizzo2006, Ice 72, InfamousPrince, Jennifergates, John, Khosein84, Koavf, Lugnuts, Mat wang, MikeAllen, Mild Bill Hiccup, Mr.Linderman, Newworldinline, Nightscream, Raze, Rcsprinter123, Rich Farmbrough, Ryulong, SefHerman, Ser Amantio di Nicolao, Shining.Star, Sofffie7, Starswept, Storiessomewhere, SummerPhD, Tbhotch, Tenebrae, TheValentineBros, WikHead, Woohookitty, 120 anonymous edits

The Avengers (2012 film) *Source*: http://en.wikipedia.org/w/index.php?oldid=459678733 *Contributors*: -5-, 19jduryea, @pple, AdamDeanHall, Airplaneman, Akerans, Alakazam, Alphius, Americanhero, Anakhin, Antovolk, Anythingspossibleforapossible, Arimis, Art1991, Artoasis, Barsoomian, Bassam Jallad, Bencey, Bobynboy, BornonJune8, Bovineboy2008, Boycool42,

Byakuya Truelight, CBcleaner, Calabe1992, Calmer Waters, Cartoon Boy, CityOfSilver, Cliff smith, ComicFan123, CommonsDelinker, Contractor815, Cumbiagermen, Darkwarriorblake, Deadlyreaper, Delovelyjenn, Dewey Finn, Dictabeard, DigiFluid, Disney22, Drbreznjev, Eagc7, Eamonn81, Edgar181, English06, Erik, EurekaLott, Famousdog, Fanaction2031, Fandraltastic, Faramarz, Faster2010, Fhb3, Foretboy3000, Fortdj33, Franklin Jebaraj, FromtheWordsofBR, Fuhghettaboutit, GAndy, Gamegeek99, GoingBatty, Golden pigeon, Guidorulz, Hans Dunkelberg, Heartsndaggers, Heenan73, Hellboy42, Humble user, Hydracyclops, InfamousPrince, Ivor Stoughton, J Greb, JDspeeder1, JLaTondre, Jaros428, Jasca Ducato, Jauerback, Jclemens, Jedi94, Jerky Chid, Jhenderson777, Jimscrooge, JosiahSandhu, Jp8636, Jsharpminor, Killerinstinct9, Killy mcgee, KingBable123, Kirujoy, Kjacket0, Kraichaikaeo, LaCp93, Lacon432, Levdr1lostpassword, Likitdi, Live Light, Lord Brixton, MC10, Marek69, Markm62, Markunator, Matanui1326, Materialscientist, Matthewakisan, Mephistophelian, MichaelQSchmidt, MikeAllen, Mild Bill Hiccup, Millahnna, MillerLogan, Milomilk, Milwaukee Patriot, Mistery Spectre, Mlaurore2, Mr.Fennoy75, MrWii000, Mvincec, Nenov Digga, Nightscream, Nodnarb42, Nokaduthodil, Nullveer, ONEder Boy, Oknazevad, Orange Suede Sofa, Osubuckeyeguy, Pedro Felipe, Planewalker Dave, Playhouse76, Polisher of Cobwebs, Pshent, QAZproWSX, R'n'B, Rdfox 76, Redranger241, Regge robban2, Reyk, Richiekim, Rio de Janiero God, Rusted AutoParts, SBAAM, Sakletare, Scientific29, ScottSteiner, Sessie24, Silversurfer06, Simpsonguy1987, SirJibby, Sjones23, SkitvsSketch, Slon02, Some jerk on the Internet, SteveyCap, Suitmonster, Sullross, TMC1982, Tenebrae, The Iceman2288, TheHip14, Thinking of England, ThuranX, Tikopowii, Timekeeper12345, TriiipleThreat, Trogga, Trusilver, Twitdiac380, Valkyrie Red, Victory93, Vrenator, WhatGuy, WikiEditor44, WolfRisingSun, Wolverinewing, Woofygoodbird, World Cinema Writer, Writ Keeper, Xeworlebi, Zntrip, Zythe, Δ, 616 anonymous edits

Opposite Sex (TV series) *Source*: http://en.wikipedia.org/w/index.php?oldid=454333744 *Contributors*: Bearcat, Bovineboy2008, Condorjoe, CoolKatt number 99999, Crystallina, Deliriousandlost, Doczilla, Dravecky, Earthtomars, Fitfatfighter, Jennifero4u, Jh0367, John of Reading, Koavf, Kyellan, LilHelpa, MJBurrage, Madchester, Mr. Chicago, Njjh201, ONEder Boy, Pinkadelica, QuasyBoy, Rainybluesky, Rjwilmsi, Ryright, Searcher 1990, Sisyph, Spartaz, TonyTheTiger, Windsok, 15 anonymous edits

Image Sources, Licenses and Contributors

File:Captain America- The First Avenger Comic-Con Panel 2b.jpg *Source*: http://en.wikipedia.org/w/index.php?title=File:Captain_America-_The_First_Avenger_Comic-Con_Panel_2b.jpg *License*: Creative Commons Attribution-Sharealike 2.0 *Contributors*: Gryffindor

File:StanLeeChrisEvansCCJuly2011.jpg *Source*: http://en.wikipedia.org/w/index.php?title=File:StanLeeChrisEvansCCJuly2011.jpg *License*: Creative Commons Attribution-Sharealike 2.0 *Contributors*: Frederik Hermann

File:Not Another Teen Movie poster.jpg *Source*: http://en.wikipedia.org/w/index.php?title=File:Not_Another_Teen_Movie_poster.jpg *License*: Fair Use *Contributors*: *drew, J.delanoy, Melesse, Nehrams2020, Oneiros, Project FMF, Skier Dude, 2 anonymous edits

File:TPSposter.jpg *Source*: http://en.wikipedia.org/w/index.php?title=File:TPSposter.jpg *License*: Fair Use *Contributors*: Armbrust, Debresser, Johnmc, Nehrams2020, Nqnpipnr, Quentin X, Sfan00 IMG, Skier Dude

File:Cellular poster.JPG *Source*: http://en.wikipedia.org/w/index.php?title=File:Cellular_poster.JPG *License*: Fair Use *Contributors*: *drew, Nehrams2020, Sfan00 IMG, Xezbeth

File:Fierce people ver2.jpg *Source*: http://en.wikipedia.org/w/index.php?title=File:Fierce_people_ver2.jpg *License*: Fair Use *Contributors*: User:Grandpafootsoldier

File:Fantastic four poster.jpg *Source*: http://en.wikipedia.org/w/index.php?title=File:Fantastic_four_poster.jpg *License*: Fair Use *Contributors*: 17Drew, Cryptic, Fortdj33, J Greb, JYolkowski, Nehrams2020, Oden, RedSpruce, Rje, Spidey104, Tennisbm224

File:London (2005 film) Poster.jpg *Source*: http://en.wikipedia.org/w/index.php?title=File:London_(2005_film)_Poster.jpg *License*: Fair Use *Contributors*: Rockfang

File:London soundtrack.jpg *Source*: http://en.wikipedia.org/w/index.php?title=File:London_soundtrack.jpg *License*: unknown *Contributors*: Skier Dude, Solaris008

File:TMNTposterA.jpg *Source*: http://en.wikipedia.org/w/index.php?title=File:TMNTposterA.jpg *License*: Fair Use *Contributors*: Alaric Deschain, Trogga, Wknight94

File:Sunshine poster.jpg *Source*: http://en.wikipedia.org/w/index.php?title=File:Sunshine_poster.jpg *License*: Fair Use *Contributors*: Armbrust, Erik, Sfan00 IMG

Image:Sunshine 2007.jpg *Source*: http://en.wikipedia.org/w/index.php?title=File:Sunshine_2007.jpg *License*: Fair Use *Contributors*: Erik, Million Little Gods

Image:Sunshine spacesuit.jpg *Source*: http://en.wikipedia.org/w/index.php?title=File:Sunshine_spacesuit.jpg *License*: Fair Use *Contributors*: Alientraveller, Erik, Hellbus, 2 anonymous edits

File:Fantastic Four 2 Poster.jpg *Source*: http://en.wikipedia.org/w/index.php?title=File:Fantastic_Four_2_Poster.jpg *License*: Fair Use *Contributors*: Fortdj33, InfamousPrince

File:Fantastic 4 II (Jessica Alba getting makeup done 2).jpg *Source*: http://en.wikipedia.org/w/index.php?title=File:Fantastic_4_II_(Jessica_Alba_getting_makeup_done_2).jpg *License*: Creative Commons Attribution 2.0 *Contributors*: Davis Hepnar

File:Nanny-diaries-poster.jpg *Source*: http://en.wikipedia.org/w/index.php?title=File:Nanny-diaries-poster.jpg *License*: Fair Use *Contributors*: Nehrams2020

File:Battle-for-terra-poster.jpg *Source*: http://en.wikipedia.org/w/index.php?title=File:Battle-for-terra-poster.jpg *License*: Fair Use *Contributors*: Courcelles, JQF, Skier Dude

File:Street KingsMP08.jpg *Source*: http://en.wikipedia.org/w/index.php?title=File:Street_KingsMP08.jpg *License*: Fair Use *Contributors*: AvicAWB, Nehrams2020, Sfan00 IMG

File:The Loss of a Teardrop Diamond Poster.jpg *Source*: http://en.wikipedia.org/w/index.php?title=File:The_Loss_of_a_Teardrop_Diamond_Poster.jpg *License*: Fair Use *Contributors*: InfamousPrince, Sfan00 IMG

File:Pushposter08.jpg *Source*: http://en.wikipedia.org/w/index.php?title=File:Pushposter08.jpg *License*: Fair Use *Contributors*: BE Design

File:TheLosers2010Poster.jpg *Source*: http://en.wikipedia.org/w/index.php?title=File:TheLosers2010Poster.jpg *License*: Fair Use *Contributors*: AvicAWB, InfamousPrince

File:Star empty.svg *Source*: http://en.wikipedia.org/w/index.php?title=File:Star_empty.svg *License*: Creative Commons Attribution-Sharealike 2.5 *Contributors*: User:Conti from the original images by User:RedHotHeat

File:Scott Pilgrim vs. the World teaser.jpg *Source*: http://en.wikipedia.org/w/index.php?title=File:Scott_Pilgrim_vs._the_World_teaser.jpg *License*: Fair Use *Contributors*: Daboyle250, Marcus Brute, Silvergoat, Trogga, 1 anonymous edits

File:Michael Cera as Captain America by Gage Skidmore.jpg *Source*: http://en.wikipedia.org/w/index.php?title=File:Michael_Cera_as_Captain_America_by_Gage_Skidmore.jpg *License*: Creative Commons Attribution-Sharealike 3.0 *Contributors*: Gage Skidmore

File:Puncture Poster.jpg *Source*: http://en.wikipedia.org/w/index.php?title=File:Puncture_Poster.jpg *License*: Fair Use *Contributors*: InfamousPrince, Sfan00 IMG

File:Captain America The First Avenger poster.jpg *Source*: http://en.wikipedia.org/w/index.php?title=File:Captain_America_The_First_Avenger_poster.jpg *License*: Fair Use *Contributors*: AvicAWB, Calmer Waters, Diannaa, Fortdj33, Robman180, Salavat, Sven Manguard, TriiipleThreat

File:Captain America- The First Avenger Comic-Con Panel 2.jpg *Source*: http://en.wikipedia.org/w/index.php?title=File:Captain_America-_The_First_Avenger_Comic-Con_Panel_2.jpg *License*: Creative Commons Attribution-Sharealike 2.0 *Contributors*: rwoan

File:Captain america set.JPG *Source*: http://en.wikipedia.org/w/index.php?title=File:Captain_america_set.JPG *License*: Creative Commons Zero *Contributors*: FormerIP (talk). Original uploader was FormerIP at en.wikipedia

File:Skinny Steve.jpg *Source*: http://en.wikipedia.org/w/index.php?title=File:Skinny_Steve.jpg *License*: Fair Use *Contributors*: TriiipleThreat

File:Captain America The First Avenger premiere.jpg *Source*: http://en.wikipedia.org/w/index.php?title=File:Captain_America_The_First_Avenger_premiere.jpg *License*: Creative Commons Attribution 2.0 *Contributors*: Marco Visser

File:What's Your Number? Poster.jpg *Source*: http://en.wikipedia.org/w/index.php?title=File:What's_Your_Number?_Poster.jpg *License*: Fair Use *Contributors*: InfamousPrince

File:TheAvengers2012Poster.jpg *Source*: http://en.wikipedia.org/w/index.php?title=File:TheAvengers2012Poster.jpg *License*: Fair Use *Contributors*: Fortdj33, InfamousPrince, Sfan00 IMG, 1 anonymous edits

File:The Avengers Cast 2010 Comic-Con.jpg *Source*: http://en.wikipedia.org/w/index.php?title=File:The_Avengers_Cast_2010_Comic-Con.jpg *License*: Creative Commons Attribution-Sharealike 2.0 *Contributors*: rwoan

File:Joss Whedon by Gage Skidmore 3.jpg *Source*: http://en.wikipedia.org/w/index.php?title=File:Joss_Whedon_by_Gage_Skidmore_3.jpg *License*: Creative Commons Attribution-Sharealike 3.0 *Contributors*: Gage Skidmore

Image:US Army on the set of The Avengers 3.jpg *Source*: http://en.wikipedia.org/w/index.php?title=File:US_Army_on_the_set_of_The_Avengers_3.jpg *License*: Public Domain *Contributors*: w:United States ArmyUnited States Army

Image:Avengers Park Avenue film set.jpg *Source*: http://en.wikipedia.org/w/index.php?title=File:Avengers_Park_Avenue_film_set.jpg *License*: Creative Commons Attribution-Sharealike 2.0 *Contributors*: Eric Schmalzbauer

File:20111015 NYCC-6.jpg *Source*: http://en.wikipedia.org/w/index.php?title=File:20111015_NYCC-6.jpg *License*: Creative Commons Attribution 2.0 *Contributors*: Marnie Joyce

Image:OppositeSexTV.png *Source*: http://en.wikipedia.org/w/index.php?title=File:OppositeSexTV.png *License*: Fair Use *Contributors*: Deliriousandlost, Jh0367

License

CPSIA information can be obtained
at www.ICGtesting.com
Printed in the USA
BVHW011446130119
537705BV00009B/42/P